a Dash of
DRASH

TORAH WITH A FOCUS ON IMAGINATIVE
MIDRASHIC INTERPRETATION

KEREN HANNAH PRYOR

a Dash of DRASH

TORAH WITH A FOCUS ON IMAGINATIVE MIDRASHIC INTERPRETATION

KEREN HANNAH PRYOR

Copyright © 2021 Keren Hannah Pryor. All rights reserved.
Publication rights First Fruits of Zion, Inc.
Details: ffoz.org/copyright

Publisher grants permission to reference short quotations (less than 400 words) in reviews, magazines, newspapers, web sites, or other publications in accordance with the citation standards at ffoz.org/copyright. Requests for permission to reproduce more than 400 words can be made at ffoz.org/contact.

First Fruits of Zion is a 501(c)(3) registered nonprofit educational organization.

Printed in the United States of America

ISBN: 978-1-941534-57-1

Unless otherwise noted, Scriptural quotations are from The Holy Bible, English Standard Version, copyright © 2001 by Crossway Bibles, a division of Good News Publishers. Used by permission. All rights reserved.

Cover design: Avner Wolff
Author photo: Sarah Walk, Sarah Cusson Photography

Quantity discounts are available on bulk purchases of this book for educational, fundraising, or event purposes. Special versions or book excerpts to fit specific needs are available from First Fruits of Zion.

First Fruits of Zion

Israel / United States

PO Box 649, Marshfield, Missouri 65706-0649 USA
Phone: (417) 468-2741   Web: ffoz.org

Comments and questions: ffoz.org/contact

LEARN MORE
ffoz.org

ב"ה

In blessed memory of Dodi,

my beloved husband, Dwight A. Pryor (ז"ל),

דויד פריאור

who embodied and reflected

the precious light of the Word of God.

CONTENTS

Introduction 1

GENESIS 3
    B'reisheet – "In the Beginning" 5
    Noach – "Noah" 9
    Lech Lecha – "Go Forth" 13
    Vayera – "And He Appeared" 17
    Chayei Sarah – "Sarah's Life" 21
    Toldot – "Generations" 25
    Vayetze – "And He Went Out" 31
    Vayishlach – "And He Sent" 35
    Vayeshev – "And He Dwelt" 39
    Miketz – "At the End" 43
    Vayigash – "And He Came Near" 47
    Vayechi – "And He Lived" 51

EXODUS 59
    Shemot – "Names" 61
    Va'era – "And I Appeared" 65
    Bo – "Come" 69
    Beshalach – "When He Sent" 73
    Yitro – "Jethro" 77
    Mishpatim – "Judgments" 81
    Terumah – "Heave Offering" 85
    Tetzaveh – "You Shall Command" 91
    Ki Tisa – "When You Take" 95
    Vayak'hel – "And He Assembled" 99
    Pekudei – "Accounts" 103

LEVITICUS ... 109
- Vayikra – "And He Called" ... 111
- Tzav – "Command" ... 115
- Sh'mini – "Eighth" ... 121
- Tazria – "Conceived" ... 127
- Metzora – "Leper" ... 131
- Acharei Mot – "After the Death" ... 135
- Kedoshim – "Holy" ... 141
- Emor – "Say" ... 147
- Behar – "On Mount Sinai" ... 153
- Bechukotai – "In My Statutes" ... 159

NUMBERS ... 167
- Bamidbar – "In the Wilderness" ... 169
- Nasso – "Make an Accounting" ... 175
- Beha'alotcha – "When You Set Up" ... 181
- Shelach – "Send Thou" ... 185
- Korach – "Korah" ... 191
- Chukat – "Statute" ... 197
- Balak – "Balak" ... 203
- Pinchas – "Phinehas" ... 207
- Mattot – "Tribes" ... 211
- Massei – "Journeys" ... 215

DEUTERONOMY ... 221
- Devarim – " Words" ... 223
- Va'etchanan – "And I Besought" ... 229
- Ekev – "Because" ... 235
- Re'eh – "See" ... 241
- Shoftim – "Judges" ... 245
- Ki Tetze – "When You Go" ... 249
- Ki Tavo – "When You Come" ... 253
- Nitzavim – "You Are Standing" ... 257
- Vayelech – "And He Went" ... 261
- Ha'azinu – "Give Ear" ... 265
- Vezot ha'Bracha – "And This Is the Blessing" ... 269

INTRODUCTION

WHAT IS DRASH, AND WHY BOTHER WITH IT?

> Once you begin to understand Holy Writ, reading the text again and again, probing deeper and deeper, illumination flashes forth like flames from a coal, assuming many different forms and shades. For infinite are the facets of Torah.
>
> —Moshe Chaim Luzzato

Our aim in *A Dash of Drash* is to approach each parashah from a different perspective—that of imaginative application (midrash). We will be encouraged to ask different questions and seek deeper answers. All of which should enrich our understanding of the Word, and Yeshua himself as the Living Word. I hope that as a result, our desire for spiritual growth will be nourished, and our daily living inspired.

Hebraic tradition recognizes four major levels of interpretation of Torah text—referred to by the acronym PARDeS (orchard):

1. *Peshat* (simple) - the plain, primary meaning; the "face value" of the text.
2. *Remez* (clue) - the allegorical; linking concepts and ideas.
3. *Drash* (to explain, to inquire) - the level of homiletic, personal application.
4. *Sod* (secret) - the esoteric or mystical level; searching for more intimate meaning.

Each level, while it remains within the constraints of biblical truth and ethical morality, complements the other. The aim of PARDeS interpretation is the exploration of the many layers inherent in the biblical text.

The collective life of every society is composed of a series of narratives—layers superimposed one upon the other that blend to form a composite whole. Similarly, each of our individual lives is an intricate and often beautiful weaving together of the narratives of our past, our present, our joys and fears, hopes and dreams.

Thus, in answer to the questions, "Why should we concern ourselves with the *drash* perspective of biblical text? What does the homiletic view of the Scriptures offer, in addition to the factual, historical, plain meaning of the text?" Nehama Leibowitz, beloved teacher of Torah in Israel from the early 1940s until her passing, assured, "The homiletical explanation [midrash] is simply another and deeper level of the text."[1]

Aryeh Newman, the proficient translator into English of Leibowitz's excellent Hebrew Torah studies, elaborates:

> The Creator, who knows the thoughts of man, chose to communicate the highest truth on which his world was built through sublime artistry—investing every word and letter with infinite depths of meaning. The Torah, according to the traditional view, is no mere literal recording of historical events, a chronicle of facts, historical or otherwise, but a highly selective manual of morals and lessons.[2]

We do need to be aware of the fact that there is a fine line between enjoying and exploring the creative midrashic interpretations and exploiting the text to say anything we want it to. At the same time, we need to hold onto the integrity of the former without allowing fear of the latter to hold us back.

In the art of cooking, an informed dash of one or two of the wide variety of aromatic spices adds flavor and character to an already good dish—turmeric in rice, cumin and garlic in lamb, coriander in curry, chili and cilantro in salsa. Likewise, a dash of *drash* adds interest and pleasure and contributes to a good, healthy study of Torah. May you enjoy the spiritual gastronomic adventure.

GENESIS

B'REISHEET

בראשית – "In the Beginning"

GENESIS 1:1–6:8

"The creation of the Universe is also the creation of time." Thus states Professor Moshe Kaveh, the President of Bar Ilan University in Tel Aviv, in his commentary on this first parashah, or portion, of the Torah.[3] This is a remarkable notion—in creating the universe, God created time. "In the beginning," therefore, also can be rendered "at the start of time."

GOD AND TIME

The Hebrew name that God revealed to Moshe at the burning bush is *yod-hei-vav-hei. Ehyeh asher ehyeh.* I am, I was, I will be. He was, he is, and he will be. He is outside the constriction and limits of time. He had no beginning, but from him, all that is created came forth. In him, all that is had its beginning.

"It thus follows, as the night the day," as William Shakespeare said, or rather "as the morning follows the evening" to be more biblically accurate (Genesis 1:5), that only people who are created in the image of God can know time in the present and retain memories of the past. Of all creation, only man can celebrate special days, can recall yesterday, and try to change tomorrow for the better by using today for good.

To quote Rabbi Lazer Brody, an acclaimed Torah teacher and counselor in Israel, who applies the teachings of Chasidic Rebbe Nachman of Breslev:[4] "Your *neshamah* [soul/spirit] is timeless. Your actions will affect the world long after you have left this life."[5] Our spirits are not constricted by time in the same way our present physical, time-bound bodies are. Our lives leave imprints on the world in deeper ways than we maybe realize. This concept was well illustrated in the movie classic, *It's a Wonderful Life*!

If we grasp the implications of this from an eternal perspective, we will take far more care in the way we behave and relate to others, particularly those close to us, and also in establishing our priorities in life. Rabbi Lazer concludes:

> The more we consider the long-term influences that our actions bear on our souls, the better we act. The better we act, the better we feel about ourselves, and the more we attain inner peace.[6]

THE IMAGE OF GOD

On the sixth day of creation, God said, "Let us make man in Our image (*tzelem*) and likeness (*demut*)" (Genesis 1:26). Verse 27 stresses this fact three times, "So God created man in his own image; in the image of God he created him; male and female he created them."

Nehama Leibowitz, Israel's renowned Torah teacher for many decades, refers to Professor Gutmann's commentary on the term *tzelem*:

> *Tzelem* (image) refers to the personal relationship that can only be found between "persons" ... Only as long as man is a person [growing in his unique God-given personality, and doesn't sink to the level of an animal ruled by his physical appetites] can he preserve his relationship with God.[7]

Yeshua, in answer to a question posed by a group of Pharisees regarding the validity of paying taxes to Caesar, gave a brilliant teaching based on man's unique creation in the image of God. When he saw the denarius (coin) they produced, he asked them, "Whose likeness (*tzelem*) and inscription does it have?" When they replied, "Caesar's, of course," he stunned them with the comment: "Then render to Caesar the things that are Caesar's, and to God the things that are God's."[8]

This is a clear illustration of the fact that the powerful, materialistic system of the world robs people of their uniqueness and stamps them with the hollow, look-a-like images of the Caesars, or Pharaohs, or those promulgated by multi-media advertisers.

God created human beings in glorious variety; no two of us are exactly alike. As Rabbi Brody expresses regarding our physicality: "Mankind is finally beginning to understand the unbelievable effort that God devotes in making each of us a special individual, via the discovery of DNA, RNA, chromosomal combinations and genetic maps." Also uniquely, we each have a spirit, for God is spirit (John 4:24), and it is this commonality, this stamp of likeness (*tzelem*) in us that responds to his Spirit of holiness. It is this internal image that the enemy of our souls violently, and yet often so subtly, attempts to blur and then extinguish.

In the superb collection of Jewish wisdom, *Pirkei Avot* ("*Sayings of the Fathers*") 3:14, we are reminded:

> Beloved is man since he was created in God's image; but it was by a special love that it was made known to him that he was created in God's image.

We are God's and beloved of God. He has given us the responsibility to value and cherish his image in ourselves and in one another. We are never to give up hope, but, in the spirit of Messiah, we are continually to fan the flame of the eternal "spark" of God's image within. "A bruised reed he will not break, and a smoldering wick he will not quench, until he brings justice to victory" (Matthew 12:20; Isaiah 42:3). May we persevere until we, and all people created in his image, learn to know the Father more fully and to serve and worship him in the holiness of his Spirit and in the truth of his Word.

NOACH

נח – "Noah"

GENESIS 6:9–11:32

It is difficult to imagine, or maybe not given the days in which we live, that after just ten generations from Adam, God could find only one righteous man in all the earth. The opening verse of the parashah is a glowing testimony to Noah's character. It states, "Noah walked with God" (Genesis 6:9). This is a reminder of God's walking with Adam and Eve in the garden of Eden and emphasizes the startling contrast between man's initial abode of peace and beauty in relationship with his Creator and the world of violence (*chamas*) and depravity that surrounds Noah and his family. We find a world estranged from God.

A RIGHTEOUS MAN

The verse also attributes to Noah the characteristics of "righteous and wholehearted" (*tzaddik vetamim*). Midrashic commentary takes note of the addendum "in his age," or generation, and illustrates how conflicting opinions can be formed in consideration of the same biblical text. This produces a healthy tension, which is a function of midrash, and the realization that, while one can draw one's own conclusion, there are various other points of view to consider.

In *Midrash Tanchuma*, an early medieval commentary, the question is posed:

> What is meant by "in his age"? ... It means righteous in *his* age, but not in others. To what may this be compared? If someone

> places a silver coin among copper coins, the silver appears attractive. So Noah appeared righteous in the age of the flood.

This opinion proposes that had Noah lived in a godly, righteous society, he would not have been noteworthy. It was only in comparison with the corruption surrounding him that Noah was prominent at all. The midrash continues to present another view:

> Others interpret the verse to Noah's credit. How so? He may be compared to a jar of balsam placed in a grave and giving off a goodly fragrance. Had it been inside a home, how much the more so!

Here, the emphasis is upon the fact that Noah was a righteous man *despite* the degenerate society of which he was a part. Had he lived in a God-fearing, kind, and loving environment, his devotion to God might have been all the greater. As it was, despite all the odds against him, he was a *tzaddik*—a righteous man—who served God wholeheartedly.

These two opposing views are formed from the same evidence regarding an individual. The second opinion highlights the good in Noah. This challenges us to employ a quality very much emphasized in biblical and rabbinic teaching, that of "a good eye"—having a generous and positive view of life and giving every person the benefit of the doubt. A "good eye" is the result of a "good heart" as is indicated in this apt talmudic saying:

> I am a creature [of God], and my neighbor is also his creature … We have learnt that it matters not whether one does much or little, if only he directs his heart to heaven. (b.*Brachot* 17a)

Let us be encouraged to evidence a "heaven-directed heart" in all our interactions with our fellow man.

SYMBOLS AND REALITY

The parashah is embedded with powerful symbols that carry forward into the subsequent generations of humankind the realities and deep truths of God experienced by Noah and his family.

The first is the ark, which is the dominant focus of the narrative. The logistics involved in the 120-year project are breathtaking. Noah undertook the task with unquestioning faith and obedience to the directives of God. Eventually, his working together with God provided the means by which his family and all life on land were preserved. God's Presence is with them and guides them, but they needed to take action and build the temporary home that would carry them through the ensuing deluge.[9]

The account of Noah and the flood emphasizes the transience and insecurity of this world. The flood itself illustrates that one's life is as fragile as a bird's nest in the branch of a tree, liable to collapse overnight during a strong storm. If we are to rise above the flood of darkness that threatens to engulf the "temporary shelters" of our generation, then our lives need to be wholeheartedly devoted to God. With our lives based solidly on the Word, set apart in the ark of his covenant, we can rest in the knowledge that the wings of his faithful and holy Presence cover us.

> He who dwells in the shelter of the Most High will abide in the shadow of the Almighty. He will cover you with his pinions, and under his wings you will find refuge; his faithfulness is a shield. (Psalm 91:1, 4)

Next, we see the symbols of the dove and the olive branch:

> The dove came back to him in the evening, and behold, in her mouth was a freshly plucked olive leaf. (Genesis 8:11)

These have become the prime symbols of holiness and peace. We see a beautiful illustration of perfect holiness and purity when Yeshua emerged from the water at his ritual immersion in the Jordan River, and the Holy Spirit of God descended upon him like a dove.[10]

The Talmud records that there is one outstanding example of chastity and lack of promiscuity in the animal world, and that is the dove. Rabbi Yochanan observed: "If the Torah had not been given to us, we should have learned modesty from the cat, honesty from the ant, and the virtue of chastity from the dove" (b.*Eruvin* 100b, 51). In the world of flora it is stated that hybrid plants can be produced from the grafting of all trees except the olive (Jerusalem Talmud, *Kilayim* 1:7). The dove and the olive branch are thus the perfect bearers of the good news that the devastating flood had receded. The combination of the two unique examples of purity was a powerful message to Noah that not only had the waters subsided, but also the perversion of nature that had brought it about had been washed away. There was hope for the future peace of humanity.

This hope was reflected in the rainbow. When God established a covenant with Noah and his sons, he said:

> I have set my bow in the cloud, and it shall be a sign of the covenant between me and the earth ... And the waters shall never again become a flood to destroy all flesh. (Genesis 9:13,15)

The *keshet,* the rainbow of God, is seen in the heavens above every nation, as are the sun, moon, and stars. They are set in place by the Creator of all as constant reminders of his loving faithfulness. The hearts of those who see and understand will long for his Presence and will desire to walk with him in righteousness as did their ancient ancestor Noah—the first man to be called "righteous."

LECH LECHA

לֶךְ לְךָ – "Go Forth"

GENESIS 12:1–17:27

In the portion Lech Lecha the land is brought into the biblical spotlight. We read of God's call to Abraham: "Go from your country ... to the land that I will show you" (Genesis 12:1). As the narrative progresses, we realize that God is again "making a match." He is weaving together this chosen family and the land he has chosen. We are told in *Kohelet* (Ecclesiastes), "a threefold cord is not easily broken" (4:12). The third strand, which renders this an unbreakable and eternal cord, is God's Word. He gives his covenantal promise in turn to Abraham, then Isaac, and then Jacob. We see this expressed in Isaac's blessing of Jacob:

> May he give the blessing of Abraham to you and to your offspring with you, that you may take possession of the land of your sojournings that God gave to Abraham! (Genesis 28:4)

GOD AS LANDLORD

God makes it clear, however, that his people are simply tenants in the land. He is the sole and rightful owner:

> The land shall not be sold in perpetuity, for the land is mine. For you are strangers and sojourners with me. (Leviticus 25:23)

This, by extension, is true of all the earth. God proved with the flood that humanity is not essential in the maintenance of the universe. Man is under an illusion if he thinks that the world is his playground, there simply to serve his needs and to indulge his pleasures. As Rabbi Bradley Shavit-Artson describes:

> The vast array of organic and living things serves a purpose higher than that of human whim. Together with humanity, the rest of the cosmos is a living, interlocking symphony to our Creator. We are the tenants, but God is the only *ba'al habayit* (property owner).[11]

When we lift our eyes to see his design and open our ears to hear the transcendent symphony of God in all his creation, we can respond in faith, believing. Then we are able to hear his still, small voice, saying, "Go forth," and, like our father Abraham, we can confidently walk the path to which he calls and directs us.

GOD AS BLESSER

On the one hand, we know that in all his vastness and mystery, the God of the Universe is unknowable. Our finite minds cannot begin to know him. How do we grasp a measure of understanding of his ineffable greatness? On the other hand, the realization slowly dawns in our dim gray matter that this Almighty, wondrous God longs to be known, to be approached, even to be loved.

Throughout the history of humankind, God's constant aim has been to "come down" and to build a relationship of love with his people—as a people corporately but also with each precious individual, as we see demonstrated with Abraham.

In fact, the Scriptures make it clear that he ardently pursues us all the days of our lives. To this end, he has instilled within us an ability to respond and relate to him, and the development of this capacity is what life ultimately is all about. Yeshua emphasized in his teaching that the end, the aim, of every commandment is love—to learn to love God by loving one another.

The result of love is blessing. Of all the great qualities of God demonstrated in this parashah, the one that emerges most forcefully is that he is a blesser. He is eager to bless his children and see them bless one another. In the opening verses the word "blessing" appears five times in different forms.

Benno Jacob observes in his study of Genesis that these blessings correspond to the five-fold abundance of light created on the first day. The word *ohr* ("light") also occurs five times (Genesis 1:3–5). Nehama Leibowitz points out: "Here we have a second world created with the advent of Abraham, a world of blessing [not only from God to man but] given to man by man."[12] She quotes Rashi's comment:

> The blessings are placed at your disposal (in your hand). Hitherto they have been in My hand. I blessed Adam and Noah. Henceforth you bless whom you wish.[13]

Like Abraham, those who walk in faithful obedience to the God of Israel inherit the great privilege of bestowing blessing upon others. Let us be blessers!

VAYERA

וירא – "And He Appeared"

GENESIS 18:1–22:24

This auspicious parashah opens with the dramatic phrase: "And the LORD appeared to him by the oaks of Mamre" (Genesis 18:1). Abraham had likely pitched his encampment under the oaks for the shade they provided. The trees were also an indication of a source of water. They would signal this vital fact to those traveling through the desert terrain. It was Abraham's custom to look out for sojourners and to offer them sustenance. Hospitality (*hachnasat orchim*) is an honored tradition established by Abraham and Sarah, one valued by their descendants to this day.

Although Abraham was recovering from his circumcision, he was seated "at the door of his tent in the heat of the day" and watching out for weary travelers who would need food, shelter, and rest. The text informs us that "he lifted up his eyes and looked, *vayissa einav vayar* (Genesis 18:2). This "lifting of the eyes" indicates a conscious, deliberate looking. He was not gazing lazily into the distance. Then, unexpectedly, the LORD appeared, *vayera*. Note the similarity to the verb *vayar* ("looked")—each derived from the root *reish-alef-hei*, "to see."

This focus on the eyes and seeing appears significantly throughout the parashah. Here, as a result of his active looking, Abraham sees the LORD. God appears to Abraham seven times throughout his life. On this occasion, the rabbis propose that he visited Abraham during his recuperation from his recent circumcision. This forms the basis of the Jewish *mitzvah* (good deed) of visiting the sick. Rashi records:

> Said R. Chama bar Chanina: It was the third day since Abraham had been circumcised, and the Holy One blessed be he came to inquire regarding his health.

The Ramban[14] elaborates that the LORD appeared as a reward for his obedience in undergoing the circumcision:

> This revelation constituted the reward for previous obedience to let them [Abraham, Ishmael, and all the men of his household] know that God had favorably accepted their deeds (Genesis 17:26-27). This is underscored by Chazal:[15]

> If to him who builds an altar in My name I reveal Myself and bless him (Exodus 20:24), how much more so unto Abraham who circumcised himself for My name? (*Avot DeRabbi Nathan*)

LOOKING, THEY SEE NOT

There is a remarkable parallel in Abraham's encounter with the angels in chapter 18 and Lot's encounter recorded in the following chapter. We read that the two angels arrived in Sodom in the evening. Certain facts are evident: The LORD was not with them, it was a city, not the desert, and Lot was sitting in the gate. Rabbi Hertz describes, "The gate is the passage beneath the city wall, where people [usually the elders of the city] congregate to converse, transact business, or have their disputes adjudicated."

Lot sees the visitors, *vayar*, but the conscious seeing, the "lifting of the eyes," is missing. To give him his due, once he recognized the strangers, Lot rose to greet them and, in the tradition of his uncle Abraham, offered them his hospitality. He, too, "made them a feast" (Genesis 19:3).

The shocking incident involving the men of Sodom then occurs, which highlights the reasons that warrant God's destruction of this and the surrounding cities—rampant homosexuality and violent hatred of strangers. Incomprehensibly, but possibly in desperation to protect his guests, Lot offered the mob his two virgin daughters, and said, "Do to them as you please" (Genesis 19:8). The angels saved the situation by inflicting temporary blindness upon the men attacking the house, leaving them in confusion and unable to find the door. Their eyes, which could not see "good," were blinded. This affliction clearly mirrors the spiritual blindness and complacency of the Sodomites. Although it seems that Lot tried to preserve Abrahamic values, they were not transmitted to his children. His older daughters married men of Sodom, who, in the arrogance of their selfish, hedonistic lifestyle, mocked and sneered at Lot when he attempted to warn them of the coming destruction.

There are other examples of seeing, or not, to consider in the parashah: the mysterious fate of Lot's wife when she lingers and vacillates and turns to look back, after being warned by the angels not to do so [16] (Genesis 19:17); and the situation of Hagar and Ishmael, who are banished from the safety of Abraham's camp into the wilderness of Paran as a result of their mockery of Sarah and Isaac. In the latter account, when the bread and water provided by a caring Abraham were depleted, Hagar left the boy in the shade of a shrub and moved away, unable to watch him die. They both wailed in their distress, and the LORD heard the cries of the boy, and he opened Hagar's eyes: "Then God opened her eyes, and she saw a well of water" (Genesis 21:19). The well had been there all along, but she had not seen it until enabled by God.

THE AKEIDAH ON THE MOUNT OF GOD

The *Akeidah*—the binding of Isaac—is a central theme of Judaism, as described by Abravanel:[17] "[The *Akeidah* is] the whole horn [strength] and merit of Israel before their Father in Heaven and ever on our lips in daily prayer."[18]

Abraham undergoes the exceptional test of sacrificing his "only, beloved son Isaac" to God as a burnt offering. His hand with the raised blade is halted, at the last moment, by a voice from heaven. Then the Torah tells us:

> Abraham lifted up his eyes and looked, and behold, behind him was a ram, caught in a thicket by his horns. And Abraham went and took the ram and offered it up as a burnt offering instead of his son. (Genesis 22:13)

In his relief and gratitude, Abraham names the mount *Adonai Yir'eh* (Genesis 22:14). This is usually translated, "The LORD will provide." However, *yir'eh* is from the same root *reish-alef-hei* to see, and a more literal translation is rendered by the Jewish Publication Society: "In the mount where the LORD is seen." The King James Version renders it, "In the mount where the LORD will be seen." Surely, to those who lift up their eyes, he was, is, and will be seen.

This is the mount chosen by God, where his Name will be placed forever, where his house, the *Beit HaMikdash*, the Holy Temple will stand, and where his eternal throne will be established in the last day. Standing in that very place, Yeshua recalled that Abraham had lifted his eyes from there and rejoiced at the revelation of the One who was to come, the Lamb that God would provide for the salvation of all mankind.

"He [Abraham] saw [my day] and was glad" (John 8:56). Not only were Abraham's eyes open to see the LORD, but his ears were also constantly ready to hear his voice, and he would obey without hesitation. Indeed, as a reward for his radical and faithful obedience, God blesses Abraham on that mount:

> In your offspring shall all the nations of the earth be blessed, because you have obeyed my voice. (Genesis 22:18)

CHAYEI SARAH

חיי שרה – "Sarah's Life"

GENESIS 23:1–25:18

The parashah begins with the death of Sarah and ends with the death of Abraham. Both references to their deaths declare the "years of their life" (Genesis 23:1; 25:7). They lived their lives to the full. This concept of a full life is reiterated in the haftarah, which records the death of King David. First Kings 1:1 informs us, "Now King David was old and advanced in years." *Vehamelech David zaken ba bayamim.*

The Midrash comments: "There is a man who reaches *ziknah* (who acquires wisdom with age) but is not *ba bayamim* (advanced in years) and vice versa." King David accomplished both and so did Abraham and Sarah.

The burial of Sarah is the first mention of burial in the Bible. Abraham sets the precedent of mourning and honoring the dead by interment for the generations after him. One of the greatest acts of kindness in Judaism is to take care of the burial of the body of one who dies alone without family or friends. This is an action that will bring no obvious tangible reward and is, therefore, considered the most selfless form of kindness.

DEEDS OF LOVING-KINDNESS

The chief characteristic of Abraham is the quality most esteemed in the Scriptures, that of *chesed*, loving-kindness. This trait is emphasized in a well-known maxim from *Pirkei Avot*:

> Shimon the Righteous ... used to say: The world depends on three things—*al haTorah, v'al ha'avodah, v'al gemilut chasadim*—on [study of] the Torah, and on service/ worship [of God], and on deeds of loving-kindness (*Pirkei Avot* 1:2).

Chesed is often translated as steadfast love or kindness. In chapter 24 alone, the term appears in verses 12, 14, 27, and 49. Among many other references in Scripture, we find,

> The LORD is slow to anger and abounding in steadfast love. (Numbers 14:18)

> I have trusted in your steadfast love; my heart shall rejoice in your salvation. (Psalm 13:5)

The attribute of *chesed* includes the qualities of love and kindness, but central to its meaning is that it describes love expressed in action. Love is an emotion and can be steadfast and deeply experienced. Until it is given expression as *chesed*, however, it remains closed within a person. *Gemilut chasadim*—unselfish acts of loving-kindness—are the means by which one demonstrates *chesed*.

We see this quality clearly illustrated in the classic narrative of Abraham's servant's search for a bride for Isaac. The character trait of *gemilut chasadim* was what Eliezer was seeking as he set about his task of finding the wife whom the LORD had prepared for his beloved master's son. The attributes of a mother of Israel were kindness and sensitivity, not wealth and pride. In the beautiful-of-spirit girl, who came to draw water at the well and unhesitatingly provided water for him and his many camels, he found what he was seeking.

The Apostle John captures the essence of *gemilut chasadim* in his exhortation: "Little children, let us not love in word or talk but in deed and in truth" (1 John 3:18). Rebekah's brother, Laban, illustrates the converse of John's exhortation. He quickly ran out to meet the stranger after "he saw the ring and the bracelets on his sister's arms" (Genesis 24:30). The jewelry is described in verse 22: "A golden ring of half a shekel weight, and two bracelets for her hands of ten shekels weight of gold." These token gifts from Abraham certainly caught Laban's attention. After he hurried to greet the man, Laban "stood by the camels at the fountain." It is noted that there were ten camels laden with "all sorts of choice gifts" (Genesis 24:10).

Laban then gushed with hospitality, but it was prompted by selfish motives and was not the *gemilut chasadim* of his sister. Laban's name (*lamed-vet-nun*) is pronounced *Lavan* in Hebrew, which means "white." Some of his actions indeed appear to be pure. However, one can reverse the letters of his name to read *nun-vet-lamed—Naval*—a scoundrel!

MOTHER OF ISRAEL

Rebekah would follow in the steps of Sarah, the first matriarch of the people of Israel. After the non-spectacular but significant meeting of Rebekah with her husband-to-be, when they both "lifted their eyes" and truly saw one another (Genesis 24:63-64), we read a lifetime of meaning in one verse:

> Then Isaac brought her into the tent of Sarah his mother and took Rebekah, and she became his wife, and he loved her. So Isaac was comforted after his mother's death. (Genesis 24:67)

Isaac and Rebekah demonstrate that a wedding is not the culmination but only the beginning of true love. Rabbi S.R. Hirsch comments:

> However important it is that love shall precede marriage, it is far more important that it shall continue after marriage; the Jewish view emphasizes the life-long devotion and affection after marriage.[19]

Without this committed devotion and affection, the marriage becomes a mere mirage.

Rashi enumerates three phenomena that were evident in Sarah's tent. They ceased at her death but revived when Rebekah entered and love filled the house:

1. *"A light that remained kindled from one Shabbat to the next."*
   When Shabbat is celebrated with true joy and holiness, the light of *shalom* will be felt in the home throughout the week.

2. *"A blessing sent to the dough."*
   There will always be sufficient provision, and none will go hungry. This is not dependent on wealth, but on kindness and hospitality.

3. *"A cloud attached to the tent."*
   The cloud symbolizes a spiritual purpose beyond the maintenance of a physical household. This is the highest goal towards which a family can aspire—the evidence of God's Presence in their home.[20]

TOLDOT

תולדות – "Generations"

GENESIS 25:19–28:9

A fascinating account is recorded in this week's parashah regarding the wells dug by Abraham and Isaac. Water means life, particularly in the dry, desert-like area of the Negev where they lived. The Scriptures note a clear promise of God to his people:

> You shall serve the LORD your God, and he will bless your bread and your water. (Exodus 23:25)

Isaac, as evidenced in the narrative, illustrates this truth. He is the first patriarch to establish fields of grain as well as raise flocks, and he prospers despite the prevailing famine:

> Isaac sowed in that land, and reaped in the same year a hundredfold. The LORD blessed him, and the man became rich, and gained more and more until he became very wealthy ... so that the Philistines envied him. (Genesis 26:12–14)

Envy and the inability to rejoice in the success of others are unfortunate, all-too-human characteristics. Our forefather Jacob would suffer the same envy from the sons of Laban who, on realizing that Jacob had succeeded in building up large flocks and a prosperous household of his own, declared, "from what was our father's he has gained all this wealth" (Genesis 31:1).

WELLS OF LIVING WATER

Isaac eventually must move to another area, one in which we are told, "Now the Philistines had stopped and filled with earth all the wells that his father's servants had dug in the days of Abraham his father" (Genesis 26:15). This action of the Philistines is perplexing. Why would they stop up a source of provision vital to their own sustenance?

Midrashic commentators consider that the story of the wells offers a symbolic interpretation. Nehama Leibowitz points out:

> The conduct of the Philistines can only be understood if we take these wells to signify the wells of the faith which the patriarchs caused to flow and which the forces of desolation and idolatry stopped up.[21]

When one digs a well, one penetrates beneath the surface of the ground to draw forth a fountain of living water that is hidden to the eye. This can be compared to the spirit, the *neshamah*, the life that is at the very core of a person and is not visible unless one seeks it out and draws it forth. This *neshamah* is a deposit of God's own Spirit of holiness within his children. The Prophet Joel foretells that, at the time of the redemption, God has promised: "In that day ... all the streambeds of Judah shall flow with water; and a fountain shall come forth from the house of the LORD" (Joel 3:18). God's Spirit shall be poured out "in that day" as a fountain of life-giving waters bringing cleansing, healing, and restoration.

This corresponds beautifully with the account of Yeshua's meeting with a Samaritan woman at a well dug by Jacob. He tells her:

> Everyone who drinks of this water will be thirsty again, but whoever drinks of the water that I will give him will never be thirsty forever. The water that I will give him will become in him a spring of water welling up to eternal life. (John 4:13–14)

She believes him and, together with many from her town, she drinks of the living waters Yeshua has to offer. He, as the Living Word, opens the well of salvation that offers a turning toward and a loving relationship with the Father of all. A blessed assurance is given to all who turn their hearts to the Father in repentance:

> If you turn at my reproof, behold, I will pour out my spirit
> to you; I will make my words known to you. (Proverbs 1:23)

TRAIL OF DECEPTION

The portion contains the stirring account of the struggle between the two brothers Esau and Jacob. It begins in Rebekah's womb. When she enquires of the LORD as to the reason for this fierce wrestling, he replies:

> Two nations are in your womb, and two peoples from within
> you shall be divided; the one shall be stronger than the other,
> the older shall serve the younger. (Genesis 25:23)

The struggle surfaces dramatically in the account of an old, dim-sighted Isaac conferring the blessing of the firstborn upon Jacob, who, at Rebekah's insistence, is disguised as Esau.

Esau is the epitome of the physically robust, outdoor man. He is a skilled hunter whose senses are trained, but he acts on impulse and is ruled by his passions. Quiet, studious Jacob seems the weaker brother. However, we learn in *Pirkei Avot* 4:1:

> Ben Zoma says: Who is strong? He who subdues his personal
> inclinations, as it is said: "He who is slow to anger is better
> than the strong man, and a master of his passions is better
> than the conqueror of a city [Proverbs 16:32].

We read how, on discovering he had lost the blessing, Esau was filled with hatred for Jacob, and he planned to kill him (Genesis 27:41).

We can deduce that Isaac's eyes of understanding were opened, for when he sends Jacob to find a wife from among his mother's family, he fully confirms the blessing and also confers upon him the blessing of Abraham (Genesis 28:3-4).

As we will read in the action-filled narrative of Jacob's exile to Syria and his eventual return to the land of his fathers, the ramifications of his deception of Isaac echo throughout Jacob's life. He learns and grows with each experience, and develops into a true leader and father of the nation-to-be, Israel. To summarize:

1. **Double-Dealing Deception** – After fleeing to his mother's family, Jacob has a moving reunion with his uncle Laban. Again the "white-washed scoundrel" features in the chronicles of God's people! True to form, Laban offers an initial period of profuse hospitality. When he takes note that his nephew is an industrious worker, he employs some crafty double-dealing that results in Jacob's working for him for fourteen years without just payment. Thereafter, Jacob works an additional six years, during which he builds up his own assets in preparation for the return to his homeland.

2. **Under-Cover Deception** – Under cover of darkness, on the bridal night, Laban deceives Jacob by substituting Leah in place of Jacob's beloved Rachel. In a stinging retort when confronted, Laban alludes to Jacob's substitution of Esau: "It is not so done in *our* country, to give the younger before the firstborn" (Genesis 29:26).

3. **Outer-Cover Deception** – Jacob will suffer a similar crushing shock as a result of deception when his sons present him with the signature coat of many colors of his favorite son, Joseph, which is torn and bloodstained. His older sons had concocted a story to cover up their betrayal and disposal of Joseph. They slaughtered a goat and splattered some of the blood on Joseph's coat. This is a grim reminder of the goat slaughtered to prepare the meal for Isaac, which Jacob serves his blind father dressed in Esau's garments and with his hands covered with the goat's hairy skin.

4. **Master-Servant Deception** – At the time of Jacob's dramatic re-encounter with Esau, Jacob humbles himself and refers to his older brother as master (Genesis 33:8,13,14,15) and to himself as servant (Genesis 32:4,18,20, 33:5,14). While it is a great relief that Jacob's life is spared and the reconciliation seems peaceful, there is a niggling suspicion that things are not fully as they appear between the brothers. An element of this will later resound in the encounter in

Egypt when the older brothers bow before the Egyptian master, who is, in reality, their brother Joseph dressed in foreign garb.

VAYETZE

ויצא – "And He Went Out"

GENESIS 28:10–32:3

Jacob has left Beersheva and is on his way to Haran when, unexpectedly, *vayifga bamakom*—he collides, has a physical-emotional encounter, with *the* place. He sleeps and has the first dream/vision described in the Bible—one of beautiful imagery and symbolism. Jacob awakes, filled with awe, and proclaims, "Surely the LORD is in this place, and I did not know it!" (Genesis 28:16). While having particular application to *Beit El*, the House of the LORD in Jerusalem, the depth and application of its message are meaningful to every person, at any time, and in any place. As one rabbi wrote:

> God is high above the world! Yet if a man enters a synagogue and hides behind a post and prays in a tiny whisper, the Holy One, blessed be He, listens to the prayer ... Can there be a God nearer than this, who is as near to His creatures as the mouth is to the ear?[22]

A sanctuary is a special place of meeting with God, especially as a community, but this one small chapter, of only twenty-two verses, in Genesis tells us from the beginning of the "family story" that any place where a child of God finds him/herself is a place where God will "come down" and meet with them. The "ladder" is there!

PRAYER IN THE NIGHT

In response to his encounter with God, Jacob prays the first recorded prayer in the night (Genesis 28:20–22). *Chazal* attribute each of the set daily prayers to one of the patriarchs (b.*Brachot* 26b).

1. ABRAHAM – the morning prayer, *Shacharit* (*shachar*, "dawn")
   Abraham always rose early in the morning to obey God's will, e.g., Genesis 21:1, 22:2. He would pray at daybreak, standing before God (Genesis 19:27), thereby strengthening himself to face the challenges of the day.

2. ISAAC – the afternoon prayer, *Minchah* (the afternoon sacrifice of grain and cereals in the Temple, e.g., Exodus 29:41; Leviticus 2:1)
   Isaac is described as walking in the field meditating/praying "toward evening," i.e., twilight (Genesis 24:63). In the late afternoon the physical demands of the day wind down, and one can take the opportunity to clear one's mind of worldly demands and focus on one's spiritual aspirations.

3. JACOB – the evening prayer – *Ma'ariv* (from the root word *erev*, "evening"), as we see described in this portion (Genesis 28:11).
   The darkness of night offers quiet solitude. Devoid of daytime distractions, it can be a time, as Jacob experienced, of unexpected spiritual revelation and intimate communion with God.

Rashi, the renowned medieval commentator, points out that *vayifga* (encounter) is also a root word of prayer. For example, Ruth pleaded with Naomi: "Do not entreat/pressure *(tifg'i)* me to leave you" (Ruth 1:16). Jacob's prayer was not prayed in a calm, relaxed manner. There was pressure. He was startled and overcome by this encounter. His prayer was a struggle, a plea, a necessary pressing-through of previous boundaries of his awareness.

SERVICE OF THE HEART

The common Hebrew word for prayer is *tefillah,* the root of which is p-l-l, *peh-lamed-lamed,* which means to judge, clarify, or decide. The word *plilim* is used for a court of law in the Torah (Exodus 21:22). The issues of life demand a constant clarifying of what is important—a sifting of the abundance of information and stimuli that inundate us every day. Thus, as described in *Siddur Avodat HaLev,* "Prayer is the soul's yearning to define what truly matters and to ignore the trivialities that so often masquerade as essential."

Another beautiful definition of prayer is expressed in the Overview of the Artscroll Prayer Book, *Siddur Ahavat Shalom*:[23]

> Prayer, then, is not a list of requests [for God knows our needs before we ask] it is an introspective process of discovering what one is, what one should be, and how to achieve the transformation. Indeed the commandment to pray is expressed by the Torah as a service of the heart (*lev*)[24] and not of the mouth [alone] (b.*Ta'anit* 2a).

Prayer is a means of communicating with our Father in heaven and sharing our needs but, more importantly, as Jacob illustrates, it is a means of strengthening our perception of who God is, and re-evaluating one's heart in his Presence and one's place in his purposes. In fact, to pray is to reconnect with the very purpose of life itself.

The highly esteemed first rabbi of the restored land of Israel, Rav Kook, poetically describes: "The soul is always praying. It constantly seeks to fly away to its Beloved."[25] We simply need to bring our minds and will into harmony with the deepest desire of our made-in-the-image-of-God spirit.

VAYISHLACH

וישלח – "And He Sent"

GENESIS 32:4–36:43

We are exhorted in Proverbs 3:5 to "trust in the LORD with all your heart." Rabbi Shmuel Bar Nachman, in *Midrash B'reisheet Rabbah Vayishlach 76*, informs us:

> Two people received God's assurances, yet they were afraid: the chosen one of the patriarchs (Jacob) and the chosen one of the prophets (Moses). Israel deserved to be destroyed in the time of Haman [for losing hope], but they defended their attitude by that of their ancestor, saying, "If our ancestor Jacob, who had God's assurance, was nevertheless afraid, how much the more so are we justified in feeling fear?"

TRUST OR FEAR

In God's original design, man was not created to experience fear. Fear is, therefore, not a natural human emotion—one that needs to be faced and overcome. Hatred, violence, and fear entered the human psyche as a result of sin and the brokenness, pain, and chaos it engenders. This ungodly triad rules when the heart of man is yielded to sin. Alternatively, when one's heart is yielded to the LORD and is filled with trust in him, then love, peace, and joy reign. Yeshua assured us:

> I have said these things to you, that in me you may have
> peace. In the world you will have tribulation. But take heart;
> I have overcome the world. (John 16:33)

After Jacob's solitary wrestling in the night, there is no further record in the Scriptures that he again experiences fear. It seems that part of the victory gained through his struggle was to overcome this negative emotion. However, he is still subject to the human condition and endures much further hardship and pain. We read in this Torah portion of the abduction and rape of his only daughter, Dinah. The violent retaliation of his sons against the perpetrators deeply pains Jacob. This is followed by the death in childbirth of his beloved wife, Rachel. Eventually, he must face the perceived death of his treasured son, Joseph. Jacob experiences deep sorrow, but since the night he "struggled with man and God," and also with his deepest inner self, he has learned to "trust in the LORD with all [his] heart" and has overcome the negative force of fear.

TO BE SHALEM

We read in the Torah that "Jacob arrived *shalem* (whole) in the city of Shechem in the land of Canaan" (Genesis 33:18). The Talmud describes this condition of *shalem* as being "whole in body, whole in [resources] money, whole in his Torah knowledge" (b.*Shabbat* 33b).

Rashi expounds that these three aspects are directly related to the trials Jacob had faced. Physically, he was healed from the lameness that he incurred during his struggle with the stranger; financially, he still had much wealth despite all the gifts he had given Esau, and spiritually, he had retained his boyhood learning of the ways of God, despite the twenty years of labor and living under the influence of Laban.

Even more meaningful is the consideration that the desirable state of *shalem* is not measured by quantity but in one's attitude and balanced approach to these three areas. Of prime importance is not how physically fit one is, how much money one has, or how much knowledge of the Word of God one has acquired. The pivotal question is: How do all these aspects of my life affect my character and my relationship with God and with others?

WHO IS RICH?

Pirkei Avot offers answers to the question of who is truly powerful, rich, and wise:

> Ben Zoma said: Who is wise? He who learns from every person, as it is said: "From all my teachers, I grew wise." Who is strong? He who subdues his personal inclination, as it is said, "He who is slow to anger is better than a strong man, and a master of his passions is better than a conqueror of a city." Who is rich? He who is happy with his lot, as it is said, "When you eat of the labor of your hands, you are praiseworthy, and all is well with you." "You are praiseworthy" in this world; and "all is well with you" in the World to Come. (*Pirkei Avot* 4:1)

Regarding the study of Torah, Rabbi Meir said,

> Whoever engages in Torah study for its own sake ... becomes like a steady, strengthening fountain and like an unceasing river. He becomes modest, patient, and forgiving of insult to himself. (*Pirkei Avot* 6:1)

It appears that when one is truly *shalem*, one is content and grateful for that which one has and is rich in love, joy, peace, patience, kindness, goodness, faithfulness, gentleness, and self-control. In other words, being *shalem* is to live a life abounding in the fruit of the Holy Spirit! (Galatians 5:22–23).

VAYESHEV

וישב – "And He Dwelt"

GENESIS 37:1–40:23

In Western, democratic thinking, the wide variety of choices, and the infinite number of options we are offered are what define our freedom. We are inundated with choices—from an endless array of breakfast cereals to an ever-expanding menu of TV programs. We are tempted, often subconsciously through sophisticated and clever advertising, to select the particular brand of the product offered. Where does God fit into this veritable ocean of choice?

THE FREEDOM OF CHOICE?

God asks only one thing of us: that we remember that all there is comes to us by his grace, from our first waking breath to the last flutter of our eyelids before we sleep. If we honor him as the Creator and provider of all, then we can in gratitude accept his kingship and the "yoke of his kingdom" in our life. Yeshua proclaims, as appointed King of the Father's kingdom, that the yoke is "easy and light" (Matthew 11:30). How can a yoke of commandments, which severely limits our choices, be easy and light?

We are presented with a perfect illustration of this freedom in the portion this week. Joseph was faced with a disturbing temptation in the form of Potiphar's wife. She was, no doubt, beautiful as well as powerful and could have bestowed many favors upon this young slave-attendant in her household. Joseph's freedom here is that he had no choice! He did not waver for a second, and replied, "Nor has he [Potiphar] kept back anything from me except you, because you are his wife." (Genesis 39:9). His answer expressed gratitude for his master's kindness and affirmed his Heavenly Master, who has made his will clear in every matter. God gives us the ability to choose. He created us in his image with a heart, will, and mind. If we surrender our will to his, we, in effect, return the right of choice to him in acknowledgment that he has the greater wisdom.

What rules my life? God's will or my own? This is our only real, basic life's choice, which then affects our choice in any matter that arises, whether profound or mundane. When we surrender our will and freedom of choice to the will of our Father God, then we find we truly are free to walk in his ways of redemption. *Pirkei Avot* 2:4 wisely expounds:

> [Rabban Gamliel, the son of Rabbi Judah HaNasi] used to say: "Treat His will as if it were your own will, so that He will treat your will as if it were His will. Nullify your will before His will, so that He will nullify the will of others [your enemies] before your will."

THE INTERCONNECTION OF DREAMS

We all are familiar with the famous dreams of Jacob, Joseph, and Pharaoh. Is there any connection between them? Jacob's dream described a unity between heaven and earth, with the ladder reaching to heaven with God at its head (Genesis 28:12-13). In Joseph's dreams, first, his brother' sheaves of wheat bow to his sheaf— indicating the future agricultural setting of Egypt—and then the sun, moon, and stars bow down to him, indicating the spiritual, heavenly realm. Just as Pharaoh's two dreams, of seven fat and lean cows and seven full and withered ears of corn, represented the same reality (Genesis 41:25), so can Joseph's two dreams be seen as one. At their core, his dreams reflect his father, Jacob's, dream—the interconnection of heaven and earth.

In Jacob's dream, God is the central figure. In Joseph's dreams, however, it is Joseph who is receiving the adulation. His brothers were incensed, and his father, Jacob, is perplexed by this, because, being Jews, they know that man bows down only to God. Having experienced his own dream-revelation of God, Jacob guarded (*shamar*) Joseph's dreams in his heart as he anxiously anticipated their realization (Genesis 37:10-11). The same terminology is used when Mary, the mother of

Yeshua, after witnessing the revelation of God in her life, also anxiously awaited the fulfillment in her son: "But Mary treasured up (*shamar*, "guarded") all these things, pondering them in her heart" (Luke 2:19).

MASHIACH BEN YOSEF – MESSIAH SON OF JOSEPH

We see a clear prototype of the Messiah Yeshua in Joseph. His Egyptian name, *Tzafnat-paneach*,[26] has interesting implications. *Tzafnat* means "food-man" (or bread-man) and *paneach*, "of life." Man of the bread of life! A possible Hebraic explanation of the name is "Interpreter of Secrets" or "Unraveler of the Hidden."[27]

The mystery of Joseph's dreams comes to fruition physically when he provides bread to a starving world during a disastrous famine. He was elevated to a noble position, and men, including his brothers, paid him homage. What of the cosmic, heavenly dimension of his dream? That mystery would be resolved only in *Mashiach ben Yosef*—Yeshua. He is the fullness of the combination of heaven and earth. He elevates earth to heaven as a man created on earth (*adamah*, "Adam"), and he brings heaven down to earth as the presence of God indwelling man. Paul tells us in Colossians:

> In [Messiah] are hidden all the treasures of wisdom and knowledge. (Colossians 2:3)

> For in him the whole fullness of deity dwells bodily. (Colossians 2:9)

The esteemed eighteenth-century Vilna Gaon pointed out that the twenty-fifth word of the Torah is *ohr*—light.[28] It was on the twenty-fifth day of the Hebrew month of Kislev that the victory of the Maccabees resulted in the miraculous lighting of the menorah in the cleansed and rededicated Temple. The light of God's Word dispersed the pagan Hellenistic darkness. It was in remembrance of this miracle that the Festival of Lights (Hanukkah) was instituted, which was celebrated by Yeshua himself (John 10:22).

Indeed, in this respect, we can make a connection with the celebration of the Messiah's birth—or, as some believe, his conception—on the twenty-fifth of December. The Light of the World broke into the darkness. The perfect, dynamic union of heaven and earth was accomplished. The connecting ladder was in place, and the heavenly host of angels filled the universe with song:

> Glory to God in the highest, and on earth peace among those with whom he is pleased! (Luke 2:14)

The full outworking of this great vision of redemption is still being "guarded" in our hearts, but we know that the day of *Mashiach ben David*, Messiah son of David—the King of kings—will break through in the final consummation that will establish God's perfect will of peace and unity in all the earth.

MIKETZ

מִקֵץ – "At the End"

GENESIS 41:1–44:17

The parashah describes the thirty-year-old Joseph's meteoric rise from the status of prisoner to second-in-command of the nation of Egypt. Pharaoh recognized his outstanding ability to interpret his dreams accurately, but also, he says, "Can we find a man like this, a man in whom is the Spirit of God?" (Genesis 41:38). Joseph humbly acknowledged, from the start, that the power of interpretation was not his own power but that "God will give Pharaoh an answer of peace" (Genesis 41:16). Rabbi Hertz notes that this means "an answer that will correspond to the needs of Pharaoh and his people."[29]

Not only did Joseph explain the dreams, but he also listed practical steps to be implemented in order to avert the disaster of famine from the nation as foretold in the dreams. Pharaoh realized that indeed this young, exceptional man before him was empowered and inspired by One greater than he—One in whose hands rested not only Joseph's life but also the life of his own nation.

OH, BROTHER!

Due to Joseph's successful overseeing of Egypt's survival through the famine, "all the countries" came to him to buy corn "because the famine was severe over all the earth" (Genesis 41:57). Consequently, at the height of his governance, Joseph's ten older brothers arrived in his presence seeking sustenance for the survival of their families in Canaan.

We read that they "bowed themselves before him with their faces to the ground" (Genesis 42:6). Joseph's first dream was fulfilled!

In the light of the significant events that are in the process of unfolding, the title of the portion could well indicate that "at the end" all turns out for the best, or in English vernacular: "All's well that ends well!" However, at this particular phase of the developing drama between Joseph and his brothers, the outcome is not yet known—and the tension is almost palpable. What would Joseph's reaction be to this appearance of his brothers who, with murder in their hearts, had betrayed him and sold him into slavery? They were now at his mercy, for he "saw his brothers and recognized them, but he treated them like strangers" (Genesis 42:7).

What action would he take? Joseph exercised amazing self-control and exhibited the qualities that caused him to become known in rabbinic literature as "the righteous one." David R. Blumenthal, quoting the teaching of Levi Yitzhak of Berditchev, indicates that human nature being what it is, the majority of people would leap at the chance to lord it over someone else, particularly a perceived enemy. He points out that Joseph did not do so; instead, he set a righteous example "by hiding his identity so that his brothers not be embarrassed."[30]

This kindness attributed to Joseph could also provide an answer to the question: Why, after he had risen to a position of power, did Joseph not make an effort to contact his beloved father, Jacob, but instead allowed him to suffer all those years under the misconception that his favored son was dead? He may have considered that, if he had done so, he would immediately have exposed the behavior and lies of his brothers. Joseph had indeed grown strong in spirit and character since the days when he was a talebearer against his brothers (Genesis 37:2).

TO CLING OR TO SPLIT?

In connection with the subject of marital relationships, let us reconsider the key verse mentioned above: "Joseph saw his brothers and he recognized them, but he treated them like strangers" (Genesis 42:7). Levi Yitzhak highlights the fact that in Hebrew, the words "recognize" (*vayakkirem*) and "treated them like strangers" (*vayitnakker*) are from the same root, though they have opposite meanings. This is fairly common in Semitic languages but rare in the Indo-European languages.[31] David Blumenthal gives a good example of one of these rare anomalies in English. "The best example in English is the verb 'cleave,' which can mean both 'to cling to' and 'to split.'" [32] This example, albeit serendipitously, ties in with the scenario—certainly, Joseph must have longed to "cling" to his estranged brothers, but instead, he kept his distance and maintained the "split" between them.

Another example of this word-play can be found in the renowned verse, "Therefore shall a man leave his father and his mother, and shall cleave unto his wife: and they shall be one flesh" (Genesis 2:24). The "cleaving" of husband and wife in marriage is the uniting of two beings that were designed by God to be one. At Creation, man was originally one being made in the image of God, until he "split" them in two. By God's design, much that human nature requires for its completion—physically, socially, and spiritually—is to be found in one's spouse, who can literally be seen as one's "other half." Adam and Eve were the example of God's design for the uniting of one man and one woman in the sacred mystery of marriage. Together they restore the fullness of the image of God.

In unity, just as the first couple, a husband and wife share the joys and the burdens of life. Together they carry the responsibilities of working toward the goals of building a home and raising a family and of providing loving companionship for one another. In so doing, they achieve the state indicated by the Hebrew word for marriage—*kiddushin* ("hallowing/sanctifying, making holy"). Marriage, when in accordance with God's will and intention, is, as Rabbi Hertz explains:

> The hallowing of two human beings to life's holiest purposes. In married life man finds his truest and most lasting happiness; and ... the human personality reaches its highest fulfillment. [33]

Positive "splitting" as with Adam and Eve, and that which occurs at a cellular level, for example, in the growth of a fetus, brings life and a consequent "cleaving." Negative separation and divisive "splitting" are never in harmony with God's perfect plans for his beloved children. The chief aim of the Adversary of our souls is to cause destructive separation and negation of all that God intends to be united in harmony and fullness of life. The appellation "foe" could well be an acronym for the "Force of Estrangement."

As we proceed with the narrative of Joseph and his brothers, the questions remain: Will there be reconciliation, a healing of the split, between the brothers? And how on earth can this be brought about?

VAYIGASH

ויגש – "And He Came Near"

GENESIS 44:18–47:27

Joseph was confronted once again, after a separation of twenty years, with the presence of his brothers. He is faced with a decision that carries dynamic tension. Have his brothers grown spiritually during his long absence, or are they still carrying animosity in their hearts? Have their characters matured and strengthened, or have they remained callous to the fate of their brother and the suffering of their father? If the latter is the case, perhaps Joseph will choose to remain a "stranger" to them (Genesis 42:7). He realized that this would preclude reconciliation and would mean bearing the pain of continued separation from his father.

THE CRUX OF THE MATTER

Joseph's hope lies in the gift that God has given each of his children, that of growth and change. Abraham Joshua Heschel describes it well: "The being of a person is never completed, final. Being human means being on the way, striving, waiting, hoping!"[34] We all are on the path to becoming. The key element of positive growth is another God-endowed gift—repentance. As we reach the climax of the encounter between Joseph and his brothers, Judah (Yehudah) steps forward and proceeds to pour out his heart in an appeal that brings the account to its zenith and the crux of the matter is revealed.

In sixteen verses (Genesis 44:19–34), Judah reveals that he and his brothers are in a place of recognition of their past sin and have experienced true repentance. He confesses that they had caused their father immense pain once before, with the loss of a beloved son, and they cannot bear to inflict that pain upon him again by "losing" Benjamin. Three things become clear to Joseph as Judah presents his plea:

1. His brothers love their father and hold him in high esteem.
2. They admit they have caused him grief.
3. Judah is fully prepared to offer himself as a prisoner in the place of Benjamin.

We witness here a reflection of the elements that are prominent in the lives of children of God toward our Father in heaven: love, confession, and coming before him in prayer and submission of self.

We have seen a striking prophetic association between Joseph and Mashiach ben Yosef, Messiah son of Joseph. Let us, here, briefly examine another layer of comparison. Judah can represent the sinner who has betrayed his brother and also the love of his heavenly Father and caused him great pain. By the confession of his sin, and in offering a sincere prayer of restitution, he proves that his love is still strong and that he yearns for reconciliation and the restoration of full, loving relationship.

Joseph, in this scenario, can represent both the Father and the Son, who were betrayed. His heart of love is deeply moved, and he joyfully and without reservation receives the prayer of repentance and is reconciled with his children/brothers.

BUT GOD!

There has been much debate regarding the incident of the mysterious sale of Joseph as a slave in Egypt (Genesis 37:25-30). Who sold him? Rashi suggests that a number of his brothers removed him from the pit and sold him to the Ishmaelites. Reuben was not included, as verses 29-30 make clear. The Rashbam,[35] on the other hand, proposes that the Midianites heard his cries and took him from the pit and sold him to the Ishmaelites.[36]

In one of the most dramatic scenes in the Bible, Joseph reveals his identity to his brothers by first reminding them of the fact that they were responsible for his sale as a slave. "I am your brother, Joseph, whom you sold into Egypt" (Genesis 45:4). They already have made it clear that they regretted their betrayal and actions, and he hastens to reassure them: "Now, do not be distressed or angry with yourselves because you sold me here, for God sent me before you to preserve life" (Genesis 45:5). Joseph exhibits great depth of wisdom and forgiveness with these words. One is naturally inclined to harbor much distress and anger at oneself over past sins and mistakes. Joseph here extends the comforting reassurance that true godly forgiveness is full and free, and it washes away any need for bitter recrimination—of others or oneself.

No doubt, Joseph's brothers' minds are reeling at this revelation, and Joseph explains that the hand of God had been working behind the scenes to preserve the lives of many on the earth, including those of his brothers and their families. He adds, in an allusion to the future, historic destiny of the Israelites: "to save you alive for a great deliverance" (Genesis 45:7). His crowning comment places everything in its eternal perspective: "So it was not you who sent me here, but God!" (Genesis 45:8).

VAYECHI

ויחי – "And He Lived"

GENESIS 47:28–50:26

Joseph undoubtedly is one of the most imposing characters of the Bible. His story is dramatic—a young slave, then prisoner, who experiences a sudden, unexpected rise to the grand position of governor and becomes ruler, second only to Pharaoh, over the mighty kingdom of Egypt. He lives a life of royalty, is widely honored, and wields great power and authority. He is a strong, well-respected man—and yet he unashamedly weeps. His example certainly undermines the truth of the Western adage that declares, "Big boys don't cry!"

JOSEPH: A MAN WHO WEEPS

We can recall previous occasions. First, when Joseph overheard his estranged brothers recognizing and confessing their sin against him as a boy (Genesis 42:21–24). Then again when he first saw his younger brother Benjamin, son of his mother, Rachel (Genesis 43:30), and once more when he revealed his true identity to his brothers:

> He wept aloud, so that the Egyptians heard it, and the household of Pharaoh heard it. (Genesis 45:2)

This concluding parashah of B'reisheet records further brother-to-brother and father-to-son encounters that cause Joseph to weep. It is not a weeping of self-pity, nor as a result of injury; rather, it is an expression of emotion that is too deep for words, one that stems from the aching love of the soul.

THE RIFT OF RESENTMENT

There is much to be learned in this parashah regarding family relationships. Many unnecessary and painful rifts are caused within families—between parents and children, between siblings, and even between husband and wife—due to the bitterness and resentment that builds when forgiveness is not extended for real or imaginary slights and injuries. The soul holds onto and nurtures the injury, and the heart becomes hardened toward the other person and, unless it is addressed and healed, a life-long rift can be sustained.

A central focus this week is the climactic deathbed scene when Jacob gathers his sons around his bedside to bestow his blessings upon them before he dies. We are told that Jacob's eyes were dim with age (Genesis 48:10). Rabbi Shlomo Riskin[37] quotes Resh Lakish, a talmudic sage, who suggests that Jacob's eyes were clouded over with fear and anxiety as he saw his now very Egyptian-looking sons assembled around his deathbed:

> "Perhaps invalid and improper fruit have emerged from my loins, just as Ishmael emerged from Abraham and Esau emerged from Isaac," thought Jacob. The sons replied, "Hear, O Israel [our father] the LORD is the God of love, our LORD, the God of justice, is the One God of love. Just as you love Joseph unconditionally, so do we hope that you will love us unconditionally. And the result will be that, despite external appearances, just as in your heart there is only One, so in our hearts will there be only One." (b.*Pesachim* 56a)

With grateful relief, Jacob whispers, "*Baruch shem kevod malchuto, l'olam va'ed.*" Blessed be his holy Name, his kingdom is eternal. Riskin concludes, "And so it was: all twelve sons succeed in establishing the twelve tribes of Israel."

God is a God of love, as indicated by his ineffable Name *Yod-Hei-Vav-Hei* (Y/H/V/H). *Hu hayah, hu hoveh, hu yihyeh*—He was, he is, and he will be. His Presence and his love are always with us—in our past, in the present, and will be throughout the future. As Paul points out in his letter to the Romans: "[Nothing] in all creation, will be able to separate us from the love of God in [Messiah Yeshua] our Lord" (Romans 8:39).

LEADER OF ISRAEL

Jacob's final blessing of Joseph includes referring to him as: "A son who is a fruitful bough by a fountain spring" (Genesis 49:22). In Hebrew this is *ben porat alei ayin*. Rashi comments that this phrase can also be translated as,

> A son of grace (*porat* is related to an Aramaic word meaning grace) to the eye, "To the eye," means "His gaze is directed towards the eye [of God] that sees him."

Joseph's natural grace and beauty could have been his downfall, as we saw in the incident with Potiphar's wife. However, he never became vain nor took advantage of his good looks. Jacob here emphasizes how Joseph had wisely controlled this gift the LORD had graced him with and always employed it only to the glory of God and in his service.

Despite Joseph's prominence and outstanding character, and Reuben's right as firstborn, the question still looms: "Who would Jacob choose as the leader of the family in his place?" The sons all know that their father would be directed in his choice by the LORD alone. This is established when he proclaims to Yehudah (Judah), "your brothers shall praise you; your hand shall be on the neck of your enemies; your father's sons shall bow down before you" (Genesis 49:8), or, as Hertz translates, "to you will your brothers do homage. Your hand (natural authority) and not your sword will hold sway over your enemies."[38]

Sforno[39] comments: "His wars are won by God and not by force of arms."

Prophetically, Jacob sees down through the ages that from Yehudah would come forth *Shiloh*: "To him shall be the obedience of the peoples. Binding his foal to the vine and his donkey's colt to the choice vine" (Genesis 49:11). Could this be a foretelling of the Messiah, the Lion of the tribe of Judah, who would be the redeemer of nations and yet appear humbly riding on a donkey?

When Jacob gave his final blessings, we read that he blessed each "with the blessing suitable to him" (Genesis 49:28). Jacob left the family an inheritance of family unity, but he did not enforce uniformity. The *Ohr HaChayim*[40] explains that Jacob blessed his sons in accordance with the innermost spiritual characteristic of each. *Chazal* state that each person is born with his or her own unique personality and destiny. We need to recognize the gift God has given us and to develop ourselves accordingly. Each person should aim to establish his or her inner foundation before he or she can progress in the purposes of God and move forward on the path for which he or she is destined by God.

To bestow a blessing can be compared to placing a shining crown upon someone's head. What an honor it is to convey our love and appreciation, and when necessary, our gracious forgiveness toward a member of the family or to a friend. We can see it as placing a beautiful crown of blessing upon the person's head. What added meaning is derived when we remember the words of Yeshua: "The King will answer them, 'Truly, I say to you, as you did it to one of the least of these my brothers, you did it to me'" (Matthew 25:40). Let us crown him with many crowns!

ENDNOTES

1. Nehama Leibowitz, *Studies in Bereshit / Genesis*, (Jerusalem, Israel: WZO). See introduction by Aryeh Newman, xxxi.
2. Aryeh Newman, "The Devout Jew and His Literature," *Jewish Life* vol. XXV, August 1958: 6.
3. Prof. Moshe Kaveh, president of Bar-Ilan University, Tel Aviv. *Professors on the Parasha* (Ed: Leib Moscovitz, Jerusalem, Israel; New York, NY: Urim Publications, 2005).
4. Rebbe Nachman of Breslev (1772–1810), classic teacher of Chasidic thought, great grandson of the Baal Shem Tov, the founder of Chasidism.
5. Rabbi Lazer Brody, *The Trail to Tranquility*, (Israel: Kalcom Publishers, 2007), 234.
6. Ibid., 234.
7. Nehama Leibowitz, *Studies in Bereshit/Genesis*, 2.
8. Matthew 22:21; Mark 12:17; Luke 20:25.
9. The rains that caused the flood fell for forty days. It is of interest to note that forty is considered the number that represents cleansing and purifying in the Bible. For example, there are forty measures of water in a traditional mikvah (ritual purification pool/bath) that is constructed to serve a community.
10. Matthew 3:16; Mark 1:10; Luke 3:22; John 1:32.
11. Rabbi Bradley Shavit Artson, *The Bedside Torah: Wisdom, Visions and Dreams* (New York, NY: McGraw Hill, 2001), 215.
12. Nehama Leibowitz, *Studies in Bereshit/Genesis* (Jerusalem, Israel: World Zionist Organization), 114.
13. Rashi – Rabbi Shlomo Yitzchaki (1040–1105), France. In 1475, his commentary on the Torah was the first Hebrew book printed.
14. Ramban (1194–1270, Spain), Rabbi Moshe ben Nachman, aka Nachmanides; talmudic scholar, a master of *halacha* (practical religious rulings) and ethics.
15. *Chazal* – Jewish sages of earlier centuries; an acronym *chet-zayin-lamed* for *Chachamim zichronam levracha*, meaning, "The wise of blessed memory."

16 Avivah Zornberg in *The Beginning of Desire, Reflections on Genesis* (New York, NY: Shocken Books, 1995), 162. Lev Shestov, Russian-Jewish author of *Athens and Jerusalem* holds that Greek thought is radically reflective rather than passionate; its face turned toward death rather than life. He writes: "Philosophy has always meant and wished to mean reflection ... looking backward ... [which] by its very nature, excludes the possibility and even the thought of struggle. 'Looking backward' paralyzes man."

17 Abravanel – (or Abarbanel) Don Isaac (1437–1508), Lisbon, Portugal – Venice, Italy. As well as a Bible commentator, he was Finance Minister to the kings of Portugal, Spain, and Naples. He nevertheless suffered expulsion in 1492 during the Spanish Inquisition.

18 Nehama Leibowitz, *Studies in Bereshit / Genesis*, 201.

19 J.H. Hertz, *The Pentateuch and Haftorahs* (London, England: Soncino Press, 1997), 87. Rabbi Samson Raphael Hirsch, (1808–1888), Frankfurt-on-Main, Germany. Outstanding Jewish educator and Bible commentator.

20 Avivah Zornberg, *The Beginning of Desire – Reflections on Genesis,* (New York, NY: Shocken Books, 1995), 398.

21 Nehama Leibowitz, *Studies in Bereshit / Genesis*, 259.

22 Seymour Rossel, *When a Jew Prays* (Springfield, NJ: Behrman Publishing, 1973), 152.

23 Nosson Scherman, *An Overview/Prayer, a Timeless Need*, (Artscroll Siddur, July 1984)

24 The sages note that the first letter of the Torah is a *bet* and the last one is a *lamed*. They combine as *lamed-bet* to spell *lev* (heart). Thus, all Torah, God's Word, expresses his heart and calls for a response from our hearts.

25 Rabbi Chanan Morrison, *Gold from the Land of Israel: A New Light on the Weekly Torah Portion – From the Writings of Rabbi Abraham Isaac HaKohen Kook* (Jerusalem, Israel: Urim Publications, 2006), 56.

26 See Rabbi J.H. Hertz's explanation in *The Pentateuch and Haftorahs* (Jerusalem, Israel: Soncino Press), 158.

27 Mentioned to me by Dov Chaiken, Hebrew expounder and mentor in Jerusalem.

28 Quoted by Rabbi Shlomo Riskin in his article "What Dreams Are Made Of," *Jerusalem Post*, December 3, 2004, which inspired my reflections here.

29 Rabbi Dr. J.H. Hertz, *The Pentateuch and Haftorahs*, 156.

30 David R. Blumenthal, *God at the Center, Meditations on Jewish Spirituality* (Northvale, NY: Jason Aronson, Inc., 1994), 31.

31 Ibid., 30.

32 Ibid.

33 Rabbi Dr. J.H. Hertz, *The Pentateuch and Haftorahs*, 931.

34 Abraham Joshua Heschel, *Who is Man?* (Redwood City, CA: Stanford University Press, 1965), 41.

35 Rashbam – Rabbi Shmuel ben Meir (1080–1158), a grandson of Rashi, who followed his style of commentary, viz. the *p'shat*, plain meaning of the text.

36 Nehama Leibowitz, *Studies in Bereshit/Genesis*, 495.

37 Rabbi Shlomo Riskin, *Toras Aish* commentery, *Vayechi*, 5765/2005, Vol. XII, No.15

38 Rabbi Dr. J.H. Hertz, *The Pentateuch and Haftorahs* 184.

39 Sforno—Ovadiah Sforno, Italian Bible commentator (1470–1550).

40 *Ohr HaChayim*—Bible commentary written by Chaim ibn Attar (Morocco, 1696–1743).

EXODUS

SHEMOT

שמות – "Names"

EXODUS 1:1–6:1

Names are prominent and of great significance in the biblical narrative, as indicated by the Hebrew name of the book of Exodus. The first task that God assigns to Adam in Eden is the naming of the animals and birds (Genesis 2:19). In this opening portion of Shemot, which follows the death of Joseph, we are introduced to a man who will be a central figure in the Bible and world history. He appears as a vulnerable three-month-old baby who is cast upon the waters of the Nile in a fragile, pitch-coated, woven basket in an attempt to save his life. Pharaoh's daughter drew him from the water and named him *M'sis*, an Egyptian name meaning "drawn from the water" (Exodus 2:10). We know him as Moses, in English, and *Moshe* in Hebrew, which carry a similarity in sound—the swishing of movement in water.

THE BIG FISH

In rabbinic writing there is an understanding that Messiah can be compared to a "big fish." Moses is seen as a messianic figure. The one whom God chooses to draw his people out of bondage in Egypt is himself drawn forth from the water like a "big fish." Fish are concealed, hidden from view until brought forth into the light. The identity of Yeshua as Messiah was first revealed when John the Immerser announced, "Behold the Lamb of God who takes away the sin of the world!" Then, after Yeshua immersed himself in the waters of the Jordan, the Gospel of Matthew describes how God gloriously confirms Yeshua's identity:

> Immediately he went up from the water, and behold, the heavens were opened to him, and he saw the Spirit of God descending like a dove and coming to rest on him; and behold, a voice from heaven said, "This is my beloved Son, with whom I am well pleased." (Matthew 3:16-17)

Rabbi Yitzchak Ginsburgh, in his book on Jewish thought as revealed in the Hebrew Letters,[1] indicates that the letters of "big fish" (*dag gadol*) total fifty, the value of the Hebrew letter *nun*, which in Aramaic means "fish." The *nun* has two forms: נ the initial letter, which is bent—bowed in humility as it were—and is referred to as the "servant," and the final letter ן (*nun sofit*), which is straight and upright, like a king's scepter. A compact picture of the Servant Messiah son of Joseph who returns in the end as the King Messiah son of David.[2]

In the days of Jubilee, when the King of kings, the Lamb upon the throne, inaugurates his kingdom in all the earth it will be, as Ginsburgh states:

> [As] in the verse of Isaiah with which the Rambam[3] concludes his book of Jewish Law (whose final section, The Laws of Kings culminates with the description of the coming of *Mashiach*): "They shall not hurt or destroy in all my holy mountain, for the earth will be filled with the knowledge of G-d, like the waters cover the sea" (Isaiah 11:9).

The fullness of Messiah will be revealed, and the original element created by God for mankind, the state of holiness filled with his presence and glory, will once again be established as fully as "the waters cover the seabed."

TIMIDITY OR HUMILITY?

The parashah contains the powerful account of the burning bush, where God chooses to reveal himself in a burst of supernatural fire to his unsuspecting servant, Moses. We are told that, after going out of his way to see the phenomenon, when God speaks, "Moses hid his face, for he was afraid to look at God" (Exodus 3:6).

In his writings, Rav Kook[4] poses the questions, "Was his response an appropriate display of awe and reverence? Or did it reflect a flaw in Moses' personality, a sign of unwarranted timidity?"[5] Rav Kook highlights differing answers that appear in the Talmud (*Brachot* 7a): Rabbi Yehoshua ben Korcha noted how God would later deny Moses' request to see His face (Exodus 33:23):

> In effect, God told Moses: "When I wanted [at the burning bush] you did not want. Now that you want, I do not want."

Due to Moses' initial timidity and fear, he forfeited the opportunity to see the fullness of God's face at the time he chose to reveal it.

Rabbi Yochanan, on the other hand, argued that Moses' action was praiseworthy. As a reward for hiding his face, Moses merited that his face would shine with a brilliant light as he descended from Mount Sinai (Exodus 34:29).

Moses exhibits a further timid reaction when God assigns him the great redemptive project.

> Behold, the cry of the people of Israel has come to me, and I have also seen the oppression with which the Egyptians oppress them. Come, I will send you to Pharaoh that you may bring my people, the children of Israel, out of Egypt. (Exodus 3:9–10)

We can imagine the doubts that filled Moshe's mind. He had escaped from Egypt in fear for his life, how could he return? How could he deliver God's message to his own people, let alone the mighty Pharaoh? He did not have the words, and, no doubt, he would stammer and stutter hopelessly.

THE DAY IS SHORT

An apt and wise maxim in *Pirkei Avot*, "The Sayings of the Fathers," could apply to this scenario: "Rabbi Tarphon said: The day is short, the task is great, the workmen are sluggish, and the Employer is insistent" (*Pirkei Avot* 2:20).

Rabbi S.R. Hirsch comments on the above *pasuk* (verse):

> Life is short and the task each individual must complete on earth is great, yet men are slow to complete their work ... Yet the reward we may expect is great and rich, it is a sense of God's approval and of His blessed nearness, the happy

knowledge of duty loyally discharged. Divine aid in this life and bliss in the life to come.[6]

Our "Employer," God himself, has assigned each of his servants a special mission to perform in his service. The duties and tasks involved are as varied as the individuals themselves, and each is of inestimable significance in God's overarching plan of bringing his redemption to all the earth. He constantly longs to reveal the radiance of his face to us, to clarify our purpose and calling, to offer us all the Divine aid we need and, in eternity, to heap upon us untold reward and blessing. May we have enough faith to respond!

We read in the continuing narrative that Moses fulfills his task as a humble, faithful servant of the Almighty God. He is a true forerunner of the Servant Messiah. Preceding the final great redemption, we read:

> They sing the song of Moses, the servant of God, and the song of the Lamb, saying, "Great and amazing are your deeds, O Lord God the Almighty! Just and true are your ways, O King of the nations! Who will not fear, O Lord, and glorify your name? For you alone are holy. All nations will come and worship you, for your righteous acts have been revealed." (Revelation 15:3-4)

VA'ERA

וָאֵרָא – "And I Appeared"

EXODUS 6:2–9:35

During this dramatic encounter in the wilderness of Sinai, God says to Moses: "I appeared to Abraham, to Isaac, and to Jacob, as God Almighty, but by my name the LORD I did not make myself known to them" (Exodus 6:3). The Hebrew name God used in his appearances to the patriarchs was *El Shaddai*. Now, it seems, he is giving a further understanding of Himself by announcing His ineffable Name, spelled with the four Hebrew letters *yod-hei-vav-hei* and generally pronounced today as HaShem (the Name) or Adonai, the LORD.

KNOWING GOD

The two verbs used in the above verse are forms of "appear" and "know." We realize that God has chosen to "appear" to mankind throughout history, and he desires to be known, but how can we truly know God? Knowing requires meeting and intimate communication, and this requires a place of meeting. In his grace, he has provided a path to this place. David Blumenthal, in his book *God at the Center*, refers to the teaching of Levi Yitzchak[7] who proposes that to come to any knowledge of God,

> One has no choice but to come to Him by means of three types of service: study of Torah, prayer, and acts of charity. These are, so to speak, the letters of God's Name.[8]

A name is a reflection of the character of a person. Levi Yitzchak indicates that by performing the acts of studying the Word so that it becomes part of one's very being, of worship and prayer, and in acts of kindness to others, we, in effect, are imitating God and building our character in accordance with his. We gradually come to know him and to be like him. The way to knowing God, therefore, is the path of obedient service.

Yeshua likewise states to his followers, "I do nothing on my own authority, but speak just as the Father taught me" (John 8:28). He continued by saying, "If you abide in my word, you are truly my disciples, and you will know the truth, and the truth will set you free" (John 8:31–32). He emphasizes the connection of knowledge of God and obeying his Word when he proclaims: "I do know [God] and I keep his word" (John 8:55). Yeshua also taught his disciples to pray, and he exhorted them to perform acts of kindness:

> In the same way, [as a lamp is lit and placed on a stand to give light to all in the house] let your light shine before others, so that they may see your good works and give glory to your Father who is in heaven. (Matthew 5:16)

In loving, devoted service in the Holy Place, as it were, we discover that God is faithfully waiting to receive us into the holy of holies of his Presence. It is a glorious expression and experience of love. To reach this place of "knowing" intimacy, we find it requires reaching beyond our analytical, knowing mind and dying to self-consciousness. In this freedom we can enter an intimate immersion into the One who is love.

AARON'S ROD

It is of interest to note that although verse 12 of chapter 7 tells us that Aaron's rod and those of Pharaoh's court magicians turned into snakes, the verse concludes: "Aaron's rod swallowed up their rods." Why does it not say Aaron's snake swallowed the other snakes?

A rod is a symbol of authority and discipline. For example, Psalm 23 states, "Thy rod and Thy staff, they comfort me" (Psalm 23:4). One generally leans or rests upon a staff. It is a support. A rod, on the other hand, connotes guidance and discipline. The psalmist describes that both the discipline and the support of the Good Shepherd are a comfort.

In the wilderness, later in the narrative, we read how Aaron's rod miraculously produced almond buds and blossoms. This was an indication from God that Aaron is the one who is to serve as the high priest in the *Mishkan*—the Tabernacle—the Dwelling Place of God in their midst. He is awarded the place of spiritual authority.

One of the significant pieces of furniture in the holy place of the Tabernacle is one that resembles Aaron's rod in that God instructed that it must be decorated with almond blossoms and buds. The beautiful, golden menorah, with its constantly burning lamps, fueled with pure olive oil, is a symbol of God's light-bearing, life-giving Word, which is illumined by the Holy Spirit of God. It is this Word that is the ultimate authority, one that provides discipline and direction:

> Your Word is a lamp to my feet and a light to my path." (Psalm 119:105)

At the same time, it provides hope and comfort:

> I wait for the LORD, my soul waits, and in his word I hope." (Psalm 130:5)

God's Word is the light of life. It is this Light of the World that was incarnated and made flesh in the Living Word—Yeshua, the Anointed One—Messiah. He is all in all. Light, life, Word, high priest, and it is in his authority that all the "snakes" of the world are swallowed up and made of no effect:

> [Yeshua after his resurrection] came [to his disciples] and said to them, "All authority in heaven and on earth has been given to me. Go therefore and make disciples of all nations, baptizing them in the name of the Father and of the Son and of the Holy Spirit, teaching them to observe all that I have commanded you. And behold, I am with you always, to the end of the age." (Matthew 28:18-20)

We eagerly look forward to that day, as foretold by the Prophet Zechariah:

> The LORD will be king over all the earth. On that day the LORD will be one and his name one. (Zechariah 14:9)

BO

בֹּא – "Come"

EXODUS 10:1–13:16

In the hierarchical world of Pharaoh every person is assigned a place, with the large majority in servitude to the state. According to the dictates of this type of society, it is very difficult, if not impossible, to change one's station in life. Once a slave, always a slave. To facilitate the escape of their people from the bondage of slavery in Egypt, Moses and Aaron confronted the very premise upon which Pharaoh's kingdom was based. They were claiming the values of God's kingdom, also expressed in the American Declaration of Independence, that "all men are created equal" and the Creator of all has endowed each person with "unalienable rights," among these being "life, liberty, and the pursuit of happiness." The definition of these values, however, requires serious thought.

LIFE, LIBERTY, AND HAPPINESS

A large aspect of freedom is the ability to take responsibility for one's life and actions, to make decisions and to act upon them. A slave does not have these options. He does not own his life, and he, therefore, has no liberty. His "pursuit of happiness" is severely stunted as a result. The Hebrew name for Egypt is *Mitzrayim*, which means bonds or constrictions. As slaves, the Israelites were bound and constricted in Egypt. God's people, the family of Jacob, were beaten down, deprived of freedom, without hope or a future. Their cry was a wordless cry of utter futility and despair. A pain-filled, silent howl pierced the heavens.

God heard, and "God remembered his covenant with Abraham, with Isaac, and with Jacob. God saw the people of Israel—and God knew" (Exodus 2:24–25). What did he know? It seems, in part, that the time of their redemption from Egypt had come.

The power of God is made evident throughout the land of Egypt in a spectacular series of plagues until even the highest court officials and magicians declare that this is "the finger of God" (Exodus 8:19). Pharaoh, however, remains hardened and unrelenting until the climax of the final plague touches his and every Egyptian home with the death of their first-born. Finally, he issues the command to Moses: "Go!"

A HASTY DEPARTURE

In the middle of the night the door to freedom is open, but it may soon swing shut! By morning, Pharaoh may once again rescind his decision. The Israelites, however, are prepared. They had followed God's directions as given to Moses. A specially chosen lamb had been slaughtered, and its blood applied to the doorposts and lintels of their homes.

What then transpired became established by God as the Festival of Passover (*Pesach*) "as a statute forever" (Exodus 12:14, 17). On the evening that *Mal'ach haMavet* ("the Angel of Death") passed over their homes and entered those of the Egyptians, the Israelites had roasted the lamb and eaten it in haste, together with unleavened bread (*matzah*) and bitter herbs (*maror*). At midnight they were dressed, with their belts fastened, their feet shod with sandals and their staffs in their hands (Exodus 12:11). The command went forth, and they set out on their journey to physical and spiritual freedom, together with many Egyptians who had seen the power of the true God and had chosen to join them (Exodus 12:38).

The Festival of Pesach is a wonderful reminder that slavery can be overcome, and freedom is possible and real. We need to bear in mind, however, that a hasty, hurried dash for freedom is not the ideal. It is bound to be incomplete. A rushed, physical escape does not mean that one's soul and mental attitudes are altered and set free. Physical release and spiritual freedom do not automatically ensure inner peace and "happiness."

Midrash *Shemot Rabbah* addresses the fact of the rushed exodus from Egypt:

> In the Messianic era, ["when the LORD has bared his holy arm before the eyes of all the nations, and all the ends of the earth shall see the salvation of our God"] we are told, "You will not depart in haste, nor will you leave in flight." (Isaiah 52:10, 12)

The exodus from Egypt demonstrated that it is God's will that human beings be freed from bondage, able to stand upright with the liberty to make choices and take responsibility for their lives and actions. The reality of the limitations that accompany physical liberty is clear. As Rabbi Bradley Shavit-Artson describes: "Often ideals outstrip our ability to realize them; our dreams soar beyond our plans."[9] We are often beset with tribulations and become overwhelmed with frustration and disappointment. The "pursuit of happiness" seems futile. Again one raises a painful howl to heaven!

LAMB OF GOD

Once more, in the fullness of time, God hears man's cry of the heart, and this time he chooses the perfect, spotless Lamb—his own firstborn Son. Historically, the people of Israel are crying out for another physical liberation from the oppression of the Pharaoh-like Roman occupiers. This time, however, God desires that a deeper, more complete release from inner bondage be made available to all peoples. He offers a greater freedom in the precious shed blood of the Paschal Lamb to be applied in humility to the doorway of the heart. He cancels the effects of repented sin and makes the way for all to draw near to himself as redeemed children. The merciful Father offers the way and the opportunity to transcend physical limitations and to pursue true and lasting peace and joy through the fulfillment of his Living Word and by his Spirit of Holiness.

One like Moses—Yeshua, the Messiah of God—came as a servant. He left the glory of the fully Divine and became fully human. He took on the limitations and constrictions of physical existence to make possible the complete liberation of all humankind. He became the Passover Lamb, the striped and pierced unleavened bread, the cups of wine, the bitter herbs—all of which, if we partake, lead us into full liberation and redemption. In him, we can even now enter the "Messianic Era" without fear or haste, but with hearts filled with true hope and joy.

BESHALACH

בשלח - "When He Sent"

EXODUS 13:17–17:16

Ozi vezimrat Yah vayehi li lishu'ah.

The LORD is my strength and my song, and he has become my salvation. (Exodus 15:2)

The parashah this week contains this joyous proclamation of praise. Moses and the Israelites have just witnessed one of the great, supernatural acts of God on their behalf. The Reed Sea had parted. They had crossed through the walls of waters on the dry sea bed, and then the waters had descended to submerge and drown the pursuing forces of Egypt. The weakened, once enslaved people now realize that truly their salvation has come. The LORD has triumphed gloriously, and, finally, they are free.

Moses powerfully proclaims what will become known as "The Song at the Sea" (*Shirat haYam*)—a song that will echo throughout the ages amongst God's people. It is a song of remembrance and praise, one that is recited daily by observant Jews at the start of *Shacharit* (the morning prayer) weekly on Shabbat and annually at Passover. It is also a prophetic song as it is sung in anticipation of the great day of the full Divine Redemption. It will then be sung, together with the Song of the Lamb, by all the redeemed at the shore of another sea, a sea of "glass mingled with fire" (Revelation 15:2-4).

MOSES, ELIJAH, AND YESHUA

All repetition in the Bible is worthy of note and generally serves the purpose of emphasizing the context and a truth that is being conveyed. Our opening verse, Exodus 15:2, is the only verse that is repeated three times, once in each section of the Hebrew Scriptures (Torah, Nevi'im, Ketuvim—Torah, Prophets, and Writings). The corresponding two are found in Isaiah 12:2 and Psalm 118:14. This fact is worthy of our attention.

With reference to Isaiah, the verse states: "With joy shall you draw water from the wells of salvation." *Ush'avtem mayim besason mima'anei hayeshuah* (Isaiah 12:3). These prophetic verses in Isaiah are happily recited at the start of the weekly Havdalah service, which concludes the Shabbat and launches one into the week ahead. Havdalah ends with the song *Eliyahu haNavi*—a song of longing for the return of the Prophet Elijah, who will announce the arrival of the Messiah, the one who will raise the dead and be enthroned as King over all the earth.

In rabbinic commentary, Psalm 118 is recognized as a messianic psalm. It contains, among others, the celebrated verse: "Blessed is he who comes in the name of the LORD" (118:26). Following verse 14, the psalmist elaborates that the "stone the builders rejected has become the chief cornerstone" (22). This emphasizes the theme of building a habitation, a dwelling place, in the earth to house the *Shechinah* (the Dwelling Presence of God).

These verses were well known to the Jewish people at the time of the Second Temple. At the supernatural occurrence of the Transfiguration, the three disciples, Peter, James, and John, witnessed Yeshua's meeting with Moses and Elijah on the mount. Simon Peter was overwhelmed at the sight of the representation of the Torah, Prophets, and Sacred Writings standing together in glowing and glorious unity. Surely the Day had come—the Messiah had been revealed, and his throne would be established? Something had to be done, and Peter's spontaneous response was the desire to build something!

> Peter said to Jesus, "Lord, it is good that we are here. If you wish, I will make three tents (tabernacles, habitations) here, one for you and one for Moses and one for Elijah." (Matthew 17:4)

THIS IS MY GOD!

> *Zeh Eli v'anvehu, Elohei Avi va'aromemenhu!* (Exodus 15:2)
>
> This is my God and I will praise Him, my Father is God and I will exalt Him!

Midrash Rabbah, in *Shemot Rabbah* Beshalach 23 comments on this verse:

> God said to Israel: "In this world you have said only once before Me: 'This is my God,' but in the world to come you will say it twice, for it says, 'And it shall be said on that Day: "Lo, this is our God (Elohim), for whom we have waited that He might save us; this is the LORD for whom we have waited."'" (Isaiah 25:9)

Throughout history, our Father God has desired to dwell among his people. He longs for the eyes of his children to be opened to see him, and their hearts to respond and to cry out in wonder, "Behold! This is our God!"

There are interesting interpretations of verse 2. Onkelos, the 2,000-year-old Aramaic translation of the Bible, renders it this way: "This is my God and I shall build a temple for Him." The root of the word *v'anvehu* is *naveh*, which can be translated as "habitation."[10] Hence, Rabbi S.R. Hirsch gives the simple and beautiful interpretation: "This is my God and I shall become His house." He comments:

> I shall offer myself to Him as a habitation; all my life and my being shall become a temple to His glorification, a place in which He will be revealed.[11]

Indeed, this should be the natural result of one's eyes being opened to see and one's heart singing out: "This is my God! *Zeh Eli!*"

Yeshua, as the chief cornerstone, spoke of the "temple" of his body (John 2:20-21). The Apostle Paul exhorts us in 1 Corinthians 6:19, "Or do you not know that your body is a temple of the Holy Spirit within you, whom you have from God? You are not your own."

As the redeemed Israelite slaves discovered by divine revelation, the way to become a holy people lay not in God's mighty external miracles but in their inner transformation. To this end—to gradually and with greater intensity reflect his image through our own righteous acts—we have within us the Spirit of Messiah. This is our "hope of glory" as we joyfully celebrate our salvation with a new song on our lips and anticipate that great day of the final redemption when we shall see him as he is, and we shall be like him (I John 3:2).

Let us sing with grateful hearts:

> You are my God (Elohim), and I will give thanks to you; you are my God; I will extol you. Oh give thanks to the LORD, for he is good; for his steadfast love endures forever! (Psalm 118:28-29)

YITRO

יִתְרוֹ – "Jethro"

EXODUS 18:1–20:23

As the grand narrative of Exodus unfolds, we become aware of the equally grand themes that flow through it, such as those of redemption, revelation, rebellion, and the wonder of God's Presence in the midst of his people. We also see the transformation of the chief characters, Moses, Aaron, and Miriam, as well as the character of the Israelites as a people. All growth of character takes time, as American psychoanalyst Stephen Mitchell describes:

> Selves change and are transformed continually over time … a single life is composed of many 'selves.' The movement of a river cannot be grasped in a moment. Rivers and selves, like music and the narrative, take time to happen in.[12]

The liberated "selves" of the Israelites were initially disoriented, unsure, and incapable of appreciating the processes of God at work amongst them. It required the span of a generation to prepare them and to bring them to their destination of the land promised by God to their forefathers.

THE NATURE OF A MAN

In this week's parashah, named after him, we see the appearance "center-stage" of Moses' father-in-law, Jethro. The immediate clue to the depth and integrity of this man's character is presented to us in the opening verse, "Jethro rejoiced for all the good that the LORD had done for Israel" (Exodus 18:9). Verses 7–12 reveal several facts, including:

1. Jethro is in good relationship and communication with Moses, who, after welcoming him into his tent along with his wife and their two sons, freely shares with him all the details of the redemptive acts of God in delivering the Israelites from their bondage in Egypt.
2. Jethro is good-hearted and generous of soul. He rejoices in the blessings of God upon others.
3. He is not a flatterer. He does not bolster the ego of his son-in-law by heaping praise upon him. Instead, he recognizes the good that God has done and gives him the glory.

This account is also a reflection of the character of Moses. We can safely assume that in his recounting of the exodus from Egypt, he gave God the honor, desiring none for himself. This is confirmed in the Scriptures, which tell us: "Now the man Moses was very meek (humble), more than all people who were on the face of the earth" (Numbers 12:3).

Moses' humility is tested, as Jethro observes during the ensuing days, when "the people all came to Moses *lidrosh Elohim*, "to seek God" (Exodus 18:15). To be the center of attention and to be seen to speak for God can be a cause for pride in any person. This does not seem to concern Jethro, however, for he knows Moses well. Instead, his concern and the wisdom of his experience as a leader are directed toward his son-in-law's stamina and welfare, as well as toward the good of the people.

The Midrash, in *Pirkei Avot* 5:21, also assures us of the upright character of Moses:

> He who leads the multitude to righteousness shall have no sin come into his hand, but he who leads the multitude to sin shall not get the opportunity to succeed in his repentance. Moshe was righteous and led the multitude to righteousness. The righteousness of the multitude was ascribed to him forever, as it is said, "He performed the righteousness of God and his righteous ordinances remained with Yisrael."

THE NATURE OF A PEOPLE

At the summit of Mount Sinai, we reach, as it were, the center and height of the book of Shemot/Exodus. Here, God chooses to reveal the glory of his Presence and, for the first time in history, presents the concept of a people chosen to be in a unique relationship with himself.

He says: "Now therefore, if you will indeed obey my voice and keep my covenant, you shall be my treasured possession (*segulah*) among all peoples, for all the earth is mine; and you shall be to me a kingdom of priests and a holy nation" (Exodus 19:5-6). The Hebrew word *segulah* indicates an exclusive, treasured possession, to which no-one except its owner is entitled. In the context of the relationship between a husband and wife, God was choosing Israel as his bride.

Any choice implies an option and a decision, as well as a particular purpose for the choice. Why is something chosen? For what is it chosen? The biblical text makes it clear that these descendants of Abraham, Isaac, and Jacob are chosen to be "priests/servers" and to be "holy" so that they might bear the Word and knowledge of God to "all the earth," which is his.

This covenant relationship, established at Sinai, is intended to begin and to be an example of an intimate relationship between God and all the peoples of the earth. This is expressed in the glorious description of the dedication of the First Temple by King Solomon in 1 Kings 8, and is further clarified by the Prophet Isaiah:

> The foreigners who join themselves to the LORD, to minister to him, to love the name of the LORD, and to be his servants, everyone who keeps the Sabbath and does not profane it, and holds fast my covenant—these I will bring to my holy mountain, and make them joyful in my house of prayer; ... for my house shall be called a house of prayer for all peoples. (Isaiah 56:7)

COVENANT RESPONSIBILITY

A relationship of covenant love requires two partners who have the power and choice to either affirm or negate the relationship. To enter a covenant relationship with God places great responsibility in the hands of his people. The basic requirements of that relationship are given when God speaks the "Ten Words" (Exodus 20:1-17). The first set of five acknowledge God's sovereignty and our duties toward him, and the second set outlines our responsibilities toward one another.

Is there a relational connection between the Decalogue and the reference to the dwelling of God as a House of Prayer? Prayer, *tefillah*, indicates intimate communication. To speak to God indicates an awareness of his Presence. The Apostle Paul exhorts us to "pray without ceasing" (1 Thessalonians 5:17). This is an encouragement to recognize our Father's constant presence and his faithful hand always graciously at work in our lives. He is the source of our life, our hope in times of trouble, and our faithful provider. If the meaning of our lives—our identities and purpose—is derived from God our Father, then the nurturing of our relationship with him is of primary importance. Neglected prayer reflects a neglected relationship, just as neglect to communicate in a marriage reflects a sad disconnection between the husband and wife.

Gary Thomas, in his book *Sacred Marriage*,[13] draws attention to Peter's significant exhortation: "Husbands, live with your wives in an understanding way, showing honor [esteem them as a *segulah*] to the woman as the weaker vessel, since they are heirs with you of the grace of life, so that your prayers may not be hindered" (1 Peter 3:7). This denotes that there is an association between a man's attitude toward and treatment of his wife, reflected in his communication with her, and the efficacy of his prayer—his communication with his God. If one considers prayer as a vital indication of intimate relationship with our Father in heaven, then it stands to reason that this will be reflected in the one relationship in a man's life that carries the same need and capacity for intimate communion.

We cherish and nurture the living things we see as precious and valuable, whether it is a growing child, a plant, an animal, or a relationship. When we nurture our marriage relationships, which are designed to be an earthly reflection and complementary outworking of our unity and harmony with our God, his reality will be made manifest more clearly in our lives, and he will be glorified.

As a husband and wife are able to demonstrate in deed and word that all they do stems from genuine love and a sincere concern for the other, trust will grow, and they will be enabled to offer themselves to one another more fully and selflessly. They will grow in common union and the joy of intimacy. So it is with the Beloved of our souls.

MISHPATIM

מִשְׁפָּטִים – "Judgments"

EXODUS 21:1–24:18

The parashah this week begins with eighty-four verses of clear and succinct directions given in rapid succession, all of which pertain to the lives of God's people. Immediately after relaying this list to Moses, God gives assurance of his constant Presence with them and of his protection and guidance en route to "the place I have prepared" (Exodus 23:20). An exhortation and accompanying promises also are given:

> You shall serve the LORD your God, and he will bless your bread and your water, and I will take sickness away from among you. None shall miscarry or be barren in your land; I will fulfill the number of your days. (Exodus 23:25–26)

In the context of this chapter we see that worship is linked with obedience, "Pay attention to all that I have said to you" (Exodus 23:13), and also with covenant, "You shall make no covenant with [your enemies] or with their gods" (Exodus 23:32).

COVENANT AND CLOUD – OBEDIENCE AND GLORY

Covenant is a mutual pact that requires willing and wholehearted agreement. After Moses conveys God's words to the Israelites and reads the Book of the Covenant before them, they respond: "All that the LORD has spoken we will do, and we will be obedient" (Exodus 24:7). Moses then sprinkles sacrificial blood on the altar and on the people, and says, "Behold the blood of the covenant that the LORD has made with you in accordance with all these words."

The covenant is sealed with blood, which represents life. "For the life of the flesh is in the blood; and I have given it for you upon the altar to make atonement for your souls" (Leviticus 17:11). Fresh in the minds of each Israelite family is the memory of the blood of the lamb that they daubed on the doorframe of their home in Egypt. The sign of the blood had spared their lives and signaled their freedom. They are willing to obey now, as they had then.

Once the covenant is established, Moses, Aaron, and his sons, and seventy elders ascend Mount Sinai where they witness the Presence of the LORD. In an amazing foreshadowing of the Supper of the Lamb, we are told, "They beheld God, and ate and drank" (Exodus 24:11). Yeshua perfectly recaptures this glorious experience when, at his last Passover meal in Jerusalem with his disciples, he breaks the unleavened bread representing his body and gives it to them to eat of it. Then,

> He took a cup, and when he had given thanks he gave it to them, saying, "Drink of it, all of you; for this is my blood of the covenant, which is poured out for many for the forgiveness of sins." (Matthew 26:27–28)

Again we see the Lamb and the blood; the covenant confirmed, and the Word of God celebrated.

No doubt the response of Moses and those who witnessed the glory of the LORD was one of absolute worship. This was the reason God had drawn them out of Egypt: "Let my people go that they may serve (worship) me" (Exodus 7:16). He delights in our worship. This fact should cause us to question, personally and in our congregations: Does God delight in the worship we afford him? Does he derive joy from our praise?

Chasidic rabbi Levi Yitzchak of Berditchev proposes a criterion for determining answers to those questions:

> If one sees that one's heart burns like a fire and that one feels spiritual enthusiasm always to worship him and that one has a passion and a will to worship the Creator, then it is certain that God, may He be blessed, has joy from that person's worship. ... This is why it is written "and the Glory of God was as a consuming fire"—for the sign, if one wants

to know if one has seen the Glory of God ... is "a consuming fire," that one's heart burns like fire.[14]

David Blumenthal points out that Levi Yitzchak presents a very subjective criterion as opposed to the traditional emphasis in Judaism of studying God's Word "in order to do." He indicates that it is not only the knowledge and performance of *mitzvot* (good deeds) in obedience to God's commands that give God pleasure, although these surely do, just as they bring a sense of satisfaction to the doer. In addition, it is the motivation of love in one's heart and the expression of that love in worship that brings joy to the heart of God. This presupposes the understanding that God did all he did and does all he does for us because he is filled with a "burning" love for his people—a love that is passionate and powerful. He cares as a faithful Father cares for his children and loves as a bridegroom loves his bride.

WHAT ABOUT ILLNESS?

Illness and disease, although varying in nature and degree, as well as the certainty of eventual death, are realities that are woven into the very fabric of life. Serious illness demands significant changes in lifestyle, and one is confronted with countless decisions. Central to these is how best to treat and manage the illness. Where do we find the answers? Where do we place our trust?

The Talmud records an interesting account in connection with Hezekiah, a righteous king of Judah (b.*Brachot* 10b). Hezekiah made the decision to have all the medical books in his kingdom locked away. It seems he believed that his people were relying too heavily on the remedies prescribed therein and were not turning to the God of Israel in prayer and trusting him for his guidance and healing. The sages approved of his decision. However, on the other hand, based on the verse in the parashah that if one injures his neighbor, one must "provide for his complete healing" (Exodus 21:19). They also deduce that one can turn to the medical profession for treatment (*Bava Kama* 85a). What then do we do? Look to God for healing or look to man?

Rabbi Chanan Morrison offers the view of Rav Kook, first chief rabbi of the nascent state of Israel, who explained that there are two forms of reliance on God:

> There is the normative level of trust, that God will assist us in our efforts to help ourselves. And there is the simple trust in God that He will perform a miracle, when appropriate.[15]

We can compare this to the role of a parent. When Israel was a babe newly delivered from Egypt, many spectacular miracles were necessary in order to learn to recognize God's hand. When a child is very young, a parent's intervention is very direct. As the child matures and becomes self-sufficient, however, the parent's help is necessarily more indirect. Similarly, Rav Kook taught that once we mature spiritually,

> We are able to recognize God's hand in the natural course of events and are aware that God is the source of our strength and skill, and then we are expected to utilize all of our energy and knowledge and talents, and recognize Divine assistance in our efforts.

Yeshua performed many miracles of healing, and he pronounced, "The very works that I am doing, bear witness about me that the Father has sent me" (John 5:36). He did not, however, miraculously heal every person on every occasion. We can rest in the assurance that the LORD is always there to be our strength and our shield and to provide direction. He also expects us to take action in accordance with our abilities and the resources he has provided. We need to do our part, but with the constant knowledge and reassurance that: "My help comes from the LORD, who made heaven and earth" (Psalm 121:2).

TERUMAH

תרומה – "Heave Offering"

EXODUS 25:1–27:19

Parashat Terumah begins a detailed outline of God's requirements for the building of his Sanctuary. God himself designs his dwelling place on earth in the midst of his people. The blueprint of the *Mishkan*, "Tabernacle," in the wilderness also is the foundation plan for the eventual *Beit HaMikdash*, "Holy Temple," in Jerusalem. From a broader perspective, the Tabernacle is about to reveal the means whereby the people of God can move from the status of slaves in Egypt to that of a holy priesthood—servants of the Living God. In his love for his children, the heart of the Father has prepared a house that is a tangible microcosm of his eternal kingdom. This house also is a key to his plan of redemption for all humanity.

Since the destruction of the glorious Second Temple in 70 CE and the consequent absence of the physical Temple in Jerusalem, the sages of Israel have emphasized the profound spiritual truths incorporated in its construction, which continue to apply in anticipation of the building of the Third Temple as prophesied by Ezekiel:

> Learning about [the *Beit HaMikdash*, or literally "God's Holy House"] is as great as building it. (*Tanchuma* 96:14)

> Whenever man achieves insight [into God's Word], it is as if the Temple was rebuilt in his day. (b.*Brachot* 33a)

> By realizing the aims of the Temple in his life ... he has attained the underlying goal. (*Torat Olah*)

This emphasis reinforces Ezekiel's prophetic word:

> As for you, son of man, describe to the house of Israel the temple, that they may be ashamed of their iniquities; and they shall measure the plan. And if they are ashamed of all that they have done, make known to them the design of the temple, its arrangement, its exits and its entrances, that is, its whole design; and make known to them as well all its statutes and its whole design and all its laws, and write it down in their sight, so that they may observe all its laws and all its statutes and carry them out. (Ezekiel 43:10–11)

Abravanel, in his commentary on this parashah, states, "Everything recorded in the Torah is designed to provide us with a permanent source of inspiration and Divine wisdom, to perfect our souls therewith."[16]

With reference to the passage in Ezekiel, he adds:

> Were they to understand the significance of the Temple properly, they would be ashamed of their iniquities ... The very details of its construction contain the cure for their spiritual ills, if they would only look carefully. That is why the text uses the expressions *haged* (tell) and *hoda* (make known) rather than *hareh* (show), indicating that it is not the surface sense of the description that counts, but the inner, deeper meaning which must be told, elucidated, made known.[17]

THREE-PART TABERNACLE—ONE OUTER, TWO INNER

1. THE HOLY OF HOLIES

This was the inner Sanctuary of God's Holy Presence, which housed the ark of the covenant. No person could enter apart from the high priest on Yom Kippur, the Day of Atonement, after he had performed a ritual of extensive preparation.

The holy of holies can be compared to the head of a body, which contains the brain—the center of knowledge and the intellect. It also carries the organs for seeing and hearing, the means of obtaining knowledge, and the mouth, the organ of speech through which the fruits of wisdom and knowledge are imparted.

We can draw a parallel here with Messiah Yeshua, who is described as the "head" of his body of disciples:

> Speaking the truth in love, we are to grow up in every way into him who is the head, into [Messiah], from whom the whole body, ... when each part is working properly, makes bodily growth and upbuilds itself in love. (Ephesians 4:15–16)

> Holding fast to the head, from whom the whole body, nourished and knit together through its joints and ligaments, grows with a growth that is from God. (Colossians 2:19)

As the Word made flesh, Yeshua embodied the wisdom of Torah and he spoke forth the truth thereof according to the will of God our Father "who desires all people to be saved and to come to the knowledge of the truth" (1 Timothy 2:4).

With reference to the ark containing the tablets of the Torah, the focal point of the holy of holies, it is written, "They shall make an ark of acacia wood (*shittim*) (Exodus 25:10). The plural pronoun "they" is used here. In connection with the construction of the other pieces of furniture in the Tabernacle, the singular "you" is applied. A possible explanation for this distinction is that all God's people should be involved with the Torah, for his Word is intended for all. Following the "head," Yeshua, one should personally study and apply the Word as much as one is able, and also support and encourage the teaching and sharing of the Word with others, for therein is found the knowledge of God and the path of spiritual growth.

2. THE HOLY PLACE

The head commands the body to function, but it cannot operate without the heart. We can compare the holy place to the heart—the place of life and giving. This is where the communion and intimacy between God and his people take place. The furniture represents aspects of a life devoted to service and interaction.

    a. Table and Loaves (Exodus 25:23, 30)

> The Hebrew word for table is *shulchan*, which is related to the word *shaliach*, a messenger, one who is sent, from the root letters *shin-lamed-chet*, "to send." God specified that the table

be made of *shittim* wood like the ark was. A classic midrashic anthology, *Tz'enah Ur'enah*,[18] points out that the Hebrew letters of the word, *shin-tet-mem*, form an acronym for *shalom* (peace), *tohar* (purity/purification), and *machilah* (forgiveness).

God sends these blessings by means of the table and the bread of the Presence upon it. After a week, when the new bread was brought in, the bread, which miraculously remained fresh, was shared and eaten by the priests. Here we see a powerful image of the Bread of Life, the Messiah, who embodies forgiveness, purity, and peace, and who imparts the Father's blessing as we partake of his life.

b. The Golden Menorah (Exodus 25:31)

The menorah represents the light of the Torah. *Baal HaTurim*[19] notes that the letter *samech* does not appear in the passage describing the menorah, to show that the adversary, Satan (written *samech-tet-nun sofit*), does not appear where the light of the Torah shines. The God of Israel is the source of light, and there is no need for light in the holy of holies. Here, in the holy place, however, the menorah stands for the sake of the people. "The spirit of man is the lamp of the LORD" (Proverbs 20:27). When the soul of a person sees the illumination of the menorah, it is filled with delight, for it is a means of recognizing and reconnecting with its source.

Similarly, Yeshua, as the Living Torah, proclaimed, "I am the light of the world. Whoever follows me will not walk in darkness but will have the light of life" (John 8:12).

> For God, who said, "Let light shine out of darkness," has shone in our hearts to give the light of the knowledge of the glory of God in the face of [Messiah Yeshua]. (2 Corinthians 4:6)

When we see him, we see the Father, and, in him, we can reconnect with the source of our life.

c. The Altar of Incense (Exodus 30:1)

The altar stands beside the menorah, and the warmth of the flames increases the fragrance of the incense. The priest offered the incense to God in response to the blessings of the loaves and the light. Fragrance is not seen with the eye. There are no better offerings we can bring to delight our Almighty God and Father than the intangibles of our devotion, prayer, and worship, offered from a heart of love and gratitude.

3. THE OUTER COURT

The outer court also was divided into three sections: the Court of the Gentiles, the Court of the Women, and the Court of Israel.

- a. The large courtyards surrounding the Temple area were accessible to Gentiles in the understanding that God's House was intended to be "a house of prayer for all peoples" (Isaiah 56:7; Mark 11:17). Gentiles could also arrange for sacrifices or offerings to be made by the priests. From this area, it was possible to see through the gates to the Sanctuary and the altar of sacrifice.
- b. The Court of the Women was the large, general place of meeting, prayer, and celebration of the festivals for all Israelites who were not in a state of ritual impurity.
- c. The Court of Israel was the smaller court where the priests would offer sacrifices on the altar on behalf of all Israel. It was accessed from the Court of the Women by a wide staircase of fifteen steps that led up to the large bronze Nicanor gates. The steps were generally traversed by the priests and Levitical musicians.

The whole of this outer area can represent the body, which grows and strengthens as it looks to the "head" for direction. If the directions are followed in loving obedience, with thoughts "taken captive to Messiah" (2 Corinthians 10:5), then the worship of the heart will be pure and healthy and pleasing to the Father of all. Then the glory of his *Shechinah*, Dwelling Presence, will fill the House.

TETZAVEH

תצוה – "You Shall Command"

EXODUS 27:30–30:10

> Oil and perfume make the heart glad, and the sweetness of a friend comes from his earnest counsel. (Proverbs 27:9)

The parashah begins and ends with the two most important daily duties of the high priest—the lighting of the menorah (Exodus 27:20-21) and the burning of the sweet incense on the adjacent altar of incense (Exodus 30:1-10). The two activities were always combined and performed every morning and evening so that they might be a perpetual light and fragrance "before the LORD" (Exodus 30:8). The only oil used in the lighting of the menorah was *shemen zayit zach katit*, which is the first and most pure oil drawn from crushed olives. The fine, individual elements of the incense were combined and crushed with a mortar and pestle to produce the God-ordained incense for the altar.

OIL AND INCENSE

We understand that Yeshua perfectly fulfills the role of high priest, representing God to man and man to God.[20] In addition we gratefully recognize that, as the purest oil, he was pressed and poured out to provide the clearest of light to the world. Also, like the incense, he was crushed to make available to us the constant fragrance of our Father's presence.

History tells us that the First Temple, built by King Solomon, stood for 410 years and the Second Temple for 420 years. This is a total of

830, which is the numerical value of the Hebrew word *katit* (*kaf* [20] + *tav* [400] + *yod* [10] + *tav* [400]). *Katit* means crushed, pressed, or pounded. Thus, as the sages deduce, the two Temples were eventually crushed to the ground. However, the light that emanated from them—the "menorah" of God's Word together with the light of the world, Messiah Yeshua—continues to shine perpetually in the earth.

The Third Temple, as described by Ezekiel, is considered to be the one from which Messiah will reign over all the earth as King of kings for one thousand years. We read in the book of Revelation that when God's eternal kingdom finally is established at the end of days, it will not need a physical Temple. The radiance of the fullness of his Presence will permeate everywhere and will be the fragrant, everlasting light.

HOLY GARMENTS

The priestly garments are designed to set the priests apart as they perform the holy tasks of service in the *Mishkan*. The priests (*kohanim*) are those set apart as representatives of God to the people, and the high priest is the representative of God to the priests as well as the people. The Midrash compares the high priest to an angel, one who is a wholehearted servant and messenger of God (cf. Revelation 8:3-4). Therefore, *Tz'enah Ur'enah* emphasizes, "Just as an angel is pure, so must the *Kohen Gadol* be pure as he accomplishes his tasks."[21]

As with every detail of the Tabernacle, the fine details of the high priest's holy garments are imbued with meaning and illustrate truths that their Designer, the LORD of Creation, wishes to convey. There were eight garments in all.

Rabbenu Bechaye asks: "Why are only six garments enumerated in this portion, when the High Priest actually wore eight garments?" He concurs, "Because this parashah refers only to the garments in which *Moshe Rabeinu* [Moses our teacher] clothed him."

The six major garments reflect the high priest's service and intimate connection with God and the people. For example, the *choshen* (breastplate worn over the heart) carries twelve precious stones engraved with the names of the tribes of Israel (Exodus 28:29). This indicates that the people of God are His *segulah* (treasured possession) and should be valued as precious stones and carried close to one's heart. Two onyx stones set in gold are attached to the shoulder straps of the *ephod* (a robe that serves as an undergarment). These are also inscribed with the names of the tribes, six on each, and indicate that the high priest bears responsibility for the tribes before God. He carries them on his shoulders, as a father can carry his children.

The two garments not mentioned are related to his personal service to God. The *michnasayim* (trousers), donned in private, remind him that he is accountable to God for the purity and righteousness of his own life. Others see the outward service, but only God sees the inner service of the heart. The second is the *tzitz*, the golden platelet embossed with *Kadosh l'Adonai*, "Holy to the LORD" (Exodus 28:36–38), which is worn across his forehead. This is like a crown placed upon him by God himself as a mark of authority to act in his Name. It is a witness that he has indeed yielded his will and life to God's kingship and that he is, in truth, holy and set apart for God's glory.

KODESH VECHOL – HOLY AND ORDINARY

A central purpose of the Tabernacle and its design is to distinguish between what is holy and what is not. God is making a clear distinction between the sacred and the profane, the divine and the ordinary. This is not a contrast between good and evil. Rather, it is an illustration of the difference between the common and down-to-earth and the heights of the holy. There is a prescribed "highway of holiness" to follow if one desires to heed God's call and to enter his presence on the heights of the Mount.

After the exodus, when he meets them on Mount Sinai in the wilderness, God presents his people with the challenge: "For I am the LORD who brought you up out of the land of Egypt to be your God. You shall therefore be holy, for I am holy" (Leviticus 11:45, 20:26; 1 Peter 1:16). As well as the physical journey that lay ahead to reach the promised land, he is calling them to make the spiritual journey in relationship with him, which would take them from the dry, desert sands of lack of knowledge of him, through the outer courts of the Temple, and from there to enter the holy place of service and worship. Ultimately, they would step beyond the veil and into the most intimate place of his *Shechinah*, the holy of holies.

The progression of the spiritual journey and the climb it requires is portrayed in the blueprint of God's House, and the means of accomplishing the journey are provided. All that is required from his children are willing and yielded hearts—hearts filled with gratitude and longing, love and awe, and with the desire to meet with him and to bask in the light of his Presence.

To enter the unbounded peace and joy of the *Shechinah* of God requires a daily commitment. It involves being clothed with the "robe of righteousness" and one's wholehearted participation, as was required in the priestly service of the holy place. How do we do this during the mundane routine of our daily lives? The aim, as priests serving the one true God, is not to disregard the "ordinary" in favor of the sacred, but rather, to elevate the everyday and imbue it with his holiness. This is the perspective of the holy of holies: All is "holy unto the LORD." All of oneself, all of life—all for his eternal glory.

KI TISA

כִּי תִשָּׂא – "When You Take"

EXODUS 30:11–34:35

In his commentary on this parashah, Rav A.I. Kook, Chief Rabbi in pre-state Israel and a great spiritual teacher and leader, clearly stated:

> In order for a leader to succeed, he must be appreciated and valued by his followers. The leader may possess a soul greatly elevated above the people, but it is crucial that the people should be able to relate to and learn from their leader.[22]

A LESSON IN LEADERSHIP

Moses experienced the glory of God's revelation upon the summit of Mount Sinai in a manner that no ordinary man had before or has since. God called him into his Divine Presence (Exodus 24:16), and, understandably, Moses lingers there as long as he can—for forty days and nights. The newly formed people, also understandably, became anxious. Where is Moses? Is he still alive? Has their leader abandoned them? Finally, they pressured Aaron into producing a golden calf, which they proceeded to worship. An idol replaced their leader. In response, God immediately ordered Moses to leave his presence: "Go down, for your people, whom you brought up out of the land of Egypt, have corrupted themselves" (Exodus 32:7). Moses must leave the heights of revelation and intimate communion with God and, as it were, lower himself from the realm of holiness to the mundane in order to serve as a leader and teacher of the people. The Talmud records:

What does it mean, "Go down?" God told Moses, "Go down from your greatness. I only gave you pre-eminence for the sake of my people. Now they have greatly sinned—why should you be elevated?" Immediately Moses' [spiritual] strength left him.[23]

Maybe God was teaching Moses in this situation that people need a leader who is present and available, and that Moses had been "removed" for too long. Another view is offered in *Tzror HaMor*,[24] which points out that it is written, "When He finished speaking with him" (Exodus 31:18) to show that the Israelites were wrong in thinking that Moses had delayed his return unnecessarily. As soon as God finished speaking with him, Moses came down with the tablets. For this reason, God punished them.[25]

After those who had frivolously worshiped the golden calf are executed, Moses ascends the Mount for another forty days in order to intercede for Israel. He returns to the people and then again ascends for a further forty days, during which time he receives the second set of tablets.

The period of forty days is often mentioned in the Bible to indicate a specific and lengthy segment of time. It is usually a time designated for purification and preparation. The Apostolic Writings record how Yeshua, led by the Holy Spirit, withdrew to the wilderness for forty days without food.[26] There he is tested, and he overcomes the temptations of Satan. It is worth noting that this takes place before he begins his ministry to the people. Thereafter, he would withdraw for short periods, for example, to mourn John the Immerser's death (Matthew 14:13), or to escape the crowds, and likely to pray (Mark 3:13; John 6:15). Ultimately, he promises his disciples, "Behold, I am with you always, to the end of the age" (Matthew 28:20).

TWO STONE TABLETS

Moses brings down from Mount Sinai two tablets of stone inscribed with the ten central commandments of God for his people. The ten, in effect, encapsulate all God's Torah—his instruction and guidance. In Hebrew, in this passage, they are called *shnei luchot ha'edut,* the two tablets of the testimony, or witness (Exodus 34:29). *Tz'enah Ur'enah* states: "God gave Israel two tablets which bear witness to the fact that

His Presence rests among them. They were like a message from the king to his people, announcing his presence with them."[27]

Rebbenu Bechaye writes: "Why did God not write the commandments upon one tablet? Because they were to bear witness [and two witnesses are always needed in court]."[28]

Interesting observations can be made as to why the tablets were made of stone. Why not wood? Or, more appropriate to a message from the Great King, of gold? Rebbenu Bechaye provides one answer:

> The tablets were made of stone, which comes from the earth, while the writing was Divine, so that both heaven and earth would bear witness when Israel would not observe the Torah properly, as it is written [in Deuteronomy 31:28], "I will call heaven and earth as witnesses against them.[29]

Another point of interest is that the punishment for transgressing most of these commandments was death by stoning. We see an example in John 8:3-11. Yeshua is teaching in the Temple early one morning when a group of spiritual leaders brings before him a woman who had been caught in adultery. They point out that according to the Torah, they have a right to stone her. Yeshua proclaims, "Let him who is without sin cast the first stone!" Then, he silently writes on the ground with his finger. Their attention is drawn to the earth, and he, himself, is the very presence of Heaven in their midst. It is a powerful witness against them of their own sins. We can only imagine what he was writing, but a verse that would have been well known to them comes to mind:

> O LORD, the hope of Israel, all who forsake you shall be put to shame; those who turn away from you shall be written in the earth, for they have forsaken the LORD, the fountain of living water. (Jeremiah 17:13)

Was he writing their names? Astounded, one after the other, they silently leave. In loving exhortation, while upholding the truth of the commandment, Yeshua bids the woman, "Go, and sin no more."

SEEING THE LIGHT

The Midrash recounts a story of the Roman Emperor Hadrian, a powerful leader who certainly knew the need for public appearances before the people. Hadrian asked Rabbi Yehoshua, "You say that your God created the sky and the earth. Why does he not reveal himself, say twice a year, so that mankind will fear him?" "Look at the sun," said Rabbi Yehoshua. "How can I possibly look at the sun?" asked Hadrian. "If you cannot look at the sun, which is merely one of God's servants," replied Rabbi Yehoshua, "how then do you expect to look at God himself, who gives off so much more light?"[30]

We read in the parashah that when Moses pleads with God to fully show him his glory, God replies, "You cannot see my face and live" (Exodus 33:20). However, once Moses is shielded in the cleft of a rock, God presents him with a partial revelation of himself. Moses can only bow to the ground in worship as he hears the LORD proclaim a number of his attributes, which have been incorporated into the prayers and worship of God's people ever since:

> The LORD, the LORD, a God merciful and gracious, slow to anger, and abounding in steadfast love and faithfulness, keeping steadfast love for thousands, forgiving iniquity and transgression and sin, but who will by no means clear the guilty, visiting the iniquity of the fathers upon the children and the children's children, to the third and the fourth generation [until they repent]. (Exodus 34:6–7)

VAYAK'HEL

ויקהל – "And He Assembled"

EXODUS 35:1–38:20

The focus of the biblical narrative returns once again to the Mishkan—the Tabernacle in the wilderness. This week's portion details the actual construction of the Sanctuary. Rabbi Ari Kahn[31] considers that the Sanctuary is a "sign of healing in the aftermath of the Golden Calf tragedy." As opposed to the gold of the man-designed idol, the gold of the God-designed objects reflects his glory.

BUILD ME A SANCTUARY

As the people of God reach out to him in building a Sanctuary, his joyous response is to come down and fill the earthly structure with some of heaven—with the radiance of his *Shechinah*. History reveals, with the tragic destruction of the First and Second Temples, that the physical structure alone is not sufficient to guarantee the presence of the *Shechinah*.

After Israel's exile in Babylon, following the fall of the First Temple, the people return to the land under the leadership of Ezra and Zerubavel to build the Second Temple. Rebuilding is a difficult task, but with divine enabling and great perseverance, they succeeded. We read that at its completion they "celebrated the dedication of this house of God with joy … for the LORD had made them joyful, and turned the heart of the king of Assyria to them, so that he aided them in the work of the house of the God, the God of Israel" (Ezra 6:16, 22).

On reading the account more closely, however, we realize that something is missing. Rabbi Kahn poses the following question: "Where is the cloud, the heavenly expression that God had allowed his Presence to return and fill the structure? Regarding God's response, the verses offer a deafening silence."[32] He quotes the opinion of a talmudic sage, Resh Lakish:

> The reason the Divine Presence did not dwell in the Second Temple was that the majority of Jews did not care enough to return and take part in the challenge of the building of the Temple and, by the same token, of the entire land.[33]

In this week's parashah we see how all the people respond with "willing and generous" hearts to Moses' appeal for help and contributions toward the building of the Tabernacle. Also, at the call of King David for donations to aid in the building of the First Temple, "more than enough" was given:

> Then the people rejoiced because these had given willingly,
> for with a whole heart they had offered freely to the LORD;
> David the king also rejoiced greatly. (1 Chronicles 29:9)

In contrast, at the call and opportunity to build the Second Temple, most of the exiles chose to remain in the comfort of their own homes in the prosperous environment of Babylon rather than undertake the arduous challenge of rebuilding the House of God and restoring the glory of his Presence.

THE WORD AND THE SPIRIT

Every aspect of the Tabernacle requires consecration—a conscious, wholehearted dedication and yielding to the will and purposes of God. The priest, the one who serves, must be consecrated. The vessels and every ingredient and item used must be consecrated as holy to Adonai. Nothing half-hearted or compromised can stand in the powerful light of his consuming fire.

The Light of his Presence and the Word of Truth are represented in the Sanctuary by the golden menorah. It is designed as the vessel that enables the Light of Truth to shine on earth—the "lamp" of his Word, tended diligently with priestly service. The element that fuels that light and enables it to shine is the purest of olive oil. The same oil is used for anointing the priest and the king. An interesting parable on the olive tree is recorded in the book of Judges:

> The trees went forth to anoint a king over them, and they said to the olive tree, "Reign over us!" But the olive tree said to them, "Shall I leave my abundance, by which gods and men are honored, and go hold sway over the trees?" (Judges 9:8–9)

We are reminded, by this combined effort of the lamps and the oil, that although we may possess the vitally necessary and beautiful vessel of the Word, it cannot shine forth the radiant life of God without the empowering of the Holy Spirit.

The seven flames of the menorah reflect the seven Hebrew words spoken by the Prophet Zechariah: *Lo vechayil velo vechoach ki im beRuchi.* "'Not by might, nor by power, but by My Spirit,' says the LORD of hosts" (Zechariah 4:6). Therein lies the strength of his people! The only true power that supplies the light that gives life is the infilling and the anointing of his Spirit of Holiness.

In the revelation to the Apostle John, we see Yeshua the Messiah identified as the Light of the World. He is the Living Word through whom those who live in darkness "without God and without hope in the world" (Ephesians 2:12) can be drawn into the Sanctuary of God. He is dressed in priestly garments. His face is brilliant, and his eyes are blazing like flames. It appears that he is speaking to John, just as God spoke to Moses, in the holy place of the Tent of Meeting, evidenced by the presence of the menorah of seven lamps (Revelation 1:12–18).

THE LIGHT RETURNS

> God said, "The little lights of your menorah are more precious to me than the lights of all the stars I have placed in the sky." (Anonymous)

According to the Midrash,[34] the windows of the Temple were constructed narrow on the inside and wider on the outside rather than the reverse, which would allow more natural light into a dwelling. This demonstrated that a supernatural light went forth from the Temple to the world.

We read in the Gospel of John that Yeshua was in the Temple to honor the Festival of Dedication—Hanukkah.[35] The Hebrew word *Chanukah* means dedication or consecration. The message of Hanukkah relates to Zechariah's prophecy (4:6) in that it was only through the miracle of God's help that the Maccabees, a small band of Jewish fighters, overcame the might of the Greco-Syrian enemy against overwhelming odds. The darkness of the edicts given by their leader, Antiochus Epiphanes, in his attempts to extinguish the light of the Torah, was dispelled.

The desecrated Temple was rededicated to the glory of God through another miracle—the rekindling of the menorah lights. Once the Temple was physically cleansed of idols and restored, the Maccabees found only one cruse of oil left undefiled. This would fuel the menorah for one day, but it would require a week to process fresh oil. In faith they lit the menorah, and the flames supernaturally continued to burn for eight days. The great wonder of this miracle is that it was an indication that the Light had returned. The *Shechinah* of God again filled his House! To this day, the custom remains to light the lights of the Hanukkah menorah in a window or at the threshold of one's door, to remember that the purpose of the light is not only to delight in it ourselves but that it may shine as a warm beacon into the darkness.

PEKUDEI

פקודי – "Accounts"

EXODUS 38:21–40:38

Psalm 90 is recognized as one written by Moses, *eved Adonai*—servant of God. Verse 17 states, "Establish the work of our hands upon us; yes, establish the work of our hands!" Why the obvious repetition? We can connect this verse to a key verse in this week's parashah; one that describes Moses' survey of the construction of the Tabernacle: "Moses saw all the work, and behold, they had done it; as the LORD had commanded, so had they done it" (Exodus 39:43).

FREEDOM AND OBEDIENCE

This work of the Israelites bore two distinct characteristics:

1. They had done it. It was the work of their hands. Every small part expressed the devotion, enthusiasm, and energy expended by each person individually and the people as a whole.
2. It was done as God had commanded. All their efforts were completely yielded to the will and direction of God. Each craftsman, construction worker, garment maker, or curtain weaver, had carried out the ideas and instructions of God with great care. No one had aspired to impose their own individual stamp upon what they did. The work was all for the glory of God.

Rabbi S.R. Hirsch comments:

> This free-willed, joyous obedience—this freedom in obedience and obedience in freedom—makes one most happily aware of one's strength [and creativity] as a servant of God, precisely by subordinating one's personality completely to the will of God. This is what characterizes a human being as a servant of God.[36]

Only with the elements of freedom and obedience working together can we enjoy the full blessing of God upon our lives and the work of our hands. The LORD honors such dedicated service. Because the Tabernacle was accomplished by God's people, according to God's plan, and for his purposes, the Torah says, "Then the cloud covered the tent of meeting and the glory of the LORD filled the Tabernacle" (Exodus 40:34).

UNITY RESTORED

Parashat Pekudei concludes the book of Exodus, and it describes a summation, a goal reached. A detailed description of the Tabernacle is repeated here, emphasizing its central importance in the book. The purpose of the exodus from Egypt was to set free the people of God from the bondage of Pharaoh, the false god, and to draw them to himself "that they might serve and worship me" (e.g., Exodus 9:1).

God desired to establish an intimate, covenant relationship between himself and the people of Israel. He had chosen Israel as his bride and drawn her to himself. The betrothal ceremony was performed at Mount Sinai. The two engraved, stone tablets were the *ketubah*, the marriage contract. God then revealed that he longed to "dwell in their midst" (Exodus 25:8), which required the building of a home, a set-apart Holy House.

Then, however, the shocking and sinful worship of the golden calf took place. This incident illustrates that idolatry is adultery. The Israelites had, in effect, rejected and turned from their true beloved to embrace another. The repetition of the plan and construction of a "nuptial home" here in the final chapters of Exodus indicates that, due to his infinite capacity for compassion and forgiveness, at the wholehearted repentance of the people, the loving intimacy between God and his beloved Israel is redeemed and restored. The Home is ultimately built, and it is filled with the glory of his Presence.

An interesting messianic perspective is related by Rebbenu Bechaye, who writes that when he inhabited the Tabernacle, God said,

> Today I am causing My Presence to rest among you; if you sin, My Presence will leave you. But when Mashiach comes, My Presence will remain with you permanently. Now you see the Divine Presence through fire, but with the advent of Mashiach you will see it clearly revealed, as it is written: "For eye to eye shall they see when God returns to Zion" (Isaiah 52:8).[37]

Indeed, Messiah Yeshua was revealed in Zion, and he said, "I am with you always, to the end of the age" (Matthew 28:20). He now is present with us through the Spirit of Holiness, the *Shechinah*. The Apostle Peter proclaimed at Shavu'ot / Pentecost, after Yeshua's resurrection and the outpouring of the Spirit:

> This Jesus, God raised up, and of that we all are witnesses. Being therefore exalted at the right hand of God, and having received from the Father the promise of the Holy Spirit, he has poured out this that you yourselves are seeing and hearing. (Acts 2:32-33)

We look forward with eager anticipation to the great day of Yeshua's return as King of kings, for "we know that when he appears we shall be like him, because we shall see him as he is" (1 John 3:2). We will rejoice with him in redeemed and resurrected bodies. Now those bodies are dedicated as his dwelling place on earth, as Paul reminds us:

> Do you not know that your body is a temple of the Holy Spirit within you, whom you have from God?" (1 Corinthians 6:19)

HARMONY AND ONE-NESS

As in all his works, we are impressed with God's fine attention to detail in the blueprints and planning of the Tabernacle. A significant element of any plan is the time frame. The precise timing of God is outlined; nothing is left to the variability of circumstance. God instructs Moses: "On the first day of the first month you shall erect the tabernacle of the tent of meeting" (Exodus 40:2). We read in Exodus 40:17: "In the first month in the second year, on the first day of the month, the tabernacle was erected." No question. When God commands, and his people willingly obey, he provides and enables.

The Hebrew calendar is lunar, set according to the moon, as opposed to the Gregorian solar calendar. The new moon, which signals the first day of the Hebrew month, symbolizes a new beginning. The moon is a constant reminder of a person's ability to emerge from total darkness into a state of fullness and light. It is, therefore, also a glowing testimony to the reality of redemption from servitude. It is the emergence from the darkness of sin and alienation into the light of truth and intimate unity.

Another reflection of divine light and unity can be seen in the simple objects of the gold fasteners of the elaborate, woven covering of the Tabernacle (Exodus 40:19). Ten large colorful tapestries were joined together, in two sets of five, with fifty hook-like fasteners. The Talmud tells us that inside the holy place, the gold fasteners would sparkle against the background of the tapestries like stars twinkling in the sky (b.*Shabbat* 99a).

Rabbi Chanan Morrison, referring to the writings of Rav Kook, writes:

> In general, the design of the Tabernacle reflected the structure of the universe and its underlying unity ... When we reflect on the beautiful harmony ... we begin to be aware of the fundamental unity of the universe and all of its forces. We realize that everything is the work of the Creator, Who unites all aspects of creation in His sublime Oneness.[38]

It is fitting to conclude this study of Exodus with a blessing of Paul that reflects the harmony and One-ness of our Creator:

> The grace of the Lord [Messiah Yeshua] and the love of God and the fellowship of the Holy Spirit be with you all." (2 Corinthians 13:14)

CHAZAK CHAZAK, VENITCHAZEK
BE STRONG, BE STRONG, AND MAY WE STRENGTHEN ONE ANOTHER IN THE UNITY OF THE ONE WHO LOVES US.

ENDNOTES

1. Rabbi Yitzchak Ginsburgh, *The Alef-Beit: Jewish Thought Revealed through the Hebrew Letters* (Jerusalem, Israel: Gal Einai Publications, 1992), 209.
2. Augustine, one of the early church fathers, pointed out that the initial letters of "Yeshua the Messiah, Son of God the Savior" in Greek combine to form the word *Ichthus*, meaning "fish." That is surely why the first identifying sign used by the early believers and subsequent followers of Messiah Yeshua is the symbol of a fish.
3. Rambam, Maimonides – Rabbi Moses ben Maimon, (1135–1204). Spain – Egypt. A great post-talmudic scholar and prolific author, he was also a world-renowned authority on medicine, the Caliph of Egypt's physician, and leader of Egypt's Jewish community.
4. Rabbi Abraham Isaac HaKohen Kook, (1865–1935). Well-loved first Chief Rabbi of pre-state Israel.
5. Rabbi Chanan Morrison, *Gold from the Land of Israel*, 101.
6. Rabbi Samson Raphael Hirsch (1808–1888), *Chapters of the Fathers* (Nanuet, NY: Feldheim Publishers, 2014), 37.
7. Levi Yitzchak (1740–1810) Chasidic Rabbi, Poland, who believed that God and Torah study are for all. He organized many study groups for the common people and his teaching focused on simplicity, sincerity, and joy in prayer.
8. David R. Blumenthal, *God at the Center: Meditations on Jewish Spirituality* (San Francisco, CA: Harper & Row Publishers, 1988), 43.
9. Rabbi Bradley Shavit-Artson, *The Bedside Torah* (New York, NY: Contemporary Books, 2001), 110.
10. Referred to by Rabbi Shlomo Riskin in his article, "The Song of Moses and the Sons of Israel"; Jerusalem Post, 6 February, 1998.
11. Rabbi Samuel Raphael Hirsch, *The Pentateuch*, 206.
12. Avivah Gottlieb Zornberg, *The Particulars of Rapture: Reflections on Exodus* (New York, NY: Schocken Books, 2001), 5.
13. Gary Thomas, *Sacred Marriage* (Grand Rapids, MI: Zondevan, 2000), 75.
14. David R. Blumenthal, *God at the Center: Meditations on Jewish Spirituality*, 56.

15 Rabbi Chanan Morrison, *Gold from the Land of Israel*, 136.
16 Isaac Abravanel, *Perush* (Commentary) *on the Pentateuch, Terumah*, Venice, 1579.
17 Isaac Abravanel, *Perush on the Earlier Prophets, Ezekiel*, Pesaro, 1511.
18 *Tz'enah Ur'enah*, The Weekly Midrash, Vol. 1, 418.
19 Ibid., 419.
20 According to the book of Hebrews.
21 *Tz'enah Ur'enah*, The Weekly Midrash, Vol.1, 422.
22 Rabbi Chanan Morrison, *Gold from the Land of Israel*, 160.
23 *Brachot* 32a.
24 In 1523, the first printed edition of *Tzror HaMor*, a Bible commentary by Rabbi Avraham Sebag, was published in Venice. He had been expelled from Spain in 1492, and made the unfortunate choice of fleeing to Portugal, where he was persecuted and saw his two sons forcibly baptized and taken from him. He buried his manuscripts to save them from confiscation and destruction. (Sadly, they were never recovered.) Rabbi Sebag eventually made his way to Africa where he managed to rewrite some of his works.
25 *Tz'enah Ur'enah*, The Weekly Midrash, Vol. 1, 436.
26 Luke 4:1–2.
27 *Tz'enah Ur'enah*, The Weekly Midrash, Vol. 1, 436.
28 Ibid.
29 Ibid.
30 *Shemot Rabbah*, Ki Tisa, 26.
31 Rabbi Ari Kahn, a student of Rav Y.D. Soloveitchik, teaches at Aish HaTorah, Jerusalem, and at Bar Ilan University, Tel Aviv. This reference is to be found at Aish.com, at *Mi'Oray HaAish, Vayakhel-Pekudei*, 2005.
32 Ibid.
33 b.*Yoma* 9b.
34 *Leviticus Rabbah*, Emor, 31.
35 John 10:22–23.
36 Rabbi Samson Raphael Hirsch, *The Pentateuch and Haftorahs*, 365.
37 *Tz'enah Ur'enah*, The Weekly Midrash, Vol.1.
38 Rabbi Chanan Morrison, *Gold from the Land of Israel*, 165.

LEVITICUS

VAYIKRA

ויקרא – "And He Called"

LEVITICUS 1:1–5:26(6:7)

The flow of narrative found in the first two books of Torah, Genesis and Exodus, is interrupted with the book of Leviticus. As Rabbi S.R. Hirsch describes:

> This entire Third Book consists of instructions telling us how to meet the requirements represented by the Sanctuary of the Law; ... how to lead hallowed lives as individuals and as a nation—an endeavor to be expressed in symbolic terms by our offerings and, in practice, by our conduct.[1]

HOLY, OR NOT

The Hebrew name of the book and of this parashah is *Vayikra*, "And He Called." God has called Moses to himself once again. We see illustrated by Moses' constant response to the call of God that the primary action involved is to move from one's present place and to draw in closer proximity to his Presence. The Hebrew verb *hivdil* describes this action; one that is used from the beginning of creation: "And God divided (*hivdil*) the light from the darkness" (Genesis 1:4). This division, or separation, brings order from chaos.

Robert Alter comments:

> What enables existence and provides a framework for the development of humankind, conceived in God's image, and of human civilization is a process of division and insulation—

light from darkness, day from night, the upper waters from the lower waters, and dry land from the latter.[2]

The call to be his people, and the purpose of the study of God's Word and the aspiration to "be like him," is expressed in Leviticus 20:24-26:

> I have set you apart (*hivdil*) from all other peoples. And you shall set apart (*hivdil*) the clean from the unclean ... And you shall be holy to Me, for I the LORD am holy.

The very concept of "being holy as he is holy" radically challenges our understanding. What is made clear in Vayikra, however, is the connection between holiness and the acceptance of these categories of "clean and unclean" in the realms of human appetite, predominantly the sexual and dietary. The idea of *imitatio Dei* includes the element of *hivdil*—setting apart, clearly defining the boundaries, and the erection of shields, as it were, between that which is holy and pure to God and that which is not.

It is the call of God that gives the authority to draw near to his awesome presence. The authority, however, is accompanied by responsibility. Once called, the priests who were specifically set apart by God to serve in the Tabernacle and Temple needed to follow a careful regimen of preparation and observe a specific code of dress before entering the Holy Place of the Sanctuary. One of the two narrational incidents in the book of Leviticus tells of the instant death of Nadav and Avihu, two sons of Aaron, the high priest, who, whether in uncontrolled zeal or misplaced arrogance, brought "unauthorized fire before the LORD, which He had not commanded them" (Leviticus 10:1).

BEHIND THE VEIL

When God sent his Messiah into the world in the person of Yeshua, in what one writer describes as "His own inconceivable Self-donation,"[3] he instituted a dynamic dimension to the tripartite biblical pattern of covenant communication. God—priests—his people (Israel: a kingdom of priests, holy nation), expanded to become: Father (God, creator)—Yeshua (Messiah, redeemer, high priest)—his people (Israel: a kingdom of priests, holy nation; Jews and those grafted in from the nations).

To Yeshua was given full authority, in the heavens and on the earth, to draw all men unto the Father, who is the creator of all. This had long been the understanding of God's chosen people, highlighted in King Solomon's dedication of the First Temple, that God's dwelling place was to be a "house of prayer for *all* peoples" (Isaiah 56:7). The vision was there; Yeshua provided the way to implement the vision.

He knew that the physical Temple would fall, and the large, universal plan would be brought more sharply into focus. From the beginning, all people, not only the Levites, were created to be set apart as priests to the One true God of Israel. Yeshua came to open the door into the Temple, to part the veil into the holy of holies of God's Presence, and to prepare the way for that reality. As a result, the Sanctuary—the Tabernacle of Meeting—would be established wherever the humble would hear the call of God and would enter his Presence with hearts yearning to serve and worship him.

RESPONSE OF THE HEART

Throughout the centuries, ever since, people from all nations have heeded the call. One shining example: In the late 1600s, a poor, uneducated, young Frenchman became a lay brother in a monastery in Paris. He worked in the kitchen and called himself "a servant of servants." He determined to live every moment in "the practice of the Presence of God." We can read (in the book of the same name compiled by his abbot from Brother Lawrence's notes and letters after his death) that he indeed was able to transform his mundane chores into a glorious experience of heaven. Brother Lawrence wrote:

> The only thing I was seeking was to become wholly God's ... I removed, for the love of God, everything that was not God.
>
> When we are faithful in keeping ourselves in His Holy Presence, keeping Him always before us, this not only prevents our offering to Him as being something displeasing in His sight (at least willfully), but it also brings us a holy freedom and, if I may say so, a familiarity with God, wherein we may ask and receive the graces of which we are so desperately in need.
>
> Presenting myself before God, I ask Him to form His perfect image in my soul and to make me entirely like Himself.[4]

Another heart response is described by Frank Lambauch (1884–1970), who lived as a bearer of the gospel and literacy to many thousands in the Philippine Islands. He had two burning passions: "First, to be like Jesus. Second, to respond to God as a violin responds to the bow of the master. Open your soul and entertain the glory of God and after a while that glory will be reflected in the world about you."[5]

He describes how, as he purposed to do his part each day, "God takes care of all the rest. My part is to live in this hour in continuous inner conversation with God and in perfect responsiveness to His will. To make this hour gloriously rich."

As children and servants of God, our hearts can join with King David, the sweet psalmist of Israel, as he sang:

> One thing have I asked of the LORD, that will I seek after: that I may dwell in the house of the LORD all the days of my life, to gaze upon the beauty of the LORD and to inquire in his temple. For he will hide me in his shelter in the day of trouble; he will conceal me under the cover of his tent; he will lift me high upon a rock. And now my head shall be lifted up above my enemies all around me, and I will offer in his tent sacrifices with shouts of joy; I will sing and make melody to the LORD. (Psalm 27:4–6)

TZAV

צו – "Command"

LEVITICUS 6:1(8)–8:36

The focus of Parashat Tzav is the dedication of the Sanctuary by Moses. It is a detailed process involving the consecration of priests, anointing, and sacrifice. The consecration takes seven days, during which time the priests must remain in the precincts of the Tabernacle. The number seven indicates completion and perfection, as we see illustrated at the creation. The period is not altogether an end in itself; it is a time of preparation and a prelude to the eighth day of new action and fresh beginnings.

GRACE AND RESPONSE

An interesting facet of the ritual of anointing is described when, on each of the seven days, Moses mixes blood from the altar with anointing oil and sprinkles it upon the priests and their clothing to consecrate them. He also applies some of the mixture to their right ear lobes, right thumbs, and the big toes of their right feet. These details are given with no explanation. A corresponding clue may be found in the description of one of the sacrifices of consecration (Leviticus 8:23).

David Blumenthal points out:

> The biblical text is accompanied by signs, which indicate how it is to be chanted. When Moses slaughters the ram of consecration, the note indicated on the word "and he slaughtered" (*vayishchat*) is very ornate and very rare.[6]

The cantillation note, called a *shalshelet,* zig-zags something like a lightning bolt. It illustrates a wavering, a dilemma, an existential crisis. Moses is yielding some of his authority as a spiritual leader to his brother Aaron. While not begrudging Aaron this God-appointed honor, he nevertheless realizes that the lineage of Aaron would carry the honor of priesthood always, while his sons and future descendants would not.

Blumenthal explains that this same note occurs on only three other words in the Torah. The first is found when Lot "hesitates" (*vayitmahmah hemah*) on leaving Sodom (Genesis 19:16). The contextual contrast is Abraham's lack of hesitancy in obeying God's voice. The biblical narrative records that each time Abraham hears God's command, he *immediately* hurries to obey—no wavering. The anointing of the priest's ear could, therefore, indicate that, as priests in his service, we are to hear God's voice and be quick to obey.

The second word with a *shalshelet* occurs when Abraham's servant "prays" (*vayomar*) for a sign in choosing a wife for Isaac (Genesis 24:12). The sign was made evident through Rebekah's generous actions. She not only willingly drew water for Eliezer to drink but also did so for his camels. The anointing of the thumb can illustrate that the attitudes of our hearts are reflected in our deeds, the work of our hands. The third instance is found when Joseph "refuses" (*vayema'en*) the persistent advances of Potiphar's wife (Genesis 39:8). The defining act of his refusal is to run swiftly from the scene! The anointing of the big toe, representing the feet, perhaps teaches us that our feet should always be ready to run from evil and instead run to do good.

The sacrifices of dedication commanded by God reflect and expand upon these characteristics. The first is a sin offering (*chatat*) for which a bull is slaughtered. Its purpose is to purify and make atonement for the altar, the place of sacrifice, and meeting with God. This is the work of God. Only he can extend the powerful grace of atonement and the purification of the effects of sin. Only the males of the priestly line may eat of this sacrifice, and only within the precincts of the Sanctuary.

The second sacrifice recorded, which is the first occasion for a response of the individual to God's atoning forgiveness, is the whole burnt offering (*olah*). A ram is ritually slaughtered and wholly consumed by the fire of the altar. No portion is left to be eaten by the priests or the people. It all belongs to God, just as all of one's life should be offered up in loving gratitude for his grace and mercy toward us.

The third sacrifice is the peace offering (*shlamim*), also of a ram, part of which is burnt as an offering to God and part shared by the people. This is the first sacrifice offered as a community and denotes regular communal and covenantal contact with God.

The Midrash reasons:

> If God demands absolute justice, there can be no world.
> If God desires a world, there cannot be absolute justice.
> (*Vayikra Rabbah* 10:1)

The altar and the Sanctuary stand as an indication that in God's plan, there is gracious provision of atonement for human sinfulness and imperfection. This enables an imperfect world to survive in the sight of a just and holy God. As the process of redemption unfolds and in the light of HaMashiach, the Anointed One, the gift from God himself, we can wholeheartedly agree with David Blumenthal's conclusion:

> How strangely beautiful to see the bloody ritualistic killing of animals transformed into a strong theology of atonement, grace, and response.[7]

THE PRIEST AS BLESSER

Two core functions of the priest (kohen) are described by the Prophet Malachi: "He is the messenger of the LORD of hosts" and "the lips of a priest should guard knowledge, and people should seek instruction (Torah) from his mouth" (Malachi 2:7).

We deduce that in addition to his service in the Temple, the priest's role includes teaching and the spiritual elevation of the people.

Rav A.I. Kook points out:

> These two roles are interrelated, since the source for their spiritual influence on the people originates in the holiness of their service in the Temple.[8]

The fruit of the priests' willing obedience and worship of God is imparted as a blessing upon the people, who learn of God's ways and are encouraged to aspire to greater heights of holiness. Rav Kook makes an interesting observation regarding the priestly blessing:

There is one duty of the kohanim that combines both of these roles: the priestly blessing. This blessing is part of the Temple service, and at the same time, reflects their interaction with the people. The kohen recites the blessing with outstretched arms, a sign that their efforts to uplift the people are an extension and continuation of their holy service in the Temple.[9]

Our Father in heaven is a blesser and a giver. Our role as a priest in God's "kingdom of priests" is, therefore, a dual role of worshiping him in spirit and truth and in sharing his Word with others in blessings, both tangible and intangible. Our high priest, Yeshua, Messiah of God, lived and demonstrated the holiness of blessing and giving. In total, willing sacrifice he extended his arms, even in death, to bless and raise up all peoples as holy unto God. He made the way; let us follow and reach out our arms to be a blessing to others in both word and deed.

OBEDIENCE VERSUS SACRIFICE

The parashah concludes with the positive verse: "Aaron and his sons did all the things that the LORD had commanded by Moses" (Leviticus 8:36). However, as we turn to the haftarah [the prophetic reading connected with the parashah, in this case, Jeremiah 7:21–8:3, 9:22–24], we sadly are reminded that this loyal obedience was not upheld in following generations of the people of Israel. The Prophet Jeremiah delivers a warning in the very House of God. He announces a judgment of doom upon the Temple and the nation as a result of the pagan worship and the moral sins of the people.

Jeremiah denounced unbidden, excessive forms of sacrifice, which had become a form of self-glorification and a symbol of wealth and power, and he emphasized that what truly is pleasing to God are acts of kindness and justice. The closing verses of the haftarah echo the Prophet Hosea's description of what God desires:

> For I desire [chesed](loving-kindness and goodness) and not sacrifice; [da'at] (knowledge of and obedience to God) rather than burnt offerings. (Hosea 6:6)

After the destruction of the Temple and the exile, the people of Israel were comforted by the words of the prophets, which emphasized that "the covenantal virtues of kindness, justice, and equity are the very basis for knowing God, and for imitating His ways."[10] The loss of the sacrificial rituals, as many feared, would not permanently impair their relationship with God. The people feared that the loss of the Temple indicated the loss of the Divine Presence of God since it was God who commanded them to make the sacrifices perpetually before him. But obedience is better than sacrifice, as we see illustrated in the first sacrificial offering in the Bible. God is more pleased with Abel's obedience to his will than with the object of his sacrifice.

SH'MINI

שְׁמִינִי – "Eighth"

LEVITICUS 9:1–11:47

The Hebrew word *kashrut* is a noun that defines the dietary laws initially commanded by God in the Torah, were given further explanation through Moses and Joshua, and then were enumerated by rabbinic decisions. Kosher is the adjective that describes anything that complies with kashrut, e.g., a kosher kitchen, kosher meat. There is no doubt that Yeshua's family adhered to the standards of kashrut of their day. The basis of kashrut, as clearly outlined in the Bible, is quite simple:

1. Certain animals, birds, and fish are forbidden as food. These are listed in chapter 11 of this parashah and also in Deuteronomy chapter 14.
2. The animals that are permitted to be eaten must be slaughtered in the prescribed manner, which assures a totally painless death. The blood must then be removed by draining and salting.

WHAT IS KASHRUT?

The plethora of rules and regulations formulated over the centuries, based on these commands from God, has given rise to the complex system of kashrut found in modern-day Orthodox and Ultra-Orthodox Judaism. The additional barriers were added in an effort to ensure adherence to the commandments of God.

Why should we bother with the laws of kashrut at all? People can offer good reasons; God gave the commands. They have proven to be good for one's health and afford protection from certain diseases. They offer those who serve the God of Israel a mark of personal and group identity. David Blumenthal provides an interesting consideration: "They are part of a mystery and create a sacramental aura to all eating."[11]

Blumenthal adds a further intriguing reason, with reference to the teachings of Levi Yitzchak on the words of Nachmanides (the Ramban), another renowned medieval commentator, who said,

> The reason the Torah forbade us these animals is that … in the future the Holy One, blessed be He, will speak with each person of Israel, as it says: "Your sons and daughters shall prophesy" (Joel 2:28).[12]

Levi Yitzchak also notes, "From this we learn that … it is not fitting that the mouth which will speak with Him [and for Him] should eat forbidden foods."

According to this view, keeping kosher is a way of preparing oneself, according to God's directives, by cultivating the bodily habits that make one a fit vessel for the Divine Presence.

The name of the Hebrew letter *peh* means "mouth." The letter is in the shape of a large open mouth. The sages of Israel point out that every part of the Torah scroll text is important and carries meaning, including the shapes of the letters and the arrangements of the words, and even the spaces around the words. At the very beginning, in the space around the first letter of the Hebrew Scriptures—a *bet*—we find the shape of a large letter *peh*. This forms, in effect, a large invisible mouth from which the Word of God flows forth, an amazing illustration that the Bible is indeed breathed from the mouth of God.

בּ   פ

bet   *peh*

This serves to highlight the significance of the mouth. The words we speak are of supreme importance and can carry life or death. They can build up or break down. The mouth also is a conduit for providing life-maintaining sustenance to the body. As Blumenthal emphasizes:

What one eats, counts. What one says, counts. To eat properly, and to speak properly, is to guard the gateway of the body. Someday God will address us [face to face]. He will speak to us, and we will speak to Him. And our bodies, as well as our minds and hearts, must be ready. We must aim to be whole when He comes.[13]

FEAR OR WISDOM?

> Now, O Israel, what does the LORD, your God, ask of you, but to fear the LORD your God. (Deuteronomy 10:12)

The Scriptures reveal that the foundation of wisdom is the fear of the Almighty God: "The fear of the LORD is the beginning of wisdom, and the knowledge of the Holy One is insight" (Proverbs 9:10). We can picture fear, or reverential awe, of God as the foundation upon which the pillars of wisdom are erected that support the whole edifice or "house" of one's life.

There are, interestingly, seven verses of Scripture in which fear of God and wisdom are mentioned together. For example, Isaiah 33:6 states: "Wisdom and knowledge will be the stability of your times, ... The fear of the LORD is his treasure." In this connection, the Babylonian Talmud records a parable of a farmer faced with the waste of a storehouse filled with rotten grain:

> This is like a farmer who ordered his worker to store grain in his warehouse. Later, when his worker admitted that he had not added preservatives to the grain to prevent rot, the farmer said, "It would have been better if you had not stored the grain in the first place!"[14]

Similarly, if wisdom gained by the study of God's Word is not preserved with sincere fear of God, it will degenerate into a distortion of his will and will prove to be a great waste. The sages, therefore, state in *Pirkei Avot*: "If there is no fear of God, there is no wisdom" (3:21). At the same time, they teach, "If there is no wisdom, there is no fear of God" (2:5). This is reminiscent of the chicken and the egg—you cannot have one without the other!

TENTS AND STREAMS OF LIVING WATER

Life is a journey, an unfolding path upon which we need the direction of the LORD. Our own wisdom and intellect are not sufficient to bring us to the God-ordained destination. In the light of the eternal home that awaits us, we are but passing through our earthbound span of life. Rabbi Chanan Morrison recounts a true story that well illustrates this principle:

> A wealthy American Jew visited one of the leading Torah scholars of this generation. Upon arriving at the rabbi's home on a moshav (a small communal farming village) in Israel, the visitor was shocked to discover the saintly rabbi and his wife living in a small house with a dirt floor and shabby wood furnishings. He immediately offered to pay for improvements to be made, including respectable furniture.
>
> The rabbi turned to his guest. "And tell me, where is your furniture?"
>
> "My furniture?" responded the American Jew, baffled. "Why, I am only a visitor here. I don't travel with all my belongings."
>
> "So with me," the rabbi replied. "I am only a visitor here in this world."[15]

This is not to say that comfortable and attractive surroundings should be shunned, but the value one places upon these should be in accord with the reality of God's eternal purposes. Our existence in this world is transient, and our focus and efforts should be directed toward goals that are of lasting worth.

Rabbi A.I. Kook notes that the sages link this to the central importance and value of Torah study—of gaining the wisdom and riches offered by God in his Word. They compare the results of Torah study to that of *mayim chayim*, a purifying stream (natural, living waters of immersion):

> Why did Balaam compare the tents of Israel to streams? (Numbers 24:6) This teaches us that just as a spring raises one from [ritual] impurity to purity, so too the tents [of Torah learning] raise one from a state of culpability to a state of merit.[16]

Rav Kook deduces that the "tents" of Torah study and immersion in a mikvah of living water have similar benefits. When submerged in water, we realize that we cannot live for long in that environment—it is a temporary experience. A tent is the most transient of homes, and learning the wisdom of Torah reminds us that this material world is transitory. Our vision and aims should be set upon the eternal values and aspirations that the Word of God teaches.

As the Torah made flesh, Yeshua is a fount of Living Water; as he revealed to the woman at the well in Samaria (John 4:6–15). He later proclaimed to the great crowd gathered in the Temple courts on the last, great day of the Festival of Tabernacles as the high priest poured out the water upon the altar: "If anyone thirsts, let him come to me and drink" (John 7:37). Thus, the more we learn of the Word, the more we learn of him, the Living Torah. When we immerse ourselves more fully in him, the Living Water, he is faithful to raise us from "impurity to purity" to the glory of our Father in heaven.

TAZRIA

תזריע – "Conceived"

LEVITICUS 12:1–13:59

The blessing "Mazal tov!" is bestowed upon the bearer of good news, such as a betrothal, a wedding, or a birth. This often is translated simply as "Good luck!" However, if one considers the Hebrew word *mazal* (*mem, zayin, lamed*) as an acronym, it carries a far deeper meaning. Mem is the first letter of the Hebrew word *makom* (place), zayin begins the word *zeman* (time), and lamed initiates the word *lashon* (tongue or speech). The adjective *tov* means good or favorable. One is thereby conveying the intention that the recipient be blessed by being in a good place, at the most favorable time, and would have fitting words to speak. It is indeed a rich blessing to know one is in the right place, at the right time, with the right words to say. As the wise King Solomon expressed: "To have an apt answer is a joy to a man, and a word in season, how good it is!" (Proverbs 15:23).

IN DUE SEASON

The opening verses of the parashah this week address the issue of giving birth and the Temple ritual and sacrifices connected therewith. It is vital that the stages in the process of birth—namely conception, pregnancy, and birthing—take place "in due season." There are specific times at which conception can occur, the full development of the fetus requires a prescribed time, and the birth should ideally happen on the "due" date. When all goes well, one can indeed proclaim, "Mazal tov!" fully recognizing that it is by no means a matter of "luck." Rather, one rejoices in the understanding that another cycle in the harmony and goodness of God's creation has been accomplished.

God set the precedent at Creation. He spoke forth mighty words, filled with power, creativity, and life. Each of his creations was established in its ordained place. All was created in his perfect timing. He rejoiced with great joy as he saw it was all *tov*, good! Man was created last. As we sing joyously on Friday night in *Lechah Dodi*: "The first in thought is the last in deed." The goal is primary in thought, before the process to achieve it is carried out. They deduce that man was the most important of the creations, and God created everything for his sake. It is man who, by means of his God-given powers of reason, will come to recognize God and be drawn into an intimate, covenant relationship with him, which is God's desire and the goal of Creation.

We note again the "season" of seven in the second verse of the portion: "If a woman conceives, and bears a male child, then she shall be unclean seven days" (Leviticus 12:2). After giving birth to a boy, a woman is in a state of ritual impurity for an initial seven days. That is, she cannot enter the Temple precincts and participate in communal worship. She must be in the "right" place, where she naturally wants to be—at home with her baby. On reflection, one realizes that the first seven days of a person's life are echoed in the traditional seven days of mourning observed after a person's death. There is a season of intimate bonding after birth and a corresponding season of deep release after death. Just as in Creation, the "season of seven" must be accomplished before the new beginning.

SIGNS IN THE FLESH

When a boy is born, we read that after seven days, he is to be circumcised (Leviticus 12:3). If the baby is a girl, she enjoys a second week at home with her mother as she does not need the ritual (Leviticus 12:5). The pros and cons of circumcision are often debated. The sages tell a story of a debate between the wicked Roman ruler, Turnus Rufus, and Rabbi Akiva concerning the deeds of man and God:

> Said Turnus Rufus: "Why do you circumcise yourselves? Couldn't God have created you in that manner?"

Answered Rabbi Akiva: "Why is a child born still tied to his mother by a cord so that we must cut the cord? Could not God cause the child to be born already severed from his mother's womb? But God wanted to leave something for man to correct. Similarly, God left the foreskin for us to correct. Further, God uses this as a means of testing us to see if we will obey His commands."[17]

A focal issue in Parashat Tazria is the skin condition *tzara'at* that is related to a spiritual condition:

> When a man has on the skin of his body a swelling or an eruption or a spot, and it turns into a leprous disease [*tzara'at*] on the skin of his body, then he shall be brought to Aaron the priest or to one of his sons the priests. (Leviticus 13:2)

Tzara'at often is translated as "leprosy." Although similar in appearance, it was not the disease we know as leprosy today. A clear illustration of the condition is given in the Scriptures when Miriam challenges Moses' leadership, and she is stricken with *tzara'at*. "When the cloud removed from over the tent, behold, Miriam was leprous, as white as snow" (Numbers 12:10). Moses intercedes for her, and she is healed. She must, however, leave the camp for seven days. No doubt, she spent this time in humble and deep repentance before her heavenly Father.

An interesting aspect of *tzara'at* is that it can appear not only on the skin but also on the walls of a house and upon clothing. If one repents and takes the appropriate action, God forgives, and the condition is healed; if not, the condition can escalate. However, one must recognize a sin for what it is before one can truly repent. The Midrash intimates that Job's condition was that of *tzara'at*:

> God is merciful. He punishes with pity, as we see in the case of Job, whom God first struck through his possessions, then through his home, then through his children, and finally through his own body ... The disease would come as a result of Divine Providence, so that man would know that he has sinned and that he must repent.[18]

PRIDE AND REPENTANCE

The Scriptures record the scenarios of two other prominent Gentile rulers who came face-to-face, as it were, with the God of Israel. On both accounts we see the conflict of pride versus humility within the heart of a man. One overcomes and is restored; the other refuses to bend and incurs death.

The first instance takes place in the dramatic setting of the exodus of the Israelite slaves from Egypt. The man is Pharaoh himself—the ruler of the mighty Egyptian empire. Throughout the narrative, we see how Pharaoh stubbornly refuses to yield his will to the dictates of God, his Creator. God sends ten plagues and illustrates his power over all creation—the waters of the Nile, the insect world, the animal world, day and night, man's body. Finally, in the face of Pharaoh's ongoing pride, God demonstrates his power over life itself, and death strikes the first-born of every Egyptian household.

The second account is found in the haftarah this week, that of Na'aman, the commander of the Syrian army. After contracting *tzara'at*, he was informed by his captive Hebrew servant girl of the Prophet Elisha in the land of Israel, who had the power to heal the condition. In his desperation Na'aman undertakes the journey seeking to consult with the prophet. When Elisha sends a messenger to him to relay the directive to bathe seven times in the nearby Jordan River, Na'aman reacts in prideful rage. He is angry that Elisha insulted him by not personally coming out to greet him and, also, he expected a simple "wave of the hand" to cure him (2 Kings 5:11). He compares the superior appearance of the rivers in his own country to the lowly Jordan and scornfully rejects the idea of immersing himself in it.

We see a redeeming quality in the midst of Na'aman's pride and anger when he pays attention once again to the words of a servant, indicating that he is a good master. He acts on the servant's wise counsel and follows Elisha's directions. He is miraculously healed and humbly pays homage to the God of Israel. Elisha now meets with him and extends his blessing saying, "*Lech beshalom,* Go in peace." Na'aman can return in shalom and wholeness to be a living testimony to his idolatrous people of the one, true God of Israel.

METZORA

מצרע – "Leper"

LEVITICUS 14:1–15:33

The soul can suffer disease and sickness, as does the physical body. Often the two are related, and the physical condition can have its roots in the soul or spirit of the afflicted. Sickness of the soul is a result of sin, as the psalmist cries out to God, "Heal me, for I have sinned against you" (Psalm 41:4).

In Parashat Metzora, the "sickness of the soul" described is the sin of evil speech, *lashon hara*, which usually takes the form of speaking ill of others as in gossip or slander, or in lying, as we see illustrated in the haftarah. The danger of this "disease" is that, in the mind of the sinner, he may be convinced that he did not sin because he performed no action; he "merely spoke." Consequently, he does not repent.

The sages ask the question: "Which is the more deadly weapon, an arrow or a sword?"

> An arrow is much worse, for a sword can only kill those within reach, while an arrow can kill those at a distance. For this reason the prophet calls slanderous talk "an arrow shot out" (Jeremiah 9:7) for it can kill over a long distance, just like an arrow.[19]

TAMING THE TONGUE

One who suffers from the disease *tzara'at* is called a *metzora*. This appellation can be seen as the contraction of two Hebrew words *motzi ra*, which mean "bring forth what is evil." The outward condition is a consequence of speaking out evil thoughts one has harbored in one's heart against another. It can be viewed as the gracious mercy of God that the appearance of the condition is an indication that one has indeed "sinned against You, God." It is, therefore, a clear invitation to repent and be healed. The *metzora* is hopefully shocked into awareness of the seriousness of his sin and will be quick to take the necessary action to redress it.

The Scriptures make it very clear that the "fruit" of the tongue can be sweet and bring much good, or bitter and bring forth much evil. An example: "Death and life are in the power of the tongue, and those who love it will eat its fruits" (Proverbs 18:21). Or, as one translation renders it: "The tongue has the power of life and death, and those who love to talk will have to eat their own words" (GWT).

The power of speech is a great gift, bestowed upon his beloved children by our Father-Creator. If one positively "loves" and values this gift of the tongue, and uses it to speak according to his Word and truth, many are the rewards. If, however, the tongue becomes an instrument of negativity and vain, foolish words, the "wages of sin" are sadly incurred. The only cure for the disease of the tongue is a clear recognition of its presence, and repentance—a renouncing of the sin and a determination to "tame the tongue" and to use it only for good and to the glory of God.

We read in the parashah that a *metzora* cannot be healed without the intervention of a kohen (priest). Once the kohen proclaims that the individual is pure, a "cleansing" ceremony is performed. The *metzora* can then return to the community, where he enters a mikvah for ritual immersion and offers a sacrifice in the Temple. The elements involved in the cleansing ceremony alert us to the details of the condition and its cause.

Two kosher birds are brought. Midrashic commentary offers:

> God commanded that he bring birds, who sing and chirp with their mouths, to atone for the evil which his mouth spoke.[20]

The kohen also brings wood of a cedar tree and a bunch of hyssop. The strong cedars grow to great heights and are often a symbol of pride, whereas the hyssop is the lowliest of shrubs. These indicate that pride is at the root of evil talk, and the *metzora* needs to humble himself like the hyssop. In this regard, another element is the crimson thread, the dye of which comes from a particular worm. If the *metzora* remembers that, next to God, he is but a "worm," he can retain humility and be healed!

The kohen ritually slaughters one bird and adds its blood to a bowl of "living water," i.e., water from a spring or a flowing stream. This is a startling, clear picture of the cleansing power of our high priest, Yeshua, who himself comes to the sinner, who is alone and isolated in his sin. He brings healing and cleansing in the ultimate sacrifice of his own blood, together with the Living Water of the Word made flesh in him. He then sets one's soul free, as the kohen does the second bird, to soar and sing forth praises to the Almighty God.

PURITY OF TIME AND SOUL

> The sun sets, and then he is ritually clean. He may then eat the sacred offerings that are his portion. (Leviticus 22:7)

Rabbi A.I. Kook points out an interesting interpretation of this verse found in the Talmud:

> The sun sets, and then it—the day—is clean [i.e., completed]. The Sages explained that the day must be completely over before the individual may partake of his offering [then his healing is complete].[21]

Rav Kook asks, "Why emphasize that the day must be clean?" He explains that there are two levels of purification referred to in the Talmud: purifying the day (*tehar yoma*) and purifying the individual (*tehar gavra*). How are the two related? He answers:

> Our goal in life should be to grow spiritually and become closer to our Creator. When we sin, we stray from our overall objective. We have also misused time that could have been utilized for spiritual growth. A full [and fruitful] life is one in which our days have been employed towards this one principal objective.[22]

A major outcome of the sin of gossip, slander, and improper, unguarded speech is the damage caused in personal relationships, whether with family and friends or even with strangers. Rav Kook teaches that two distinct efforts need to be made to make restitution once a person repents of this sin. Correcting one's behavior is vital, but this of itself does not restore a damaged relationship to its proper state. He says, "The relationship will remain fragile until I have made an additional effort to rebuild the ties of affection and friendship."[23]

A key step in the first stage of this dual process of repentance and restoration is the mikvah—immersion in living water—as we see in the case of the *metzora*. This is, of course, a prominent theme throughout Scripture and is highlighted in the New Testament, e.g., the baptism (immersion for repentance) of John, which Yeshua honors, and through which he is honored by God, his Father (Luke 3:21–22). Also, the immersion of three thousand in the Temple precincts (Acts 2:41). The mikvah is the outward demonstration of repentance. The sinner, as it were, dies to the "old," negative character trait and sinful deeds and rises from the water a cleansed, "new" or "renewed" person. A fresh start is made just as the sun sets on the "old" day, and a new day begins.

This is what the sages call *tehar yoma*, the purification of the day. The old must fade away and be let go of before the new day can be embraced. This understanding adds an extra dimension to the adage: "Let not the sun go down on your anger"! If we can live each day with this awareness then, as Rav Kook concludes, "The day has not been lost to sin. With the setting of the sun, we begin a new day and make a new start."

The second stage of restoration is achieved, as when the *metzora* "may then eat of the sacred offerings," when the individual is restored to personal and communal worship in the House of God. He once again can draw close to God in awe and love, for his relationship with him is healed and restored.

To restore damaged relationships with others also requires specific action. One needs to bring the offerings of vulnerability and forgiveness to the other. In this, we are enabled by the One who has extended full forgiveness to us. We then can joyfully anticipate the restoration and redemption of any rift in the relationship and enjoy the accompanying blessings intended for his children by our Father in heaven.

> It is the act of forgiveness that opens up the only possible way to think creatively about the future at all. (Father Desmond Wilson)

ACHAREI MOT

אחרי מות – "After the Death"

LEVITICUS 16:1–18:30

> Tell Aaron your brother not to come at any time into the Holy Place inside the veil, before the mercy seat that is on the ark, so that he may not die. (Leviticus 16:2)

The opening verses cause us to confront the reality of our mortality. The text continues with a description of the rituals of Yom Kippur, the Day of Atonement, the holiest day of the biblical calendar. The Torah reading in synagogues on Yom Kippur is comprised of verses 4 through 34 of this chapter. The essential elements connected with Yom Kippur, on both a personal and communal level, are self-scrutiny, cleansing, and renewal of life in relationship with one's Creator and with others.

THE GLORY OF HIS PRESENCE

This portion, Acharei Mot, is read when the land of Israel today is experiencing the warmth and beauty of springtime:

> The rain is over and gone. The flowers appear on the earth, the time of singing has come, and the voice of the turtledove is heard in our land. (Song of Songs 2:11-12)

It is six months after the previous Yom Kippur and six months before the next. This suggests that this time of new life, together with the redemptive freedom celebrated at Passover, also is an appropriate time for intentional self-reflection and atonement—a "spring-cleaning" of the soul.

The necessary rituals that Aaron, as high priest, must undertake before entering the holy of holies are initiated with the sacrifices of a bull for a purification offering and a ram for a burnt offering. The Midrash considers:

> The bull recalls the merit of Abraham's offering in Genesis 18:7.
>
> The ram is a reminder of Isaac's readiness to be sacrificed in Genesis 22:13. (*Leviticus Rabbah* 21:11)[24]

These sin offerings reinforce the understanding that even the high priest, one especially appointed and consecrated by God, as well as all the *kohanim* (priests), are only human and subject to the weaknesses and challenges of all people. When he enters the inner Sanctuary of the holy of holies, the high priest comes into God's Presence not as a supernaturally pious person, but as the representative of a flawed community and a people who are aspiring to holiness. He fully identifies with those whose prayers, hopes, and tears he brings before the Almighty.

On the other hand, the awe and solemnity of the occasion and the high esteem afforded the high priest are emphasized in Leviticus 16:17: "No one may be in the tent of meeting." The Babylonian Talmud says, in Tractate Yoma, that even the angels who were always in the holy of holies would go out before the entrance of the high priest.[25]

God had set in place all the details of his preparation and the rituals involved before Aaron was to enter. It was literally a matter of life or death. The opening verse of the parashah states, "after the death of the two sons of Aaron, when they drew near before the LORD and died" (Leviticus 16:1). We can surmise from this that, perhaps in their zeal, they drew too near in a manner not prescribed by God. Maybe they entered the holy of holies inappropriately dressed? This consideration offers insight as to God's command regarding the garments of Aaron as high priest.

On the Day of Atonement he sets aside the beautiful golden garments regularly worn when performing his service in the Temple and, after immersing himself in a mikvah, he dons four simple, white linen garments. This action is filled with significance. The high priest is anointed to be, in effect, the holiest person on earth. He is the only one allowed to enter the Presence of God in the innermost Sanctuary of the Temple—the one who represents all the people before God and who represents God before the people. He is honored in the eyes of God and man, and his special priestly "garments of glory" reflect this. On this day, however, before entering the holy of holies, he must set these aside for garments of humble, white linen. This signals that the highest position and honor one can attain in this world is as nothing when one enters the glory of God's Presence. Nothing man can achieve or accomplish is a cause for pride. Human beings can take no credit for wealth amassed, learning gained, or work produced. It all fades into insignificance in the radiance and the greatness of the Almighty God.

TORAH AND LIFE

A key verse in the parashah highlights the centrality of God's Word in people's lives:

> You shall therefore keep my statutes and my rules; if a person does them, he shall live by them. (Leviticus 18:5)

God does not want us to die for him. He desires, and in fact commands, that we live for him. "Choose life!" (Deuteronomy 30:19). He is not a despot who "lays down the law" and demands unwilling and unquestioning obedience, at the pain of death. He is an eternally loving Father, who after redeeming his children from a culture of slavery and death, gives them the gift of his eternal Word to lead and guide and to draw them into all truth.

The timelessness of his truth was incarnated in the glorious gift of his Son, the Word made flesh who "dwelt among us ... full of grace and truth "(John 1:14). Yeshua, as the bearer of salvation for all humanity, made flesh the radiance of the glory of the Father. He defined the commandments of God and filled them full of meaning by his very being.

What a privilege to draw near to the Holy Scriptures in the light of Yeshua and what joy to learn to walk in our Father's ways. As recorded in the writings of early church scholar Athanasius of Alexandria, *The Life of Anthony*: "[Don't be impressed by emperors] rather wonder that God wrote the Law [Torah] for men and has spoken to us through his own Son."

It is little wonder that the psalmist declared with all his heart:

> Your truth has preserved my life! O how I love Your Torah, it is my meditation all the day. I have more understanding than all my teachers. I hold back my feet from every evil way, in order to keep your word. (Psalm 119:92, 97, 99, 101)

IN SICKNESS AND IN HEALTH

The attitude of our hearts toward the Beloved of our souls is reflected in the words that often are proclaimed in wedding vows to an earthly beloved: "Do you promise to love, honor, and obey, in richness and poorness, in sickness and in health?" This infers that one's commitment to love, honor, and obey our spouse is not dependent on external conditions. No matter the state of the outward circumstances, the inner devotion of the heart will stand true and unwavering. This was proclaimed by the people of Israel at Sinai, with the words, "All that the LORD has spoken we will do, and we will be obedient" (Exodus 24:7). Yeshua echoed this attitude of heart when he said to his disciples, "If you love me, you will keep my commandments" (John 14:15).

Sara Yoheved Rigler, a Jewish author in Jerusalem, has written an amazing biography of Chaya Sara Kramer (1925-2005) and her husband, Rabbi Yaakov Moshe Kramer, z"l, who were considered one of the most saintly couples in Israel of their generation. Chaya Sara, then in her early twenties, was the only one of her family who survived the Holocaust. Even after enduring the living hell of Auschwitz, she was able to say, "A bad place has nothing to do with bad things happening to you. All that really matters is what issues from you."

Sara Rigler writes,

> No wonder Rebbetzin Chaya Sara was always smiling, despite her barrenness, despite her poverty, despite the grueling hardship of her daily life. She was performing mitzvot [good deeds—actions in willing obedience to God and his Word]. ... She would project her own light, even in the darkness of hell. Blessings poured from Rebbetzin Chaya Sara like water gushing from a spring after the winter rains. ... Yet, Chaya Sara always attributed all to God—the Blessed Holy One—and retained an awesome humility.[26]

Another touching account of devotion to God and his Word was recorded by Rabbi A.L. Scheinbaum,[27] who remembers when he visited the dean of his yeshivah, Rav Baruch Sorotzkin, z"l, in the hospital where he was undergoing treatment for a debilitating disease. He was suffering excruciating pain, yet he remained undaunted and continued to study Torah. Shortly before his death, his son visited him and found him in a wheelchair, in obvious pain, hunched over a biblical text. "Why are you learning now?" his son asked him. "When else will I be able to learn?" answered the saintly leader of the yeshiva.

KEDOSHIM

קְדוֹשִׁים – "Holy"

LEVITICUS 19:1–20:27

> You shall not hate your brother in your heart, but you shall reason frankly with your neighbor, lest you incur sin because of him. (Leviticus 19:17)

The Hebrew word *hochiach* (rebuke, reprove) denotes giving correction or, as Rabbi S.R. Hirsch describes:

> [Reproof is] making someone aware of an unpleasant fact about himself; to explain to him that he has been guilty of an intellectual error, or that he has strayed from the path of morality.[28]

REBUKE IN LOVE

In so doing, we do not risk harboring any resentment or anger against him. An equally negative reaction is to complain of it to friends. Neither action brings release and healing as the cause of the anger remains unchanged. If one cares at all for oneself, and for the other, the grievance must be addressed and confronted. By bringing the matter into the light and helping him to recognize and understand what he has done, we are demonstrating that we care for our neighbor and that we do not "hate him in our heart." Hirsch adds, "Bearing a grudge in silence bespeaks an ignoble character."[29] He points to a clear example of this in 2 Samuel 13:22, "And Absalom spoke to Amnon neither bad nor good, for Absalom hated Amnon."

The Midrash reinforces this idea in stating that the commandment *hocheach tochiach* ("rebuke him again and again") indicates that "as a rule, we should not remain silent but should repeatedly, again and again, if necessary, remonstrate with our brother or sister if we see them commit a sinful, harmful action, no matter the magnitude ... so that the sinner may, if possible, gain insight into his conduct and mend his ways" (b.*Bava Metzia* 31a).

The Talmud states even more strongly that even if one's own conduct is blameless, if one does not do what is possible to help others not to go astray, one is considered an accomplice in their guilt (b.*Shabbat* 54a–55a). This applies in one's family, regarding one's fellow citizens, and even the whole world. If we shy away from confrontation, when it is healthy and necessary, or if we take revenge or bear a grudge, we are "taking the sin upon ourselves." Engaging in confrontation in a critical, negative, unloving manner also misses the mark. Healthy reproof is accomplished in a non-judgmental, non-condemnatory way, with a heart attitude of compassion and forgiveness.

Healthy, humble confrontation usually is difficult. To open one's heart and willingly be transparent and vulnerable takes courage. One may be rejected. One's offer of reconciliation may be refused. However, to hold onto one's anger and resentment and to harden one's heart against another person is to risk incurring the sin of *sinat chinam*, baseless or groundless hatred. The Babylonian Talmud, in b.*Yoma* 9b, points out that the Second Temple was destroyed on account of this sin and states, "The offense of groundless hatred is equivalent to the three sins of idolatry, sexual immorality, and murder," which caused the fall of the First Temple.

Rabbi Joseph Telushkin comments:

> People guilty of "groundless hatred" never repent because they never acknowledge their sin ... they will justify their own personal hatreds ... no one repents of its commission or roots it out of his or her heart.[30]

To root it out of one's heart requires action—the action of *hocheach*! Any person who sincerely seeks to serve God will appreciate correction.

As King Solomon expressed: "It is better for a man to hear the rebuke of the wise than to hear the song of fools" (Ecclesiastes 7:5).

Loving confrontation and "rebuke" is what the LORD our God calls us to in order to ground and establish healthy, godly relationships; relationships that are founded upon and filled with his loving-kindness; relationships that are bathed in the light of his truth.

LOVE THE STRANGER

The Word of God teaches that the most noble, fundamental attitude one can have toward God and man is *ahavah*—love. Rabbi Hirsch emphasizes that this requirement of love is not dependent upon our neighbor's person or his personality. Hirsch maintains that at all times, and in every case, whether he is a close friend or a criminal, "we are to rejoice in his happiness as if it were our own, grieve over his suffering as if it were our own, assist as eagerly in advancing his welfare as if we were working to advance our own, and keep trouble away from him as if we ourselves were threatened by it."[31]

We see an amplification of the commandment to love in this parashah:

> You shall treat the stranger who sojourns with you as the native among you, and you shall love him as yourself... I am the LORD your God. (Leviticus 19:34)

This command is accompanied with the reminder, "for you were strangers in the land of Egypt." The stranger in a society is often viewed with suspicion and merely tolerated. Israel's experience as strangers in Egypt, when their human rights were betrayed, and they suffered enslavement and affliction, should serve as a constant basis for fair treatment of the stranger. More than extending fair and just treatment, God expects his people to love the stranger as we love ourselves.

God sets his personal seal, as it were, upon the command by declaring at the end of the verse, "I am the LORD your God!" Because we honor God as our Father, we honor every human being who is created in his image. He himself is love, and his Word sets this love as the goal and standard for his children.

Yeshua extended this commandment of love still further:

> Love your enemies and pray for those who persecute you, so that you may be sons of your Father who is in heaven; for he makes his sun rise on the evil and on the good, and sends rain on the just and on the unjust. (Matthew 5:44-45)

BE HOLY

The portion opens with the powerful injunction: "You shall be holy, for I the LORD your God am holy." His people are *kedoshim* (holy ones) for God is *kadosh, kadosh, kadosh*!

Among the challenging and significant questions that arise upon reflection of this awesome reality are: "What is holiness?" and "How on earth can I be holy?" Perhaps what comes to mind is the picture of a saint, somewhat ephemeral, in a state of meditative bliss raised above the lowly material level of his fellow humans. We are quickly brought down to earth, however, as we read the words immediately following the initial proclamation:

> Every one of you shall revere his mother and his father, and you shall keep my Sabbaths: I am the LORD your God. (Leviticus 19:3)

The parashah continues to list further "down to earth" requirements for holiness, and we come to understand Rabbi Hirsch's comments:

> Kedusha (holiness) results when a morally free human being has complete dominion over all his energies and inclinations and over the enticements and tendencies associated with these and places them in the service of God ... in order to accomplish the will of God on earth.[32]

Yeshua clarified this concept in his answer to the question by a scribe as to which was the greatest commandment:

> You shall love the Lord your God with all your heart, and with all your soul, and with all your mind. And ... you shall love your neighbor as yourself. (Matthew 22:37, 39)

When we love God with all our hearts, our strongest desire will be to please him and to honor his Name. The way he has given us to do this is the process of holiness, a continual growth in sanctification, a daily growing in awareness and intimate knowledge of him. As a result, we grow in faith and trust and are enabled to live more fully in loving obedience to his will, which is perfect. We then can say, "Not my will, but Thine be done!"

The most immediate, tangible means of expressing our love for him is the demonstration of our love toward our "neighbors"—our spouse, family, and fellow man, whether friend or stranger. Every true act of justice, selflessness, and brotherly love flows from this love—the holy love of God.

The elements of how to build a life and a community that express this love are found in his Word—the inspired teaching and guidance of God. The power to do so is given by his *Ruach HaKodesh*—his Spirit of Holiness. The fullness and demonstration of his Word, and of walking in its truth by the Holy Spirit, was given to us by God himself in the form of his Son, Yeshua the Messiah, who said,

> A new [renewed] commandment I give to you, that you love one another: just as I have loved you, you also are to love one another. By this all people will know that you are my disciples, if you have love for one another [if you keep on showing love among yourselves]. (John 13:34–35)

EMOR

אֱמֹר – "Say"

LEVITICUS 21:1–24:23

From chapter 17 through the end of the book of Leviticus/Vayikra, with the exception of chapter 26, the chapters begin with the phrase, "And the LORD said to Moses," an echo of the opening verse of the book. This repetition seems to reinforce the fact that these are the undisputed words of God himself.

The first Hebrew verse of this portion contains a rather clumsy reiteration of forms of the word *emor* (say): the LORD said (*vayomer*) to Moses, "Speak (*emor*) to the sons of Aaron, and say (*v'amarta*) to them ..." (Leviticus 21:1). One can deliberate on the reason for this seeming redundancy. Maybe God is emphasizing that Moses must direct these words only to the priests, the sons of Aaron?

Rashi, the renowned medieval commentator, offers the opinion that this is a means of enjoining the priests, in turn, to speak of these words to their children and to others. Just as God spoke to Moses and taught him, and Moses, in turn, taught them, so they are to teach their children and students.

Another related Hebrew word that connotes telling or communicating is *daber*. A prime example of the use of *daber* (*dibrot*, plural) is *Aseret HaDibrot*—the Ten Commandments, or literally translated: the Ten Words.

Rabbi S.R. Hirsch explains the difference between *daber* and *emor*. While *daber* denotes the concise statement of an idea, *emor* implies the instilling of an idea into the mind and spirit of another. This indicates that the latter requires a more interactive form of communication, while the former is putting ideas into words regardless of whether or not the listener accepts them. He continues:

> Therefore, in the parlance of Jewish law, *daber* is always the concise statement of the law as given to us in the Written Torah (*Torah shebichtav*), while *emor* indicates the complete explanation that has been handed down to us through the Oral Torah (*Torah Sheb'al Peh*).[33]

WRITTEN AND ORAL TORAH

The Written Torah, the inspired and recorded Word of God, has remained the bed-rock of Judaism as well as Christianity. In Judaism, the Oral Torah also is revered as the explanation of the Torah, which is silent on many important subjects. The sages believed that God communicated many of the missing details to Moses, who passed them on to Joshua, who transmitted them to his successor. So it continued in a vital process of "saying" and teaching and debate that has continued to the present day.

Rabbi Joseph Telushkin highlights the importance of the tradition of orally passing on the written Word of God from generation to generation:

> Teaching the Torah orally, the rabbis knew, compelled students to maintain close relationships with teachers, and they considered teachers, not books, to be the best conveyors of [the truth of] Jewish tradition.[34]

He quotes the British-Jewish scholar and writer Hyam Maccoby:

> [This is] the keynote of the Talmud. God is a good Father who wants his children to grow up and achieve independence. He has given them his Torah [guidance, instruction], but now he wants them to develop it.[35]

The oral transmission of the teachings of the Written Torah and the rabbinic commentary thereon were eventually redacted under the direction of Rabbi Yehudah HaNasi circa 200 CE. After uprisings in Roman-controlled Palestine, namely the Great Revolt and the Bar Kochba rebellion, when over a million Jews were killed, including thousands of rabbis and their students, Rabbi Yehudah HaNasi feared that the Oral Torah would be lost unless it was formalized in written form. He is credited with systematically codifying the Oral Torah into six Orders or major categories with a total of sixty-three subdivisions or tractates. For example, the order *Mo'ed* (Festival) includes the tractate *Shabbat*. *Nezikim* (Damages) contains ten tractates on biblically based civil and criminal law, and *Nashim* (Women) deals with relational issues and includes the tractates of *Kiddushin*, "marriage," and *Gittin*, "divorce." This codification of the Oral Torah is known as the Mishnah.

The Mishnah was studied extensively by rabbis throughout the following generations. The discussions on critical issues and the commentaries of outstanding rabbis were recorded and preserved in a series of manuscripts that, together with the Mishnah, became known as the Talmud (from the word *lamad*, "study"). Those recorded in Palestine, circa 400 CE, became known as the Palestinian Talmud, or in Hebrew: *Talmud Yerushalmi* (Jerusalem Talmud). Another more extensive collection was compiled more than a century later by the large and learned rabbinic community in Babylon. This is known as the Babylonian Talmud or *Talmud Bavli*, and due to Babylonian Jews having greater resources, and enjoying a more stable political situation than their counterparts in Israel, the Babylonian Talmud naturally became the more dominant Talmud and is considered to be the greater authority of the two.

The later rabbinic teachings and discussions are commonly known as the Gemara, which is the Aramaic word for "teaching." Rabbi Telushkin gives further explanation:

> The rabbis whose views are cited in the Mishnah are known as the *Tannaim* (Aramaic for teachers), while the rabbis quoted in the Gemarah are known as the *Amoraim* (explainers or interpreters).[36]

In Judaism, the Ultra-Orthodox and Orthodox place great authority on the Mishnah and the Gemara, and both believe that these texts are necessary to practice the written Torah. The more liberal Conservative communities and, in particular, the Reform branch of Judaism do not hold any legal authority to the Oral Torah nor the written Torah in many areas.

Orthodox Judaism considers the Torah the immutable Word of God, as has mainstream Christianity. The latter, however, considers the Apostolic Writings (New Testament) as part of the absolute Word of God (*Devar Adonai*). Scholars have raised some questions, however, as to whether the epistles would more correctly fall into the category of talmudic-style teaching and commentary.

MIDRASHIC INTERPRETATION – SAY TO ONE ANOTHER

Midrash is a category of rabbinic literature. It is divided into *midrash aggada* (sermonic applications of the biblical text) and *midrash halachah* (rules of living that are derived from it). The sages of Israel always believed that every word of the Torah was from God and therefore was of great significance. A seemingly superfluous word, such as in the opening verse of this parashah, would be carefully considered to seek understanding of what new idea or nuance the author wished to convey by placing it there. In doing so, they would employ the medium of midrash.

If pursued "for the sake of Heaven," midrash offers a creative, imaginative, God-inspired stream of thought to which any sincere student of his Word can contribute.

As free and expansive as midrash may be, there are necessary and recognized constraints in place to prevent it from digressing into heresy or blasphemy. The beauty of midrash is that anyone with a heart that honors God and his Word, and who is hungry to know more of him and to communicate that knowledge with others, is eligible to participate. For example, it is an edifying tradition that anyone present at the Shabbat table who so wishes, including children, is encouraged to share their *drash* on that week's Torah portion.

Rabbi Telushkin relates an instance when one of his friends was teaching a Torah study at a home for the aged. The subject was the account in Genesis 19 that describes how Lot and his family were fleeing from the destruction of Sodom, where they had lived. The group was discussing the verse, "But Lot's wife, behind him, looked back, and she became a pillar of salt" (Genesis 19:26) and were considering what possible relevance it could have in relation to our lives today.

An eighty-five-year-old woman broke into the discussion. "Don't you understand what it means? When you are always looking backward, you become inorganic!"[37] Great wisdom! While, of course, we honor the godly traditions of the past and learn from them, she understood that being bound to the past, always looking back and depending on memories to give reality to the present day, "freezes" one's life. In effect, it robs one of life by locking one in the past. Although this lesson becomes more vital the older one becomes, it can be applied at any stage of life.

The story also clearly illustrates the importance of "saying"—of communicating and sharing and passing on the timeless truths contained in the precious Word of God. Books are valuable and indispensable, but real life abounds in face-to-face meetings and communicating words of truth and life one to another.

BEHAR

בהר – "On Mount Sinai"

LEVITICUS 25:1–26:2

God makes an intriguing statement in the opening chapter of this parashah:

> The land shall not be sold in perpetuity, for the land is mine. For you are strangers and sojourners with me. (Leviticus 25:23)

CITIZENS OR STRANGERS?

He has accomplished a mighty feat in bringing his people to the land he had promised them, and the God of Israel is now making it unequivocally clear that the land remains his. They are to remain "strangers and sojourners," as were their forefathers Abraham, Isaac, and Jacob. The final two words of the verse, "with me," present us with a clue to the solution of the paradox. He is indicating that the *goal* of their miraculous arrival and possession of the land of promise was not the land itself, it is rather to be viewed as the place God had chosen as *his* dwelling place. It was a place to be "with God." Their unwavering focus and devotion were to remain primarily and fully upon the One who promised—the Landowner himself.

God did not give the revelation of himself and the gift of his Torah in "the land flowing with milk and honey," but in the wilderness at Mount Sinai. This was to be a reminder that the true home of their hearts was not the land itself but the kingdom over which he was King.

Before their love for and commitment to the land promised as their eternal inheritance, they were to be loyal citizens of the kingdom of heaven. This poses a similar challenge to us today, as it has through the centuries since Sinai: Where does the deepest loyalty of our hearts lie? Of which kingdom are we a citizen?

Once we have entered the kingdom of God and have wholeheartedly accepted his kingship, conferred upon Yeshua our Messiah, we, too, are set free from the Pharaohs of this world. In the embrace of our Father in heaven no other power may legitimately lay claim to our lives. In a very real sense we become "strangers" in this world. We can no longer identify with the ideals and rules of any society that conflict with the ways and commandments of God, our new Master. Lawrence S. Kushner summed it up well:

> The measure by which one feels oneself distant, alien, a stranger in this world of lies, by that measure does one feel close to Heaven. And the opposite is also true.[38]

The mastery of the world is an illusion. Reality is measured in relation to one's proximity to Heaven—to God. The goal of *teshuvah*, of repentance, is to turn away from the bondages of this world, from the slave-drivers who "lord it over" their subjects and to enter the freedom and peace of serving one's true Master, the Father and Creator of all.

THREE COVENANTS

In the Holy Scriptures we find evidence of three foundational covenants established by God with Abraham and his descendants. These are woven together, each giving meaning and fullness to the other, and they forge a strong cord of connection between God and his people.

In a brief overview:

1. THE ABRAHAMIC COVENANT

This is given by grace, one cannot earn it. It is received in faith; one trusts and believes in the Giver and accepts his terms. God chooses us. Just as God first chose Abraham, who lived in a pagan society of idol worshipers, so he chooses each individual and offers the opportunity to be joined to Abraham's family, his "household of faith." This covenant, extended to Isaac and Jacob, includes the promise of the land—the place where God would choose to establish his Name forever.

2. THE MOSAIC COVENANT

This covenant was instituted at Mount Sinai with Abraham's household, the family of Israel. It forged them into a nation or kingdom, with God as their King. God, as a bridegroom lovingly offers his chosen bride a *ketubah* (marriage document), presented his newly formed people with his Word. It was an expression of his love and commitment and included both blessing and chastisement. The covenant is received by consent and requires willing, loving obedience.

3. THE RENEWED COVENANT

At Mount Zion, in the city of His dwelling, Jerusalem, God once again broke into history. As prophesied by Ezekiel: "I will give you a new heart, and a new spirit I will put within you. And I will remove the heart of stone from your flesh and give you a heart of flesh. And I will put my Spirit within you, and cause you to walk in my statutes and be careful to obey my rules" (Ezekiel 36:26-27). The astounding factor here was that, in the person of his Son and Messiah, Yeshua, God renewed and expanded his covenant people to include the "whosoever will come" from all the nations (Acts 10:43-46).

We see that, at Mount Sinai, the family of Abraham, Isaac, and Jacob became a covenant people of God—a peculiar and particular nation. Indications were simultaneously given that this covenant would be extended to all who would receive it. The shofar would be sounded and echoed throughout the centuries as "good news" to all people who had ears to hear its call. *Shemot Rabbah* 5:9 comments on Exodus 20:18:

> "And all the people witnessed the thunderings": Rabbi Yochanan said that God's voice, as it was uttered, split up into seventy voices, in seventy languages, so that all the nations should understand.

Elsewhere, the sages say that the words issuing forth from the LORD could be seen visually as a fiery substance that traveled around the camp and rested upon each individual (*Song of Songs Rabbah* 1:13).

The book of Acts, in chapter 2, vividly describes the gathering of Yeshua's disciples at the Temple in Jerusalem to celebrate the Festival of Shavu'ot, which marked the giving of the Torah at Mount Sinai. What then occurred at Mount Zion was a powerful re-enactment and realization of the events at Sinai. They experienced the cloud of God's Presence, the shaking of the mount, the appearance of the flames of his Spirit of Holiness. They were surrounded and filled with His glory, and, as overflowing vessels, they spoke forth the Word of God in the tongues of the seventy nations.

Now, in the Son and by the power of the Holy Spirit, all men could receive, and all men could walk in the ways of blessing contained in the Word of the Father. The gate of grace was opened for all to enter the family of Abraham, Isaac, and Israel by faith. In the Master Yeshua, all can now walk after him in willing obedience to the laws of the kingdom of God. All can ascend upon the highway of holiness to Zion, the City of the Great King.

THE WORD AND THE SPIRIT

The Word of God and the Spirit of God are inseparably united; they exist in perfect harmony. Yeshua, the Word made flesh, proclaimed that all he did was in the power of the Spirit. When his mission on earth was accomplished, he ascended to the Father so that the gift of the Spirit of Holiness could be poured out to dwell within God's people:

> This Jesus God raised up ... Being therefore exalted at the right hand of God, and having received from the Father the promise of the Holy Spirit, he has poured out this that you yourselves are seeing and hearing. (Acts 2:32-33)

The interaction of the Spirit and the Word results in harmony and peace—shalom: true completion and perfection. One gives expression and meaning to the other. They certainly are never in opposition. They work together to bring life to the will of the Father—to allow his eternal glory to shine in the darkness. They prepare and show the way and provide all that is necessary to establish the blessing of the kingdom of God on earth.

On our part, as chosen and beloved of God, all that is required of us is to have ears to hear his call to covenant intimacy and, in response to his Spirit, to believe and trust in his Word with humble, grateful, caring, and obedient hearts. We then are enabled to dwell in the light of our Father's blessing and to reflect it powerfully into the lives of others.

BECHUKOTAI

בְּחֻקֹּתַי – "In My Statutes"

LEVITICUS 26:3–27:34

If you walk in my statutes (*bechukotai*) and observe my commandments (*mitzvot*) and do them ... I will walk among you and be your God. (Leviticus 26:3, 12)

But if in spite of this you will not listen to me, but walk contrary to me, then I will walk contrary to you in fury, and I myself will discipline you sevenfold for your sins. (Leviticus 26:27–28)

The repetition of the verb "walk" in the opening section of this final portion in the book of Vayikra emphasizes the concept of movement in relation to obeying the statutes and commandments of God. There is a movement and change that occurs in one's spirit in accord with the physical choices one makes and the direction one takes in life. It is a move closer toward or further away from God.

BLESSINGS AND CHASTISEMENTS

When our actions are based on loving obedience to his expressed will, we walk in harmony and intimacy of relationship with him. He walks with us and talks with us, just as he did in the garden with his beloved Adam and Eve. If we choose to rebel and disobey his will, our walking away results in the removal of his Presence. Estrangement occurs, and distance is created. The result of our sin of self-will is separation from the blessings of his Presence. We are exiled from the garden. Our hearts may become stubborn and hardened in their disobedience, and our eyes become blinded and our ears deaf to his voice, but his love far exceeds his righteous anger. Rather than abandoning us to our self-chosen, hopeless path without him, he chastises us "seven times" for our sins in an effort to draw us back to himself.

This way of chastisement, repentance, and restoration is a major theme woven throughout the Scriptures. For example:

> Behold, blessed is the one whom God reproves; therefore despise not the discipline of the Almighty. For he wounds, but he binds up; he shatters, but his hands heal. He will deliver you from six troubles; in seven no evil shall touch you. (Job 5:17–19)

> My son, do not despise the LORD's discipline or be weary of his reproof, for the LORD reproves him whom he loves, as a father the son in whom he delights. (Proverbs 3:11-12)

> Know then in your heart that, as a man disciplines his son, the LORD your God disciplines you. So you shall keep the commandments of the LORD your God by walking in his ways and by fearing him. (Deuteronomy 8:5-6)

One may ask, "Why seven times of trouble?" The number seven, in biblical numerology, denotes completion and perfection. We may, therefore, deduce that our faithful and loving Father will discipline us as often as necessary to bring us to the completion in relationship with him for which we were created. He will not give up after seven attempts.

Simon Peter posed the question, "Lord, how often will my brother sin against me, and I forgive him?" And Yeshua answered: "I do not say to you seven times, but seventy-seven times." (Matthew 18:21-22). Or seventy-seven thousand times. As many as it takes!

The writer of Hebrews sums it up perfectly:

> He disciplines us for our good, that we may share his holiness. For the moment all discipline seems painful rather than pleasant, but later it yields the peaceful fruit of righteousness to those who have been trained by it. Therefore lift your drooping hands and strengthen your weak knees, and make

straight paths for your feet, so that what is lame may not be put out of joint but rather be healed. (Hebrews 12:10-13)

HOW THEN DO WE WALK?

In light of the above, the question is raised: "How then do we walk in his statutes and keep his commandments?" How do our actions comply with God's will? Walking indicates forward movement. It's a conscious action, one step following the previous step, and each step brings us closer to our final destination. The key to the journey is to ensure that one is moving in the right direction. Each step is, therefore, an action that brings us into greater fulfillment of our identity as a child of the Holy God, or it can lead us further away.

David Blumenthal comments on the writings of Levi Yitzchak regarding the definition of a "spiritual" act, or an action performed according to the will of God:

> To qualify as spiritual, an act must be done only because God commanded it ... a deed must be an act of obedience, of servanthood. The only justification for doing any religious deed is that God wants us to do it.[39]

This is a difficult concept to grasp for those immersed in the modern, independent, "My way or the highway!" approach to living. Everything is judged based on "What do I think is right?" "What suits me?" The "little I" attempts to overrule the "Great I AM" and then wonders why it is suffering in a ditch of disappointment and despair.

David the Psalmist, the sweet singer of Israel, depicts the beauty, serenity, and strength of the bond between a shepherd and his sheep as he leads them to green pastures and still waters. He describes the LORD as the shepherd and, by extension, all who know his voice and follow him are his flock. The Good Shepherd leads us in "paths of righteousness for his Name's sake." Even though we walk through valleys darkened by "the shadow of death," we need have no fear, for the Shepherd is with us. His "rod and staff" comfort and protect us.

The rod and staff are tools used by a shepherd for guidance and correction and for protection and prevention of harmful attacks by predators. A sheep that needs correction might not understand the sharp prod that will prevent it from taking the wrong path. However, if it humbly responds to the shepherd's rod, it will remain on the sure path, safe from harm and secure in the shepherd's care.

THE LAND SHALL YIELD ITS PRODUCE

This parashah alerts us to the importance in God's eyes of the geographical entity of the land of Israel. In contrast, to this day, the exact location of Mount Sinai remains in dispute. The modern-day Torah commentary *Etz Hayim* makes an astute observation:

> Sinai is not [primarily] a geographic location. It is a symbol of Israel's awareness of having stood in the Presence of God and of having come to understand what God required of them. Whenever a person hears the commanding voice of God and commits himself or herself to live by that voice, that person can be considered to be standing at Sinai.[40]

God's voice speaks continually through his Word and his Spirit, and he constantly communicates with us in a multitude of ways through the natural world if only we have eyes to see and ears to hear.

We can be servants of God wherever we are, but God always has a special purpose for his people living in his land. When the majority were no longer recognizable as his people, and the nation considered itself to be like all other nations, they no longer fulfilled their calling to sanctify God's Name. As we see in Israel's history, the result of such rebellion and disobedience to the call of God was exile from the land. It became desolate, and its cities were laid waste. Indeed, God said, "I myself will devastate the land, so that your enemies who come to settle in it shall be appalled at it" (Leviticus 26:32).

If, while in exile and separated from God and the land, the people repented and their uncircumcised heart was humbled, and they made amends for their iniquity, God also said,

> Then will I remember my covenant with Jacob, and I will remember my covenant with Isaac and my covenant with Abraham, and I will remember the land. (Leviticus 26:42)

> I will give you your rains in their season, and the land shall yield its increase, and the trees of the field shall yield their fruit. (Leviticus 26:4)

What a joy and privilege to have witnessed in our generations the restoration of his covenant people to the land, and to have seen the desolate land blossom as a rose. The fields are filled with abundant fruitfulness, and the trees clap their hands and rejoice. May we do the same!

CHAZAK CHAZAK, VENITCHAZEK
BE STRONG, BE STRONG, AND MAY WE STRENGTHEN ONE ANOTHER IN THE UNITY OF THE ONE WHO LOVES US.

ENDNOTES

1. Samson Raphael Hirsch, *The Pentateuch* (New York, NY: Judaica Press, 1986), 507.
2. Robert Alter, *The Five Books of Moses* (New York, NY: W.W. Norton & Company, 2004), 541.
3. Marva Dawn, *The Sense of the Call* (Grand Rapids, MI: Eerdmans Publishing, 2006), 12.
4. Richard J. Foster & James B. Smith, eds. *Devotional Classics* (San Francisco, CA: HarperSanFrancisco, 1993).
5. Ibid.
6. David R. Blumenthal, *God at the Center: Meditations on Jewish Spirituality*, 78.
7. Ibid., 79.
8. Rabbi Chanan Morrison, *Gold from the Land of Israel*, 188.
9. Ibid.
10. *Etz Hayim: Torah and Commentary,* (New York, NY: The Jewish Publication Society, 1999), 626.
11. David. R. Blumenthal, *God at the Center: Meditations on Jewish Spirituality*, 81.
12. Ibid., 81.
13. Ibid., 82.
14. b. *Shabbat* 31.
15. Rabbi Chanan Morrison, *Gold from the Land of Israel*, 190.
16. Ibid., 191.
17. *Tz'enah Ur'enah, The Weekly Midrash*, Vol. 1, 590.
18. Ibid., 592.
19. Ibid., 597.
20. Ibid., 594.
21. Rabbi Chanan Morrison, *Gold from the Land of Israel*, 195.
22. Ibid., 196.
23. Ibid.

24 *Tz'enah Ur'enah, The Weekly Midrash*, Vol.1, 601.

25 Ibid.

26 Sara Yoheved Rigler, *Holy Woman: The Road to Greatness of Rebbetzin Chaya Sara Kramer* (New York, NY: Mezorah Publications, 2006), 91.

27 Rabbi A.L Scheinbaum, *Peninim on the Torah: An Anthology of Thought Provoking Ideas, Practical Insights, and Review Questions & Answers on the Weekly Parsha* (Cleveland, OH: Hebrew Academy of Cleveland, 2016), 204.

28 Rabbi Samson Raphael Hirsch, *The Pentateuch, Tiryat Zvi*, 455.

29 Ibid.

30 Rabbi Joseph Telushkin, *The Book of Jewish Values: A Day-by-Day Guide to Ethical Living* (New York, NY: Random House, 2000), 68.

31 Rabbi Samson Raphael Hirsch, *The Pentateuch*, 455.

32 Ibid., 451.

33 Ibid., 468.

34 Rabbi Joseph Telushkin, *Jewish Literacy: The Most Important Things to Know About the Jewish Religion, Its People and Its History* (New York, NY: HarperCollins Publishers, 1991), 151.

35 Ibid., 156.

36 Ibid., 153.

37 Ibid., 157.

38 L.S. Kushner and Kerry M. Olitzky, *Sparks beneath the Surface: A Spiritual Commentary on the Torah* (Lanham, MD: Jason Aronson, Inc., 1977).

39 David R. Blumenthal, *God at the Center: Meditations on Jewish Spirituality*, 100.

40 *Etz Hayim, Torah and Commentary*, 34, 757.

NUMBERS

BAMIDBAR

בְּמִדְבַּר – "In the Wilderness"

NUMBERS 1:1–4:20

The book of Bamidbar/Numbers describes the journey of the people of Israel from Mount Sinai to the banks of the Jordan in Moab, across from Jericho. The journey amounts to almost forty years of wandering through this wilderness area, which becomes, in effect, a training ground, a type of boot camp. It is a place where all natural resources are removed, including food and water, and the Israelites need to have complete trust in their Redeemer. They must learn that he is willing and able to supply all their needs. The family of Jacob, chosen of God, now faces the challenge to grow and mature in their new status as the nation of Israel.

Any resentment must be replaced with willing obedience, complaining with grateful praise, and suspicion with trust. Fear and any accompanying seeds of hatred must be overcome by divine love. In the light of God's revelation, the traits ingrained by harsh slavery need to be recognized, worked through, and triumphed over. Then the bound slaves will stand erect and walk forward in the true freedom of their distinct identity as sons and daughters of the Almighty and Holy God.

As the narrative unfolds and culminates in the fear-based refusal to enter the land of promise, we find that the first generation dies in the wilderness. It is the second generation, under the leadership transferred from Moses to Joshua, who enters victoriously into their destiny as the people of Israel reunited with the land of Israel.

TAKE A CENSUS

As indicated by the English name, Numbers, a theme of numbering or counting is evident in this book, one that is echoed periodically throughout the Scriptures. At the start of this parashah, God instructs Moses to count the Israelites:

> Take a census of all the congregation of the people of Israel, by clans, by fathers' houses, according to the number of names, every male, head by head. From twenty years old and upward, all in Israel who are able to go to war. (Numbers 1:2-3)

What may appear as a rag-tag band of escaped slaves, wandering aimlessly through a deserted hostile wilderness, is immediately brought to order, arranged in their camps, and enlisted in the army of God. The harsh reality is that they will be encountering antagonistic enemies and armies, and preparation and training are necessary. Only within God's framework of discipline and order will they be strengthened and enabled to gain the victory.

God had already presented the blueprint of his order in the Torah given at Sinai. A renowned Renaissance commentator, the Maharal of Prague, describes the Torah as the *seder olam*, the order of the world.[1] The study and implementation of Torah can thus be seen as "universe maintenance." Rabbi J.H. Hertz emphasizes the importance of establishing this order:

> Israel—God's army—however great in numbers, is nothing unless order and discipline reign in the midst thereof. Order is Heaven's first law.[2]

The census, taken at the start of Bamidbar, serves to impart this perspective to the Israelites. Although the Levites, set apart to serve as guardians and priests of the Tabernacle, are not counted, and neither are the women, babies, and youth under twenty, they all receive a prophetic vision of God's purposes and calling upon their lives as his people. If they walk in the ways prepared by God for his children, individually and collectively, they will be assured of victory in battle, and they will walk in his blessing and provision. Their lives will prosper and be fruitful, and even the place they inhabit will be blessed—"the desert will blossom as a rose."

This is demonstrated when, as they are nearing their destination, Balak, the king of Moab, summons the false prophet Balaam to curse the people of Israel whom he fears. From one of the high places, Balaam surveys the great camp with the Tabernacle at its center, and he can utter only a blessing:

> How lovely are your tents, O Jacob, your encampments, O Israel. Like palm-groves that stretch afar, like gardens beside a river, like aloes that the LORD has planted, like cedar trees beside the waters. (Numbers 24:5-6)

The fearful band of slaves has indeed become an ordered, fruitful oasis in the desert—a garden reflecting the beauty and harmony of their God.

FROM REBELLION TO RELATIONSHIP

The wilderness trek of the Israelites is as much a spiritual journey as a physical one. They have been rescued from the ruthless and depersonalizing whip of Pharaoh, which had reduced their lives to a terrifying and meaningless existence. Now their Redeemer has wooed them into the quiet, open spaces of the desert where he speaks to them and draws them into a relationship of covenant love. He longs to dwell with them and to delight in them as a bridegroom over his beloved bride. He is as a faithful, devoted husband to his people Israel. If they remain close to his side, he will be their constant, loving protector and provider.

However, this transition from the meaninglessness of slavery to the responsibility and rewards of covenantal relationship is not instant or painless. The people of Israel personify the struggles and temptations, failures, and rebellion of every individual who is chosen and drawn into relationship with the beloved of our souls.

All who respond to his gracious mercy and receive the yoke of the kingdom of God are his people, as described in the first epistle of Peter:

> But you are a chosen race, a royal priesthood, a holy nation, a people for his own possession, that you may proclaim the excellencies of him who called you out of darkness into his marvelous light. Once you were not a people, but now you are God's people; once you had not received mercy, but now you have received mercy. (1 Peter 2:9-10)

The wilderness journey illustrates that life is a succession of choices to be made at every turn, in every situation. It all crystallizes into one clear, translucent truth—God's will is transcendent, his Word is truth, and his ways are perfect. The only clear choice we have at all times is expressed in Yeshua's life-defining declaration: "Father ... not my will, but yours, be done" (Luke 22:42).

In the person of his uniquely begotten Son, the Father revealed to humanity the perfect image of himself, in which all are created. Yeshua, in his complete humility and perfect yielding to the will of the Father, raised high the standard of the kingdom's righteousness, peace, and joy. He also made the way clear for all God's children to follow after him in loving obedience and enjoy the richness of relationship with our Father, the creator of all.

FIRST FRUITS – SET APART UNTO GOD

The Festival of Shavu'ot/Pentecost is also called *Zeman Matan Torateinu*, the Time of the Giving of our Torah. When the Temple was standing, the people of Israel would bring the first fruits of their harvest up to Jerusalem in joyous procession as an offering of gratitude to the giver of all things. Today we can offer grateful praise for our Messiah-Redeemer, who died on our behalf and was raised from the grave as a "first-fruits" of resurrection life:

> But in fact [Messiah] has been raised from the dead, the first-fruits of those who have fallen asleep. (1 Corinthians 15:20)

> Every good gift and every perfect gift is from above, coming down from the Father of lights, with whom there is no variation or shadow due to change. Of his own will he brought us forth by the word of truth, that we should be a kind of firstfruits of his creatures. (James 1:17–18)

God met with his people at Mount Sinai at the first Shavu'ot, and again at Mount Zion, where he presented another great gift. With Yeshua, the Torah Incarnate, now enthroned at his right hand, God poured upon the disciples gathered in the Temple courts the infilling presence of his Holy Spirit. The gift is freely given to all who receive—the

Spirit of Holiness, who leads into all truth, provides guidance and counsel, and imparts insight into the Word of God.

At Shavu'ot, we celebrate the giver of these perfect gifts. What better way to do so than by the study of his Word, in the light of the Living Word and the anointing of the Holy Spirit? In so doing, we become better equipped to serve our Father and Lord in establishing the order of his kingdom in our own lives and in the world:

> But we ought always to give thanks to God for you, brothers beloved by the Lord, because God chose you as the firstfruits to be saved, through sanctification by the Spirit and belief in the truth. (2 Thessalonians 2:13)

NASSO

נשא – "Make an Accounting"

NUMBERS 4:21–7:89

The parashah addresses overarching aspects of the collective destiny of the people of Israel. Prominent elements are the erection and dedication of the Mishkan (Tabernacle of Meeting), the dwelling of the *Shechinah* of God. God's instructions are all of great consequence in the ongoing preparation of the nation for their entry into the land promised by God to their forefathers. Interspersed among the historically significant issues, we find clear reminders that God is equally concerned about the daily affairs of each individual. While carefully detailing matters regarding their national aspirations, commands also are given regarding right relationships within the family and with the materialistic world. Only when these matters are in good order can the people march forward and successfully fulfill their collective destiny.

THE INFLUENCE OF GOOD AND EVIL

As nothing in Torah is seen as random or coincidental, the sages take note of the juxtaposition of subjects that are addressed. In this portion we see an interesting juxtaposition of the subjects of abstinence and adultery in the laws of the *Nazir* and the *sotah*, the wayward wife.

The late Rabbi Yosef Leib Bloch commented that this offers an insight into human nature. When one witnesses the effects of sin, in this case, the punishment and degradation of an adulterous wife, and the tragic results of wrong choices in life, one can hopefully be influenced to turn away from sin. On the other hand, Rabbi Bloch points out that a display of evil, in whatever form, can be "a catalyst for the spectator himself to turn to evil. The dark side of a human being, the iniquitous nature that remains concealed within the innermost recesses of one's mind, can apparently be aroused to sin."[3]

Maimonides, the brilliant medieval philosopher, physician, and teacher, stated that it is the nature of man to gravitate toward and be influenced by the philosophies and behavior of those around him. We all know the power of peer pressure and how we can be affected by our environment. Rabbi A.I. Scheinbaum emphasizes a significant lesson:

> He who performs a sin is guilty not only of his own sin, but also of influencing others to follow suit.[4]

The effect of one's sin not only harms oneself but has inevitable, although often invisible, repercussions in the lives of those around us, for which we also are held accountable. The damage reaches further than we realize, indeed sometimes from generation to generation. The negative effects of the sin of adultery are obvious in the deep hurt of the spouse and any children involved; also of consequence is the demeaning of the value of covenant relationship and the resulting negative influence in the minds of others. It causes the destruction and degrading of all that God designed and intended to be "lifted up" and holy. All sin can be seen in this light as adultery toward God. The most serious effect of any sin is that it separates us from God's Presence, and his Name, rather than being exalted and sanctified in our lives, is dishonored and shamed.

The antidote for "adultery" toward God, in whatever form, is offered in the example of the *Nazir*. The Nazirite, by making a vow of abstinence for a set period of time, chose to disassociate him or herself from the society around them in specific ways. They separated themselves from the non-essentials of enjoyment of "wine and fine dining" and grooming—"no razor shall touch his head" (Numbers 6:5). They also avoided a dead body and did not attend funerals. The main focus was not self-denial or weakening of the body as food and water were allowed. Rather, it was to recognize one's limitations and weaknesses and to draw closer to God. They were separated unto God:

> All the days of his separation he is holy to the LORD. (Numbers 6:8)

At the conclusion of the set period of abstinence, the *Nazir* brings a sin offering to the Temple, in recognition (a) of the fact that he has refrained from the blessings of good things that God has given to be enjoyed and (b) of any inherent sin within himself that might cause separation from God, resulting in death rather than life.

As God's set-apart people, all our words and actions reflect upon our Father and his Word. The Name of God, rather than being sanctified by the love, grace, and humility one expresses, is profaned by one's sin and anger. We are ambassadors of the Almighty God. Wherever we are and whatever we do, may we glorify his precious Name and not diminish it.

THE INDIVIDUAL MATTERS

> When a man or woman commits any of the sins that people commit by breaking faith with the LORD, and that person realizes his guilt, he shall confess his sin that he has committed. And he shall make full restitution. (Numbers 5:6–7)

When Yeshua answers the question regarding the most important mitzvah (commandment), he clearly connects the attitude one holds toward one's fellow human beings, and the resulting actions toward them, with one's attitude toward God himself. He highlights the connection by saying, in effect, that the love you demonstrate toward your neighbor illustrates your love for God (Matthew 22:36–40).

The Scripture verses above (Numbers 5:6–7) emphasize the importance of recognizing the wrong committed when one fails to act in a loving manner toward another. This is inevitable as we strive for the healing of our broken human condition. One also needs to recognize that any unloving act against another, in thought, word, or deed, is a "breaking of faith with the LORD." As our negative act diminishes the image of God in the other person, so it affects the One in whose image they are made. In his mercy, God offers us, as his redeemed people, a means of *teshuvah*, repentance—a way to turn from the wrong we recognize. By confession and restitution, we can be restored in relationship with him and then, hopefully, with one another.

The Midrash records that four people were tested by God to determine whether they had truly recognized and repented of their sin and could therefore receive pardon. All four failed the initial test.

1. The first was Adam.

    God asked him, "Have you eaten of the tree?" Adam replied, "The woman You gave me, she gave me from the tree" (Genesis 3:11–12). By this answer, he evidenced no sign of remorse or personal accountability; rather, he blamed God and Eve.

2. The second was Cain.

    God asked, "Where is Abel, your brother?" (Genesis 4:9). Cain replied, "I do not know, am I my brother's keeper?" He lied to God and also refused accountability and responsibility for his brother.

3. The third was the evil prophet Balaam.

    God asked him, "Who are these men with you?" (Numbers 22:9). He replied, "Balak, son of Tzipor, king of Moab, has sent to me." Balaam knew it was his own decision to go against the will of God to serve a worldly king, but he attempted to shift the responsibility onto Balak.

4. The fourth was King Hezekiah.

    When the king proudly showed the messengers of the Babylonian king all the sacred treasures in the Temple, God asked a similar question through the Prophet Isaiah: "Who are these men, and from where do they come?" (Isaiah 39:3). Hezekiah replied with some conceit, "They come to me from a distant country, from *Bavel*—Babylon." Isaiah then prophesied the invasion of the Babylonian army, the looting of the Temple, the destruction of Jerusalem, and the exile of the people.[5]

In the inestimable love of our Creator, God extends his grace and mercy toward us, along with every breath we are granted. We are extended renewed opportunity to repent of every transgression that separates us, and we are enabled to draw close to his presence once again.

THE LORD, YOUR BLESSER

The jewel of *Birkat haKohanim*, the Priestly Blessing, is found in Parashat Nasso (Numbers 6:24–26). The full blessing consists of three lines, each of which contains the name of the LORD, and carries two blessings—a total of six. This perfect vessel of blessing culminates in the final word *shalom*. The peace of God embraces all blessing, and *shalom* is his ultimate will for his people Israel. It is the hallmark of his kingdom, which will spread to all corners of the earth.

True *shalom*, as the full meaning of the word implies, incorporates *shalem*, wholeness and completion. The desire and will to aspire to the completeness and unity found in God is the foundation for peace in this world. David the psalmist describes: "Behold, how good and how pleasant it is for brethren to dwell together in unity!" (Psalm 133:1). By recognizing his image in one another, and in every human being, and determining to seek out and embrace this holy aspect of the Divine in the other, we gradually build one another up in our Father's blessing of "one-ness"—of unity and harmony—of shalom.

Yeshua proclaimed in his seminal teaching on the Mount of Beatitudes in Galilee:

> Blessed are the peacemakers, for they shall be called the sons of God. (Matthew 5:9)

In the *Sar Shalom*, the Prince of Peace, we become a new order of priests, of servants of God. As those anointed with the oil of the Spirit of Holiness, as was Aaron the high priest (who is described in rabbinic literature as *Rodef Shalom*, the Pursuer of Peace),[6] we can extend the cup of blessing to others. As his children, we can act as messengers of our Father and King in heaven and shine the light of his blessing and peace into a depressed and meaningless world.

BEHA'ALOTCHA

בהעלותך – "When You Set Up"

NUMBERS 8:1–12:16

The central piece of furniture in the Holy Place of the Mishkan (Tabernacle) was the menorah—the seven-branched candelabra. It was eye-catching due to its size, the beauty of its design, and the seven flames that provided light for the Sanctuary. This Sanctuary was the holy place of God's first physical dwelling place on earth—his House. It was the place where man and God could meet in intimate communion, and Aaron, the high priest, carefully tended it. Aaron was miraculously appointed and anointed for the task, and he was permeated with the vision of what the Sanctuary represented—a world of peace and perfection, filled with the *Shechinah* of God.

SHINE THE LIGHT

The menorah symbolized a return to the intimacy of the garden of Eden and offered the hope and vision of eventual and universal peace and harmony. It pointed to an eternity infused with the delight and Oneness of the Divine Presence of God. The holy place also offered a further picture of encouragement to his people. Each home, when established on the vision and reality offered by the God of Israel, could become a *mikdash me'at*—a small tabernacle of meeting. The family could create and build their home as a sanctuary filled with his light and presence and the beauty of holiness: a place of peace, radiating his glory.

At the heart of Judaism is embedded this desire to build a home that honors God and, like Abraham's tent, would be a witness to his truth and kingship. Likewise, Christian pastor and author, Bill Johnson, highlights the impact of a godly home:

> When relationships are good and the boundaries of godly discipline are intact, there is no limit to the influence of the godly home. [Our goal, as a healthy, intentional family, should be] to mingle and associate with the lost, but don't take on their values or habits. That way we, as both salt and light, have our proper effect of preserving and exposing in order to bring them into their destiny.[7]

The haftarah connected with the parashah is drawn from the vivid prophetic writings of Zechariah. The prophet's vision speaks of the means by which this goal of a godly home can be achieved. It is reflected in the seven flames of the menorah and the seven corresponding words spoken by God to Zechariah, which translate as, "Not by might, nor by power, but by My Spirit, says the LORD of hosts" (Zechariah 4:6).

The menorah is a symbol of the light of his Word of truth, and here God emphasizes the fact that his Holy Spirit is the oil that enables the light to shine with life. In the same way, if we are to shine forth his life with clarity and power, it can only be by the same Spirit of Holiness he has imparted to us through our high priest, Yeshua. In this same power we are called and can work toward fulfilling the greater prophetic vision revealed in his Word.

PROPHETIC VISION

When Adam and Eve were exiled from *Gan Eden*, the garden of Eden, they each carried a curse. The curse upon Adam, the male, resulted in his need to labor and produce sustenance from a stubborn earth, which also was cursed on his account (Genesis 3:17). Eve, the female, would suffer the physical conditions related to childbirth, and her desire would be for her husband, and he would rule over her (Genesis 3:16). "Desire for her husband" sounds like a good thing. However, in any unhealthy society still operating under the curse of sin, where God's love and grace are not functioning, a woman is in a position of extreme vulnerability. The all too common experiences of abuse and deep emotional pain are inevitable when the man inordinately "rules" and "lords it over" the woman. The force of estrangement sets in, and relationships and families become spiritually and emotionally paralyzed.

It is of vital importance that the people of God, the members of the household of faith, continue in our commitment to the prophetic vision of a redeemed and healed world. It is, and always has been, the will of our Father in heaven to reverse the curse and to restore humanity and the earth itself to the state and purpose for which they were created. Paul confirms in his letter to the Romans:

> For the creation waits with eager longing for the revealing of the sons of God, ... [because] the creation itself will be set free from its bondage to corruption and obtain the freedom of the glory of the children of God. (Romans 8:19, 21)

Central to the purposes of God in his dealings with humankind is redemption from the curse incurred by Adam and Eve, which continues from generation to generation. The focus of his kingdom on earth is the restoration of the delight and harmony of relationship with him and with one another enjoyed in the garden. The prophetic promise offered, which is our hope, is that the joy of "oneness" with God we can anticipate in *Olam Haba*, the World to Come, will be of even greater depth and intensity than man was capable of knowing in the beginning. Just as light shines more brightly after darkness, and relief is all the sweeter when the pain ceases, so the healed and renewed earth will be all the more glorious:

> As it is written, "What no eye has seen, nor ear heard, nor the heart of man imagined, what God has prepared for those who love him." (1 Corinthians 2:9)

PRESENT ACTION

All God's acts of redemption are executed with this healing and restoration in mind. This also is the purpose to which he calls his people. In Hebraic thinking this is described as *tikkun olam*, repairing the world. The *tikkun*, healing and repairing what is bent, broken, and damaged by sin, must begin in our own hearts and our relationship with our Father and with those he places in our lives. Every choice we are given each day—each thought we think, every word we say, any action we take—will either contribute to *tikkun olam*, which reverses the curse upon humanity or will contribute toward and further the curse. Each of our lives, therefore, has the potential to become a powerful daily blessing in accord with the will of God to restore his love, kindness, and presence in the world or not.

This option is unrelated to the circumstances in which we find ourselves. Joseph, unfairly imprisoned in Egypt, acted to bring peace and establish order in the prison (Genesis 39:22-23). Later, God raised him up to do the same in the whole country and the known world. Our prime example is Yeshua himself. Although without sin, he suffered and bore our pain so that we might be set free from the curse of sin. After he was mocked and whipped without mercy by the Roman soldiers, he carried the crossbeam to his place of execution. He was, no doubt, suffering extreme pain and exhaustion, but he paused to speak with the women who were weeping for him at the roadside. He shared a message of repentance. In effect, "Weep not for me. May your tears be tears of repentance. Return to your God and Father, restore your relationship and enter your true identity as his beloved child."

When our vision remains clear—to be a light in the world that receives its light from the Tree of Life, the Word of God, illuminated in our Messiah—we can go forward empowered by the Holy Spirit, and we can face our destiny and future challenges with courage and faith. We can indeed follow closely after the one who lived, illustrated, and embodied the Word of God, and said, "I am the way, the truth, and the life" (John 14:6). "Follow me!"

SHELACH

שלח – "Send Thou"

NUMBERS 13:1–15:41

The sad fate of *dor hamidbar*, the wilderness generation, is sealed in the dramatic episode described at the start of the parashah. We know it as "The Sin of the Spies." In the later unfolding of the narrative we learn that, due to the negative report of ten of the twelve spies, the whole generation is destined to wander and die in the desert. Only Joshua and Caleb survived. They were the two spies, or scouts, who had relayed a positive report and encouraged the people to press forward with God into the land he had promised. They ultimately led the new generation forward in the victorious claiming of their inheritance.

SCOUT THE LAND

The serious nature of the sin of the spies induces us to examine it more closely and to learn the lessons we may derive from it. Rabbi Shlomo Riskin refers to a midrash cited by Rashi in *Tanchuma* 5:

> What is the connection between this biblical segment of the scouts and the biblical segment of Miriam [found at the conclusion of last week's portion]? It is the fact that she was punished for speaking evil against her brother Moses, and these wicked "leaders" saw and did not internalize the lesson.[8]

The sin of *lashon hara* (evil speech) is highlighted here. Rabbi Riskin considers the attitude that could have prompted the negative speech:

From this perspective, the transgression of Miriam was not so much to slander as her inability to recognize the unique stature of Moses; if Moses' relationship to God was not unique, then the Five Books of Moses' revelation likewise would lose its unique status.[9]

The true transgression, then, is disregard for the Word of God. Although God had made it clear, Miriam did not recognize the God-conferred uniqueness of her brother Moses, and the ten spies did not recognize the God-conferred uniqueness of the land of Israel. Riskin points out:

> The scouts investigated the Land as any would-be settlers would investigate any land they hoped to inhabit; they were blind to the very special relationship God had to this land, and were deaf to His promise that His people were able to conquer it.[10]

Joshua and Caleb, on the other hand, shared the faith of Moses and understood, as had their forefathers Abraham, Isaac, and Jacob, that one does not view the things of God with a natural eye but with eyes of faith. As the Apostle Paul describes:

> We look not to the things that are seen but to the things that are unseen. For the things that are seen are transient, but the things that are unseen are eternal. For we walk by faith, not by sight. Yes, we are of good courage. (2 Corinthians 4:18, 5:7–8)

The spies were sent to scout the land for practical, strategic information regarding the fertility of the land, the strength of the people, and the defense of the cities. Moses knew it was a good and prosperous land because God had said so. Had the faith of the spies been strong enough, they could have "seen through" the daunting physical realities. However, their attitudes of unbelief, fear, and frustration were revealed, and as a result, they found the faults they were looking for. Despite the positive proclamations and exhortations of Joshua and Caleb, leaders of the tribes of Ephraim and Judah, respectively, the Israelites preferred to rely on the reports of the group of ten spies rather than to place their trust in the Word of God. This reaction affirms the wise saying: "All is in the hands of God, except the fear of God." Man's basic choice in any circumstance is to "fear" God—to have faith and trust in His Word and character—or to harbor fear of man. The latter stops us in our tracks and causes us to wander aimlessly in the desert, while the reverent fear of God enables us to walk forward and to claim the inheritance of his promises to us.

Two interesting points to note: 1) The Levites were not included and did not participate in either the sin of the golden calf or the sin of the spies. Some commentators hold, therefore, that they all entered the land; and 2) We are seeing a true modern miracle in our days through the restoration of the State of Israel and the return of the Jewish people to their land.

THE ANTIDOTE OF TZITZIT

The *Shma* is the proclamation of faith in the One true God of Israel. Devout Jews utter it as part of the morning and evening prayers, and it is the first prayer taught to Jewish children. The opening passage of the *Shma* declares the unity of God, the acceptance of the yoke of his Kingship, and our all-encompassing love for him—body, soul, and spirit (Deuteronomy 6:4–9).

In the second section rewards for the fulfillment of commandments and punishments for transgressions are mentioned and an affirmation of our acceptance of God's Word and commandments (Deuteronomy 11:13–21).

The sages added a third paragraph to the *Shma*—the passage regarding the wearing of tzitzit (fringes) on the corners of one's garment, which is found in this week's portion (Numbers 15:37–41). Why was this commandment deemed important enough to be a part of the *Shma*?

Significantly, the passage on tzitzit occurs at the end of the parashah. God, as it were, offers an effective antidote to the toxic effects of the sin of the ten spies, which was caused by the focus of their eyes on evil and an attitude of prideful disobedience in their hearts. Wisdom states: "The eye sees, the heart desires, and the person executes." In contrast, the purpose God gives for wearing tzitzit is "for you to look at and remember all the commandments of the LORD, to do them, not to follow after your own heart and your own eyes, which you are inclined to whore after. So you shall remember and do all my commandments, and be holy to your God" (Numbers 15:39–40).

Rashi notes that the Hebrew word *tzitzit* has the numerical equivalent of six hundred. The fringes contain eight threads and five knots, a sum of thirteen. This totals 613, which is a reminder of the 613 commandments that are written in the Torah. In regularly looking upon the tzitzit attached to one's clothing, one is constantly reminded of the nearness of the Word of God, the reality of the supernatural, and the realm of faith. One also is reminded to be aware of the earthly influences that draw one to sin against God, and they thereby lose their power. The fear of God is reinforced, and the fear of man and the lusts of the flesh are overcome. The passing temptations of the flesh, the eyes, and pride, are conquered in loving obedience to our Father, and the eternal life of faith is enjoyed in the present:

> For all that is in the world—the desires of the flesh and the desires of the eyes and pride of life—is not from the Father but is from the world. And the world is passing away along with its desires, but whoever does the will of God abides forever. (1 John 2:16–17)

The Gospel of Luke records the account of a woman who had suffered a hemorrhage for twelve years and was physically spent and financially depleted as a result. She had heard of the healing power of Yeshua, the messianic miracle-worker from Nazareth. When an opportunity arose, she drew near to him in a crowd and in trembling desperation broke a rule of society:

> [She] came up behind him, and touched the fringe [tzitzit] of his garment; and immediately her flow of blood ceased. (Luke 8:44 RSV)

Yeshua realized that power had been drawn from him, and he confronted her, and commended her by saying, "Daughter, your faith has made you well; go in peace" (Mark 5:34).

TECHELET – ENDLESS SKY

Today, tzitzit are attached to the corners of the tallit—prayer shawl. In everyday use they are worn, traditionally by Jewish males over the age of thirteen, on a light, cotton vest-like undergarment called a *tallit katan* ("small tallit"). When donning the large tallit before prayer, a beautiful blessing is uttered:

> How precious is your steadfast love, O God! The children of mankind take refuge in the shadow of your wings. They feast on the abundance of your house, and you give them drink from the river of your delights. For with you is the fountain of life; in your light do we see light. Oh, continue your steadfast love to those who know you, and your righteousness to the upright of heart! (Psalm 36:7-10)

It is written that each of the four corners of the garment is to have three white strands and one strand of blue. The particular blue of the one strand at each corner is called *techelet*. The sages comment that techelet "resembles the sea, the sea resembles the heavens, and the heavens resemble the Throne of Glory."[11]

White is commonly associated with the purity and righteousness of God, and the *techelet* blue of the endless sky signifies his majesty and sovereignty over the earth, as well as his constant gracious presence with us. The combination of the two should, therefore, encourage one to greater holiness as one walks in his ways.

For centuries, since the exile from Israel in 70 CE, the strands of the tzitzit were all white as the species of sea snail found along the coast of Israel that produced the dye for techelet had disappeared. Since the restoration of the modern nation, it has once again been found, and kosher *techelet* is once again obtainable.

The four strands of the tzitzit are threaded through a hole in the corner and knotted, this results in eight strands. Four sets of eight make a total of thirty-two, the number that spells the Hebrew word *lev*, which means "heart." This is a significant pointer that part of the purpose of tzitzit is a reminder to love and serve the LORD with all one's heart.

In connection with tzitzit, Rabbi Shlomo Riskin refers to a teaching on the parashah given by his mentor, the renowned author and teacher Rabbi Joseph Soloveitchik, which refers to the blue and white flag of the reborn nation:

> White represents clarity, logic, rational truth; blue, symbolizing the infinity of the oceans and the heavens, represents longing, infinity, mystery, the supra-rational. Torah, the Land of Israel and the People of Israel are a combination of logic and love, natural and supernatural, mathematical reason and miraculous romance.[12]

KORACH

קורח – "Korah"

NUMBERS 16:1–18:32

The parashah this week includes paradigmatic examples of rebellion, its causes, and its consequences. The principal rebels are Korach, who is a member of the same family of Levi as Moses and Aaron, and Dathan and Aviram, of the tribe of Reuben. Korach, Dathan, and Aviram join forces to challenge the leadership of Moses and Aaron on a spiritual and administrative level. How do they instigate their rebellion? Primarily, we discover, through the use of words.

THE ROOTS OF REBELLION

The generation of the wilderness, *dor hamidbar*, is characterized by words. The Hebrew word *midbar* can be read *mi dibur*, "from speech." First, they experience the revelation of God and hear his words to them. They also receive his teaching, instruction, and guidance through Moses. Now, however, we see the poisonous fruit of ingratitude and dissatisfaction emerging as words of resentment and rebellion. Fear and envy breed anger, which leads to resentment, which eventually manifests in some form of rebellion. This negativity can be communicated effectively to others via words.

We can find the seeds of Korach's rebellion in the watershed episode of the sin of the spies, which resulted in the condemnation of the whole generation to wander and die in the desert. Korach had experienced the miraculous acts of God in the exodus from Egypt, at Sinai, and in the provision of manna and water. He also had witnessed the fear and negativity of the ten spies, and the consequent failure of the Israelites to overcome and move forward into the land promised them by God.

Chasidic commentator Levi Yitzhak interpreted Korach's subsequent despair and rebellion as an indication that, while he accepted the miraculous presence of God and the intensity of his power, he could not apply that reality to everyday life:

> He knew that it is possible to live under God in the world of the word, but he questioned whether one can live under God in the world of individual action. Korach ... made a common double error: first in identifying the peaks [of spiritual experience] as more real than the valleys; and, second, in assuming that, in the valleys, humankind is free to do as it sees fit, even in the Name of God.[13]

Korach accepted God's miraculous Word but rejected its application in the mundane world of activity. In effect, he assumed he had a right to take the law into his own hands. Levi Yitzhak comments that this reaction constitutes "trying to outguess God's designs. Rather ... spirituality is living at the peaks *and* in the valleys; spirituality is hearing the Word *and* [living it] in obedient servanthood."[14]

This tendency to rebel against the revealed will and word of God is endemic to humanity. David Blumenthal comments on the teaching of Levi Yitzhak:

> In the area of everyday, we accept too glibly the right to act on God's behalf, and, when we fail, we doubt God and His design. Servanthood is living in the world of action and following humbly His will; it is not living only in the world of the Word and arrogating that Word to ourselves.[15]

CONTAGIOUS CONFLICT

Dathan and Aviram were members of the tribe of Reuben, the firstborn of Jacob. The camp of Reuben was situated alongside the tents of Korach the Levite, and they were thus easily drawn into the rebellion. Their resentment stemmed from the fact that the birthright had been taken from Reuben and conferred upon Joseph, who had received a double portion from Jacob through his sons Ephraim and Manasseh. Moses' closest servant was Joshua, of the tribe of Ephraim. He was destined to be the future leader. A Reubenite would have enjoyed that prestigious position. Dathan and Aviram and On (a fellow Reubenite who it seems later repented and was spared) joined Korach. Their ambitions, however, were not for priestly honors; they were hoping to replace Moses as political leaders of the nation.

The mutinous action began when Korach, together with 250 well-known leaders from among the tribes, approached the Tent of Meeting and challenged Moses and Aaron's authority. "When Moses heard it, he fell on his face" (Numbers 16:4). His reaction was not one of fear but of humility before God, and he was, no doubt, trusting him for wisdom as to how to respond. Moses indeed displays wisdom by instigating positive action and also by deferring the issue until the next morning (Numbers 16:5). By breaking up the crowd and sending the individuals to prepare in their tents for the next morning's incense offering, he hoped the rebels would have time to reflect and repent. The incense offering was to be performed only by the high priest, Aaron, and was a symbolic expression of complete devotion to the Torah and will of God. Moses, thereby, placed in God's hands the decision of accepting or rejecting their claim to his position of leadership and honor.

The next morning dawned on a succession of dramatic events and encounters with the power of God. Moses and Aaron were again on their faces, interceding that the righteous of the congregation be spared. God commanded that the people move away from the tents of the three instigators. They obeyed and left the rebels standing outside their tents. Miraculously, "the earth opened its mouth and swallowed them up, with their households and all the people who belonged to Korach and all their goods" (Numbers 16:32).

Simultaneously, "fire came out from the LORD" (Numbers 16:35) and consumed the 250 co-conspirators who were offering incense at the Tent of Meeting in place of Aaron. God then commanded that the copper censers used in the prideful act be crafted as a covering for the altar. In the future, when anyone brought an offering to the altar his reflection in the beaten copper would be a vivid reminder of the fate of those who rebelled against God. They could remember the serious consequence of stirring up self-centered conflict, whether in spiritual or mundane matters. The offenders were struck by both heaven and earth. The supernatural fire came from heaven, and the mundane earth swallowed them.

We see, in almost unbelievable stubbornness of heart, that the very next day, supporters of the rebels rose up in accusation against Moses and Aaron, saying, "You have killed the people of the LORD" (Numbers 16:41). Immediately, a plague broke out among them, and they began to die. Punishment again fit the crime. The plague highlights the unseen, contagious nature of dissatisfaction and complaint. It spreads from mouth to mouth as criticism and accusation are poured forth from person to person like ever-widening ripples in a pond. This could be a component of God's warning to the people that they separate themselves from the dissenters. Just as viruses are airborne and can contaminate those in the vicinity, so too, dissatisfaction is spread to others from those in rebellion against God. It is in the very air around them!

INCENSE AND LIGHT

As a result of the plague, 4,700 people died before Aaron was able to offer incense and make atonement for them. Note that the atonement, like the punishment, matched the sin. The negative words were carried in the air from person to person; now, the incense permeated the air with its sweet fragrance as though to banish the toxic effects still hovering in the aftermath. The special, God-designed incense contained eleven spices that combined to produce its singularly beautiful scent. Later in history, when the Temple stood in Jerusalem, it was said that the fragrant incense from the Holy Place so filled the air that the women of the city did not need to wear perfume.

In Hebraic literature the incense is likened to a very precious possession—*da'at Elohim*, knowledge of God. This knowledge is linked with the Final Redemption and the establishing of God's kingdom in all the earth. It is written that in the days when King Messiah reigns from Jerusalem, the earth will be filled and permeated with the light and fragrance of the knowledge of God as the waters cover the sea (Isaiah 11:9).

In the holy place, the altar of incense is placed adjacent to the menorah, the golden vessel of light. The two were lit in sequence by the high priest. The menorah represents the Word of God—the Tree of Life, which brings the light of wisdom and understanding to those who seek after *da'at Elohim*. The light of the menorah illuminates the way to the altar of incense, the sweet fragrance of which represents the fruits of this precious, intimate knowledge. This knowledge cannot be grasped with the hand but is gentle, invisible, and yet can penetrate like perfume into every dark, hidden corner. How privileged we are, as those serving the Almighty today, to have access to both the light and this valuable incense and to spread its shining aroma wherever he places us:

> But thanks be to God, who in [Messiah] always leads us in triumphal procession, and through us spreads the fragrance of the knowledge of him everywhere. (2 Corinthians 2:14)

CHUKAT

חוקת – "Statute"

NUMBERS 19:1–22:1

This is the law when a person dies in a tent. (Numbers 19:14)

The subject of ritual impurity (*tumah*) is addressed in this parashah, with a specific focus on impurity derived from contact with a dead person. Regarding the verse above, midrashic commentary pauses at the word "tent" and connects it with the beginning of the verse, "This is the law." Throughout the biblical narrative there is a correlation between tents and the study of Torah. The obvious example is the Tabernacle—the Tent of Meeting, which housed the Presence of God and the symbols of his Word: the ark of the covenant and the menorah.

THE TENTS OF TORAH

We can trace this association to the beginning of the family of God, to our forefathers who lived in tents. Abraham's tent was always open to welcome strangers and weary travelers. He and Sarah kindly would offer them physical nourishment and refreshment. In addition, as they were bearers of the truth and message of the One true God of the universe who had sent them forth as his emissaries, the couple would also assuredly have shared their knowledge and graciously taught the ways of God to all who would hear.

In the beautiful first romance of the Bible we read how, when Isaac received his *bashert*—his God-chosen bride—he brought her into his mother Sarah's tent, "and took Rebekah, and she became his wife, and he loved her" (Genesis 24:67). This happily indicates that their covenant union was established and consummated there. We also know that Isaac was the son of Abraham and Sarah, raised in the ways of God. In order to love and to grow in love, Isaac would share the truth and beauty of their knowledge of God with Rebekah in the tent of Sarah. This afforded her a depth of knowledge that was lacking in her previous home, the household of Laban.

In the case of the brothers Jacob and Esau, we see that Esau was a macho, outdoor man and a skillful hunter, while Jacob was "a quiet man, dwelling in tents" (Genesis 25:27). Jacob took heed of the principle, "keep your father's commandment, and forsake not your mother's teaching" (Proverbs 6:20). He devotedly studied the teachings of God passed down from his grandfather, Abraham.

Thus, regarding those who toil in the "tents" in the study of Torah, the Talmud records:

> From where do we learn that Torah study is only truly absorbed by one who "kills himself" over it? As it says, "This is the Torah—when a person dies [to self] in the tent [of Torah learning]." (b.*Brachot* 63b)

SACRIFICIAL STUDY

To devote one's life to the study of the Word and teaching of God requires a high degree of self-sacrifice and commitment. Rabbi Chanan Morrison, in his adaptation of the teachings of Rav Avraham Yitzchak Kook, makes the comparison between those who provide for the physical needs of society and those who go beyond the call of duty to provide for the spiritual needs of the people:

> The purpose of society is to provide reasonable living conditions, without excessive hardship, for its citizens.[16]

To achieve this goal, some are prepared to work long, irregular hours and accept any inherent dangers connected with their occupations, such as firefighters, soldiers, police officers, bus drivers, security guards, doctors, and nurses. Without their services, the stability and security of the community would be threatened, and the populace would accordingly suffer more violence and discomfort.

Rav Kook proposes that, likewise, those who are willing to dedicate their lives to Torah study, the study of the Word of God, are guardians of the souls of the people:

> Just as a soldier cannot properly perform his service for the nation without a willingness for self-sacrifice, so too, Torah scholars must totally dedicate themselves to their mission. ... The breadth and depth of knowledge required for Torah scholarship necessitates long and intensive hours of study. ... Only by overcoming the desire for creature comforts and "the easy life"—by demonstrating their willingness to "kill themselves" in the tents of Torah—do these scholars prove their worthiness to lead the nation [Israel, the people of God] in attaining its spiritual aspirations.[17]

We cannot all devote ourselves to such a high level of study of the Word. However, we cannot walk in obedience to the will of our Father if we do not know it. The guide of life must first be studied before applying it with increasing personal effect and benefit. The teachings of the LORD are given "that you shall learn them and be careful to do them" (Deuteronomy 5:1). The sages reiterate,

> The way of the wicked is darkness (Proverbs 4:19). They, on the other hand, who occupy themselves with Torah have light everywhere ..., as it is said: "Thy Word is a lamp unto my feet, and a light to my path" (Psalm 119:105).[18]

WATER AND ASHES

The parashah opens with the verse, "This is the statute (*chok*) of the law that the LORD has commanded" (Numbers 19:2). The term *chukat Torah* reflects the indispensability of a regulation. It is found in only one other place in the Scriptures—Numbers 31:21—where the purification and immersion in water of household utensils captured from the enemy are described. Both issues are mysterious. There are no clear, logical reasons given for the procedures. The only obvious similarities between them are the purpose of purification and the use of *mayim chayim*, living water.

A person or a tent that has been exposed to a dead body is considered ritually unclean, including any items within the tent. In order to be cleansed, some of the ashes of the red heifer are mixed with living water. Using a bunch of hyssop, the mixture is sprinkled upon the person or items seven times. This is done by someone who is ritually clean on the third day and the seventh day (Numbers 19:17-19). The red heifer (*parah adumah*) brings to mind the first Adam, whose name carries the meaning of both earth (*adamah*) and red (*adom*), and also the first sin, as a result of which death entered creation. It also can remind us of the sin of the golden calf, when the idol was ground to dust and mixed with water, which the people had to consume.

In the purification process described, a perfect heifer must be prepared and completely burned to ashes. Three additional items are burned together with the heifer: a log of cedarwood, a bundle of hyssop, and a cord of scarlet wool. The ritual was a reminder that man can be cleansed from the effects of death, with its implications of separation from life and what is holy. It is not the Father's will that we remain in bondage and a slave to the drives within and the constant onslaught of temptations without.

We cannot, however, be set free and remain free in our own strength. This is made possible through the elements of atonement provided by God himself in the person of his Anointed Son, our Messiah Yeshua, and his sacrificial death,. We see the symbols of his death reflected in the purification ritual: the wood of the cross/tree upon which he gave the sacrifice of his life; the hyssop of humility—he divested himself of all glory and "emptied himself, taking the form of a servant, being born in the likeness of men" (Philippians 2:7); and the scarlet cord, depicting his shed blood. The additional element of living water (*mayim chayim*) can represent, as well as the water of the Word, the new life of his supernatural resurrection—life eternal, empowered by the Spirit of Holiness.

The ashes of atonement are provided, and they can be consumed and absorbed within our very beings through the medium of living water—the water of the Word of God made available to all in the Living Word, who said:

> Whoever drinks of the water that I will give him will never be thirsty again. The water that I will give him will become in him a spring of water welling up to eternal life. (John 4:14)

Esteemed Jewish scholar and rabbi Joseph Soloveitchik provides an interesting view of the fear of death and purification from the "chains" of the impurity associated with death:

> How can a person redeem himself from death? How can he free himself from the fear of death; how can he manage to be purified from the filth that is in death? [He can free himself and be purified] through a dual process; first, through the means of immersion. [Immersion] is the organized, scientific, medical attempt whose goal is to lessen, as much as possible, the power of death. The man [who confronted death] purifies himself from death impurity in the way that all impure people purify themselves—alone.
>
> The second process is [purification of death impurity] through the sprinkling [of the waters]. This process is linked to us putting our trust in the Master of the world. [We believe] that at a certain stage in the future he will redeem us, "and the pure will sprinkle on the impure" (Numbers 19:19). The pure who will free the impure from the chains of the filth [that is death] is the LORD, as the prophet spoke, "I will sprinkle upon you pure waters, and you will be pure" (Ezekiel 36:25).
>
> Only God has the power to heal man from the terror and fear that come from the cessation [of the human being through death]. Man can never solve the mystery of death and suffering; only God will clarify this great and terrible mystery to us. Death is the most confounding phenomenon of all. It is an experience that cannot be studied in-depth, a law that no man can grasp its meaning.[19]

BALAK

בלק – "Balak"

NUMBERS 22:2–25:9

The parashah this week contains possibly the most comical incident in the Torah. At the same time, a number of the most serious issues of life are addressed. Accomplished teachers often use this combination. Humor can prepare the heart and mind to receive a compelling message of sober truth. The narrative recounts how Balaam, a recognized Mesopotamian prophet, after much deliberation and dialogue and the coming and going of envoys of the Moabite king, Balak, eventually sets out on the journey to Moab. The distance was about four hundred miles (640 km), which by horse or donkey would entail a journey of at least twenty days. And yet, Balaam has trouble making his way out of his own neighborhood. He is accompanied by two servants and a large group of Moabite dignitaries, who presumably witness the antics.

WORDS, WORDS, WORDS

Inexplicably, Balaam's donkey suddenly veers off the road into the adjacent fields. He responds by beating her in an attempt to turn her in the right direction. Instead, she enters a lane with walls on either side, and his foot is crushed against one of them. She then reaches a narrow place with no room to maneuver to the right or left. Now, even more enraged by the pain, he beats her again. The donkey simply lies down. By now, Balaam is so furious he continues to beat her with his stick. She then cries out, "What have I done to you that you have struck me these three times?" (Numbers 22:28). He is blinded in his rage and humiliation, it seems, and he dialogues with the donkey, "Because you have made a fool of me!" And he adds, "I wish I had a sword in my hand, for then I would kill you." (Numbers 22:29). The Midrash highlights an irony:

> This sorcerer, who is setting out to destroy an entire people with words, needs a sword to harm a donkey (*Tanchuma* 9).

The LORD then "uncovers Balaam's eyes," and he sees an angel standing before him with a drawn sword in his hand.[20] The humble donkey had eyes to see what the all-wise seer had not, despite his claim that his "eyes were opened" to God's revelations (Numbers 24:4,16). The angel of the LORD voices God's disapproval in no uncertain terms and proclaims that Balaam's mission is "perverse before me" (Numbers 22:32). Rather than choosing to turn back immediately, Balaam questions, "If it is evil in your sight, I will turn back." Obviously, Balaam's intent has not wavered, so the angel merely echoes Balaam's aim, "Go with the men." From this, we may learn that although God makes his wishes very clear, he does not force his will upon us. A person is allowed to go on the path he or she chooses, whether for good or evil.

NEIGHBORS – MOAB AND MIDIAN

Balak, the king of Moab, had heard the news of Israel's victory over the two mighty kings, Sichon and Og, and he was terrified. Israel had made it clear that they were coming in peace and simply desired unhindered passage through his country. Nevertheless, Balak stalled and, viewing them as the enemy, conspired to destroy them. By their sheer numbers and proven strength, the Israelites were too great to overcome physically, and he sought other means to defeat them. He displays a psychological cunning when he summons the elders of Midian (Numbers 22:4). He knew that Moses had spent much of his adult life there and was married to a Midianite woman, Zipporah, a daughter of Jethro, one of the most renowned priestly leaders. Balak enquired of the elders as to the source of Moses' power. Midrashic commentary records:

> The Midianite elders told Moab: "Moshe's power lies only in his mouth; when he prays." Said Moab: "We shall bring

Balaam, whose power is in his mouth, and he shall curse them."[21]

Balak proceeds to send the Midianite elders, together with selected Moabite elders, to Balaam with his request. The seer replies, "Lodge here tonight, and I will bring back word to you, as the LORD speaks to me." The verse then records an interesting fact: "So the princes of Moab stayed with Balaam" (Numbers 22:8). What happened to the Midianite elders? They are not mentioned again. *Tz'enah Ur'enah* comments:

> The elders of Midian said: "If he will go with us immediately, well and good; if he delays us, it is a sign that there is no truth in his words." As soon as Balaam asked them to stay overnight, the Midianite elders left him but the lords of Moab remained.[22]

Balaam lived in Aram, the birthplace of Abraham and still the abode of his brother Laban's family with whom Jacob had lived for many years. It is considered that Balaam was a grandson of Laban's. This may have been another reason why Balak, in his clever conspiring, had looked to him as an ally with inside knowledge. Midrash considers that when negotiating with Balak, Balaam could well have pointed out the common history between the forefathers of the Israelites and the king of Moab himself. Balak, a Moabite, is considered a descendent of the misinformed union of Lot and one of his daughters:

> If Avraham had not saved Lot from Sodom, then Lot and his daughters would have been destroyed, and you, Balak, would not ever have reached this world (for he was [of the issue of] Lot's daughter). ... How can we curse them, when it was their forefathers who brought us into this world?[23]

This ancestral connection, however, did not seem to deter them for even a moment.

DISCIPLES OF ABRAHAM

Although Balaam might have taken some pride in his connection with the forefathers, the sages reveal that he was the precise opposite of the righteous Abraham:

> The Mishnah says that whoever possesses the three characteristics of a good eye, a lowly spirit, and a humble soul is a disciple of our father Abraham; while one who has the three opposite characteristics is a disciple of the wicked Balaam. (*Avot* 5:22)[24]

An illustration: Abraham arose early in the morning to saddle his donkey in order to set out to obey the will of God, although it might cost him everything (Genesis 22:3). Balaam also arose in the morning and saddled his own donkey but, despite his words, his setting out and subsequent actions violated God's will and with a view to gaining riches and honor for himself.

The three righteous traits of Abraham are echoed by the Prophet Micah in the haftarah (Micah 6:8):

> He has told you, O man, what is good; and what does the LORD require of you?
>
> 1. To do justice—to walk in the balanced ways of God's goodness and truth and not to stray in paths set by one's own will,
> 2. to love kindness—to seek out the grace of God in every situation and to impart this to others, as opposed to harboring anger and seeking means to curse, and
> 3. to walk humbly with your God.

The word "humbly" is written *hatznea* in Hebrew, a variation of *tzni'ut*, "modesty." *Tzni'ut* incorporates three aspects: modesty (of outward appearance), purity of heart and motivation, and moderation of action, that is, not given to excess in any area.

We are exhorted by another descendent of Abraham, the disciple Jude, to not be influenced or distracted by those "who cause divisions, worldly people, devoid of the Spirit" such as Balak and Balaam. Instead, beloved, like our father Abraham, "building yourselves up in your most holy faith and praying in the Holy Spirit, keep yourselves in the love of God" (Jude 19–21).

PINCHAS

פנחס – "Phinehas"

NUMBERS 25:10–30:1 (29:40)

> Phinehas, the son of Eleazar, the son of Aaron the priest, ... was zealous for my sake; ... Behold, I give unto him my covenant of peace. (Numbers 25:11–12 KJV)

Shalom—Peace. The term brings to mind a state of all-encompassing harmony. It often raises an image of stillness and serenity—white sands, gently waving palms, and a glowing, sun-setting sky, or perhaps a shaded, green-hued glen traversed by a clear, bubbling brook. Beauty-filled surroundings, however, are not always the prerequisite for peace. Sometimes the deepest peace is experienced in a situation of great turmoil and conflict. An outworking of this paradox is described in the story of Pinchas.

PEACE – A COVENANT?

The harmony of true peace transcends one's physical surroundings and is established in the rest found in right relationship with God—in covenant relationship. Real, deep, and lasting peace also is found among people, one to another, when those concerned are at peace with God. We discover this truth illustrated primarily in the covenant of marriage. When a husband and wife first are fully yielded in their covenant relationship with the Father, a harmony of unity in oneness of vision and purpose is enjoyed. Then a nurturing, dynamic peace ensues—a peace that brings blessing and benefit to both. The same principle applies to family members, congregations, communities, tribes, and nations. Without God and his covenant of peace, people can form and entertain tolerant compromises, agreements, plans, truces, alliances, plots, and counter-plots, but they will not make nor find peace. Peace cannot be artificially created or found; it is a blessing that comes from the unity and outworking of the bond of covenant relationship.

Consider the challenging situation in the parashah. The Israelites have camped for many months in the environs of Moab. The Moabite king, Balak, in fear and hatred of this new nation, has tried unsuccessfully to destroy them through the curses of the powerful soothsayer Balaam. He knows he is outnumbered and cannot match the military prowess demonstrated in their previous conquests. Balak, therefore, employs a more subtle, "peaceful" tactic.

Suddenly, Moab has a more tolerant, friendly face, and the Israelites become more comfortable in their camp. There is more interaction: smiles, hellos, introductions. The women are visiting, and they are quite exotic in their bright garb, jewelry, and perfume ... and who is this god of whom they speak? Pe'or? And you are free to do what? Eyes wander, heads are turned, and hearts ensnared. The men abandon their covenant with God and embrace instead the pawns of Balak, the women of Moab, in illicit sexual relationships, and they turn to the idol Pe'or. Immorality and idolatry go hand-in-hand.

PEACE IN ACTION

The camp is in turmoil. No doubt, there are many tears shed by the Israelite women. Also, as a silent censure from God, a plague breaks out, and thousands of men die. Moses and Aaron are unusually quiet. We may assume they are interceding before God in desperation. Is there surrender without protest to these Moabites who are in conflict with the God of Israel? This passivity serves to promote the cause of the enemy and seems to shatter any hope for a peaceful, God-honoring outcome. In the midst of the disorder and confusion one man rises up in zeal for God's ways and in honor of his Name—Phinehas. He acts on behalf of their covenant with the LORD, and his valiant act restores the foundation of peace to his people.

The defiant and public act of Zimri, the prince of the tribe of Shimon, and Kosbi, the Midianite princess, was symbolic of the defection of Israel from their covenant with God to bow before the idol Pe'or. The essential act of Peoric worship was to defecate before the idol. This has more subtle implications than are initially obvious. Defecation is a natural, healthy function of the body and gives one a feeling of relief. The idol Pe'or embodied the concept of "Do whatever comes naturally. If it feels good, do it. If this is your nature, it's right to express it." Sound familiar? The nature of Pe'or worship thus encouraged "free sex." "It's natural. If you feel like it, do it with whomever, wherever, however you wish." This effectively removed sex from the context of love and sanctity in a sacred covenant union and established it more in line with a "natural urge" like defecation.

Rabbi Shlomo Riskin explains:

> This is a cultural precursor ... of much of contemporary, postmodern thought. ... Discipline has become the "hobgoblin of little minds," and self-expression takes precedence over duty to family, to country and to ideal. [It precludes] the necessity of self-sacrifice and striving, and confirms the fact that there are no absolutes with regard to what is proper and improper conduct.

Ethics are "situational," dependent upon one's situation, and every individual is a genius when it comes to justifying his desires in a subjective situation. This is the very antithesis of the Jewish/biblical ideal of "perfecting the world in the Kingship of the Divine," and the necessity of self-sacrifice in order to attain that goal.[25]

SACRIFICE? WHO, ME?

A common saying in Israel today is, *Hachayim zeh loh piknik*! "Life is not a picnic!" Praise the LORD for the occasional picnic, but in general, life is a battle, and there are few easy victories. This is more obvious in the ongoing, sometimes daily round of physical challenges, but the reality also applies to matters of the spirit and soul. Reducing spirituality to an easy-going, feel-good, secular-humanist type of faith is a tragic mistake. The spiritual journey was never considered to be a comfortable stroll, but rather a challenging, goal-oriented climb—ever-onward, ever-upward. It's a challenging journey that, more often than not, requires sacrifice, effort, and preparation.

The description in the parashah of the sacrifices required by God is read at the synagogue services on festival days. Even at times of joyful celebration, commemorating great miracles of God's revelation and power, there is a place for sacrifice. Every holiday or celebration, in fact, requires the sacrifices of our time, talents, energies, and finances in the preparation and enjoyment thereof. This is obvious, for example, in the event of a wedding or a special birthday celebration, and also on biblical festivals and holidays. Rabbi Berel Wein emphasizes:

> The Shabbat and the holidays are days of the spirit that have to be earned ... they are not cheaply obtained. Thus, on the holidays of the Hebrew calendar we read of the sacrifices in the Temple in order to remind us of the sacrifices necessary for us to achieve an inner appreciation of the holidays and their meaning. [26]

Pinchas laid his life on the line to act in the interests of God. He became "in his heroism, courage, selflessness, and denial of self-interest, the epitome of sacrifice, both physically and spiritually."[27] The LORD immediately halts the plague in affirmation of his act of sacrifice and extends to him and his descendants the eternal blessings of true peace and harmony in his service.

MATTOT

מטות – "Tribes"

NUMBERS 30:2(1)–32:42

The opening verse is unusual in that Moses is addressing his teaching to *rashei hamattot livnei Yisra'el*—the heads of the tribes of Israel—and not the people in general. The Chatam Sofer comments that the laws of vows and oaths delineated are therefore directed principally to leaders, "because people in high public office are more often tempted to make promises that they cannot keep."[28] The consequence is a loss of respect for the spoken word. Leaders, in any capacity, bear the great responsibility of setting the standard for those whom they lead.

IN THE EYES OF GOD AND MAN

We know from the very beginning, when God spoke all things into being, that words are not merely sounds. They carry weight and meaning. They have the power to hurt or to heal, to lift up and ennoble or to bring down and denigrate. The LORD takes words very seriously, and we are exhorted to do the same. Words, of course, inextricably are bound up with action. What we do, and what is perceived by our behavior in the eyes of others, has great influence. Often, as the saying goes, "Actions speak louder than words."

A large section of the parashah records the war against the Midianites. It seems regrettable that Moses' last actions on earth are connected with war. However, war and conflict are sad realities of life, and it appears that, like poverty, they will be with us until the return of Messiah. We learn from the Scriptures, however, that even in the extreme situation of war there are righteous guidelines to be applied and godly behaviors to exhibit. In the midst of the war account we find the verse, "ye shall return and be guiltless before the LORD and before Israel" (Numbers 32:22 KJV). This is addressed to those who have engaged in the bloody pursuits of battle and return to their camps. And yet, by adhering to the ethics prescribed by God, they may be seen as pure before him and the people.

Our actions are not only between God and us, they affect others. Every action we perform and behavior we practice can promote and encourage security and godliness and strengthen the society we are a part of, or it can have a negative, discouraging, and possibly destructive effect. The sages apply this concept to the "battle" of everyday life and make the extension that one's actions should be such that they do not cause others even to suspect one of sin. People, in general, are influenced by what they witness. The onus is upon us to ensure that our behavior will not be a stumbling block to others. We need to guard against any action in the spheres of our marriages, our families, businesses, communities, cities, or nations, that could cause another to harbor uncertainty, even if the suspicion aroused is unwarranted.

On the other hand, we also are encouraged to judge others favorably, to have "a good eye" when viewing the deeds of others. This principle is effectively a safeguard for one's own mind, for it precludes the environment from affecting one negatively.

May we be "pure in the eyes of God." May our words and actions be to the honor and glory of the One who gives us life and be an inspiration to those he places in our lives.

MESSENGERS OF GOD

The haftarah this week is the first of a triad called "The Haftarot of Admonition or Rebuke." They always are read on the three Shabbats following 17 Tammuz[29] and leading up to the fast day of Tisha b'Av (Ninth of Av). The latter commemorates the tragic destruction of the First and Second Temples and other historical disasters that befell the Jewish people. The three haftarot of admonition are followed by seven prophetic readings of consolation. It is comforting to note that the seven consolations are more than double the three rebukes. Such is the nature of our Father in heaven! We are reminded that, in all our dealings with others, our words of encouragement and comfort should far outweigh any correction or rebuke that is necessary.

The definition of the appellation "prophet" generally is accepted as "messenger of God," as in the Greek *prophetes*—one who speaks on behalf of God—and the Hebrew *navi*—one who proclaims [words of God]. Prophecy has two basic functions. One is foretelling, describing future events, which can be proven only once they are fulfilled. They confirm the Word of God and enable one to see the "big picture" of God's working in history. Today, we certainly need to be aware of the words of the biblical prophets and be in touch with the "signs of the times," as Yeshua exhorts in Matthew 16. The second, more immediate, function of prophecy is to offer a call to repentance and right relationship with God. The purpose of the prophetic word is to enable people to see how they are living their lives in the present. It gives a clear "wake-up call" to get back on track with God. This is illustrated in the words of Jeremiah and the other prophets of old. Their messages from God were explosive and often harsh. They were intended to shatter indifference. They would always, however, conclude with words of compassion, hope, and redemption. They shone the light of truth into the darkness and revealed the way back to God.

A PROPHET GREATER THAN ...

The first great public spokesman for God, the one who stepped into the prophetic spotlight, is Moses. The divine messages he transmitted, in fact, shifted the paradigm of reality and affected history. He illustrated how a human being, when acting according to the express will of God, has the power to affect reality by the words they speak on his behalf. However, Moses himself proclaimed, "Would that all the LORD's people were prophets, that the LORD would put his Spirit on them!" (Numbers 11:29).

As people of God, with our wills surrendered to his, we are faced with a challenge: "Are you prepared to become a vehicle for the expression of the LORD's will?" The extent of evil and injustice in the world today brings to mind the verse, "Where there is no prophetic vision the people cast off restraint, but blessed is he who keeps the law" (Proverbs 29:18).

Hopefully, we will be yielded vessels willing to speak his words of truth, rebuke, comfort, and consolation as he leads and gives the opportunity to do so.

Abraham Heschel, in his amazing two-volume set, simply called *The Prophets*, writes:

> The prophet was an individual who said NO to his society, condemning its habits and assumptions, its complacency, waywardness, and syncretism. ... His fundamental objective was to reconcile man and God. Why do the two need reconciliation? Perhaps it is due to man's false sense of sovereignty, to his abuse of freedom, to his aggressive, sprawling pride, resenting God's involvement in history![30]

Man desires to order history his way, according to his prideful self-aggrandizement. Those who have ears that are deaf to his voice cannot say, as Yeshua did, that which should be the cry of every child of God, "Not my will, but yours, be done" (Luke 22:42)!

May our Father enable us to respond joyfully to his call to participate in the outworking of his plan of redemption for Israel and the nations. May we be alert, strong, wise, and humble, standing in a profound "fear" of our Father God and with hearts filled with the love and compassion of our Messiah Yeshua.

MASSEI

מסעי – "Journeys"

NUMBERS 33:1–36:13

The portion Massei marks the close of our journey through the book of Numbers (Bamidbar). We have persevered through the dry stretches of the wilderness and hopefully have enjoyed refreshing water from the Rock.

The journey of the Israelites can more accurately be described as a "wandering." Rather than a direct, purposeful traverse from point A to point B, it appears to be a somewhat aimless rambling through the hostile desert region. This enforced wandering in exile is a familiar theme in Jewish history. In fact, the movement of exile and return is a constant motif, like the waxing and waning of the moon or the ebb and flow of the waves of the sea upon the shore. It is reflected in the life of the nation of Israel and also spiritually in each of our individual lives. It is like a dance, drawing closer to and then away from the Beloved of our souls.

GOD IN EXILE?

The wilderness wandering seems futile and a waste of time. To wander, to be in exile, to be rootless and homeless—what purpose could this serve? On closer examination, we find that it yields many important existential lessons. Chief among them is that, when your life is in God's hands, nothing happens for no reason. Everything has a purpose, according to his will and design. Another vital realization is the assurance, as the psalmist expresses: "I will be with him in trouble" (Psalm 91:15). We are not alone on our journey; God is with us in exile.

The sages reinforce the understanding that God himself goes into exile along with his people. Rabbi Natan points out,

> Wherever Israel is, the Divine Presence is there with them. When they were in Egypt, the Divine Presence was there, too. Now the Divine Presence is also with us, and when we return to Yerushalayim (Jerusalem) the Presence of God will return with us, as the verse says: And the LORD your God shall return [with] you to Yerushalayim (Deuteronomy 30:5).[31]

This is God's desire, that his people return to him and to his land, and that his name be glorified and lifted up. Then, as foretold by the Prophet Isaiah, all the nations will stream up to the mountain of his house, and "out of Zion shall go forth the [Torah], and the word of the LORD from Jerusalem" (Isaiah 2:3).

As we journey through life, and we hold fast to the LORD, we can reach out to fellow travelers who are alienated from him with the invitation, "Come let us go up" (Isaiah 2:3). There is a way from the darkness of futility into the light of his life that provides purpose and direction for the path ahead. The psalmist affirms:

> Good and upright is the LORD; therefore he instructs sinners in the way. (Psalm 25:8)

SIGNIFICANT STOPS

Moses lists the progress of the wilderness journey "by command of the LORD" (Numbers 33:2). Levi Yitzchak reflects:

> There are forty-two voyages the children of Israel took, when it says: "They camped in ..., and they camped in ..." This showed that, when the Israelites camped in a place where there was evil fear ... then they would worship God, may He be blessed, with exalted fear, fearing His power, glory and might ... and when they camped in a place where there was evil love ... then they would worship God, may He be blessed, with true love ... and so on ...[32]

This is an encouraging thought. The Israelites were by no means perfect, and yet because the presence of the Holy One accompanied them, they were able to influence the places they camped for good. In their worship and exaltation of the God of Israel, any evil they encountered could be overcome and redeemed.

David Blumenthal comments on Levi Yitzchak's observation:

> At every step in life, no matter how depressing, the Jew [the child of God] is not to look at his or her own discomfort but is to seek the remnant of the Divine element in that moment and to redeem it, gently, for God.
>
> [In so doing] homelessness ceases to be a human discomfort; it becomes an imitation of the Divine [who also is in exile]. It also places humankind in a very significant position, that of being able to help God, of being capable of participating actively in the Redemption. [33]

The Prophet Ezekiel makes a connection between this wilderness wandering and Israel's later exile among the nations, when he says, on behalf of the LORD, "I will bring you into the wilderness of the peoples" (Ezekiel 20:35).

Today we have the comfort and reassurance of his presence with us in our particular, individual exile and can place our trust in his protection and provision. We also are given the glorious hope and assurance that just as the Almighty preserved Israel and brought them up from the wilderness, so will he effect the final great Redemption when all Israel will be saved and all the nations will be blessed.

In that great day, when Yeshua returns as King of kings to reign from Jerusalem, "the earth shall be full of the knowledge of the LORD as the waters cover the sea" (Isaiah 11:9), just as the prophets said it would be!

CHAZAK CHAZAK, VENITCHAZEK

BE STRONG, BE STRONG, AND MAY WE STRENGTHEN ONE ANOTHER IN THE UNITY OF THE ONE WHO LOVES US.

ENDNOTES

1. Derech Chaim, *Masechet Avot* 2.
2. Rabbi Dr. J.H. Hertz, *The Pentateuch and Haftorahs* 2nd ed. (London, New York: Soncino, 1993), 573.
3. Rabbi A.l. Scheinbaum, *Peninim on the Torah* (New York, NY: Noble Book Press, 2001), 238.
4. Ibid., 239.
5. *Genesis Rabbah* 19:11
6. *Pirkei Avot* 1:12.
7. Bill Johnson, *Dreaming with God* (Shippensburg, PA: Destiny Image Publishers, 2006), 103.
8. Rabbi Shlomo Riskin, "The Miraculous Is Our Reality," *Jerusalem Post*, 24 June, 2005.
9. Ibid.
10. Ibid.
11. Dr. J.H.Hertz, *Pentateuch and Haftorahs*, 634.
12. Rabbi Shlomo Riskin, "The Miraculous Is Our Reality," *Jerusalem Post*, 24 June, 2005.
13. David. R. Blumenthal, *God at the Center: Meditations on Jewish Spirituality*, 117.
14. Ibid.
15. Ibid.
16. Rabbi Chanan Morrison, *Gold from the Land of Israel*, 261.
17. Ibid., 262.

    Note: Rav Kook proved to be one of the leading lights in the "tents of Torah," whose legacy is continued in *Mercaz HaRav* (the Rav's Yeshiva or Center for Torah Study) in the heart of Jerusalem. We honor the memory of the eight young students who were "toiling in the tents" when the precious lights of their lives were violently snuffed out by a PLO terrorist on 6 March, 2008.

18. *Shemot Rabbah* 36:3.

19 Rabbi Joseph Soloveitchik, *Out of the Whirlwind: Essays on Mourning, Suffering and the Human Condition* (Israel: Yediot Achronot, 2009), 95. (Translated by Jeremiah Detwiler.)

20 It is unusual for an angel to carry a sword. One wonders if this was a prophetic symbol of the death of Balaam. Not long after, he died a premature, violent death by a sword.

21 *Tz'enah Ur'enah, The Weekly Midrash*, Vol.1, 782.

22 Ibid., 783.

23 Ibid., 787.

24 Arthur Green, *The Language of Truth: The Torah Commentary of the Sefat Emet* (Philadelphia, PA: Jewish Publication Society, 1998), 257.

25 Rabbi Shlomo Riskin, chief rabbi of Ephrat, Israel; *Torah Lights: Bemidbar: Trials and Tribulations in Times of Transition*, "Pinehas, A Man of Peace" (Jerusalem, Israel: Magid Books, 2012).

26 Rabbi Berel Wein, *Toras Aish*, Vol. XI No. 42, Pinchas (Israel, 5764, 2004).

27 Ibid.

28 *Etz Hayim,* Torah and Commentary (Philadelphia, PA: The Jewish Publication Society, 2001), 941.

29 Tammuz 17 is observed as a fast day. It marks the first breach of the walls of Jerusalem by Babylonians during the time of the First Temple. (*Etz Hayim*, 968.)

30 Abraham Joshua Heschel, *The Prophets* (New York, NY: Harper & Row Publishers, 1969), xvii.

31 *Tz'enah Ur'enah, The Weekly Midrash*, Vol. 1, 815.

32 David R. Blumenthal, *God at the Center: Meditations on Jewish Spirituality*, (New York, NY: Harper and Row Publishers, 1987), 129.

33 Ibid., 130.

DEUTERONOMY

DEVARIM

דברים – "Words"

DEUTERONOMY 1:1–3:22

The Israelites are poised on the plains alongside the Jordan River overlooking the promised land. Moses knows he will not cross over with them but that God will bury him after making his final ascent upon a mountain nearby. He will die after enjoying a glorious, prophetic view of the land for which he longs, but he cannot now enter.

WORDS AND BEES

The parashah begins with the verse: "These are the words (*devarim*) that Moses spoke to all Israel" (Deuteronomy 1:1). These words launch the final book of the Torah, also named Devarim. The statement emphasizes the importance of the words Moses is about to deliver as his last discourse on earth.

Midrashic commentary draws attention to the similarity of the Hebrew words *devarim* (words) and *devorim* (bees):

> The Sages say, in *Sefer Rabasi*, that Moshe began with *eileh ha'devarim* (these are the words) because the Torah is compared to a bee, whose honey is sweet and whose sting is poisonous to men. The Torah likewise is an elixir of life to those who heed it, and a deadly poison to those who do not.[1]

This concept is reinforced later in the portion when Moses reminds the people that "the Amorites came out ... and chased you as bees do" (Deuteronomy 1:44). In a presumptuous act, contrary to Moses' instructions, the Israelites had gone out to do battle with the inhabitants of the land (Numbers 14:45), who, in response, had attacked them like a swarm of stinging bees.

Interspersed in Moses' discourse are admonitions that indeed carry the sting of rebuke. He recounts sins they had committed since leaving Egypt and during the wilderness journey. The Midrash enumerates these sins as follows:

> You spoke wickedly and said it would have been better to die in the desert; you sinned in ... [Moab], with illicit relations and with the idol Peor; you sinned immediately upon reaching the sea, when you said, "Are there no graves in Egypt then, that you took us out to kill us in the desert?"; later you spoke against the manna, which was white and good, and you said, "Our intestines will be bloated from it"; you sinned with the spies; with the dispute of Korach; and you made the Golden Calf.[2]

These total seven sins. When God says, "I will punish you seven times more for your sins" (Leviticus 26:18), it can also carry the implication, "I will punish you for your seven sins." Moses is the paradigmatic leader. Here he illustrates the importance of admonition, a warning against the propensity to sin, to maintain discipline—a key element in the successful overseeing of any endeavor. The responsibility rests upon the head, or leader, to set the standard of values and to initiate and model them, whether in the context of a family, a school, a business, a sports team, or an army battalion. The sages caution:

> If the head of the congregation ... does not warn his people,
> God punishes him even before He punishes the people.[3]

We also are informed that the discourse takes place "after he had defeated Sihon" (Deuteronomy 1:4). Moses delivers this great concluding address only after overcoming the two mighty kings, Sichon and Og. By his deeds and actions, a true leader proves to his people that he is worthy of their honor and respect. He earns the right to rebuke and correct. The people could not turn around and say, "What good did Moshe do for us, that he comes now to rebuke us?"[4]

IS HONOR DUE?

A popular saying that carries some truth is, "Give honor where honor is due." A prominent exception to this rule is, "Honor your father and mother," which is found in the commandments reviewed here by Moses (Deuteronomy 1:3).

A child's parents are physical agents of God in enabling the child to be born into this world. Ideally, each parent continues to cooperate with God in caring for and raising that child in the manner of, and according to, the directions he has imparted. In doing so, while discipline is necessary and vital, it is always undergirded by two unwavering elements: first, unconditional love that is freely and constantly expressed and, second, the warmth and reassurance of sincere encouragement. By this reflection of our Father in heaven, parents would bestow upon their children such bountiful blessing that every precious child would be well equipped to stride forward with confident expectancy on their journey through life.

Sadly, this ideal is not often realized. However, children are told to honor their parents—no matter if they deserve their respect. Parents remain God's agents, and it is to him that they are answerable, and with him rests their reward or punishment. In the haftarah, we see that God regards Israel as "children I have reared and brought up" (Isaiah 1:2). The same applies to all humanity to whom he has given life. God, the Father of all, is the first "parent" to whom our honor and obedience are due.

In his discourse, as is the case throughout his tenure of leadership, Moses demonstrates the qualities of a good parent who clearly reflects the Father of all. His words of rebuke are minimal when considered alongside his words of caring instruction and loving assurance.

CALL THE WITNESSES

An important factor Moses brings to the people's remembrance is how he, in effect, had established the first law-courts by appointing judges amongst them. The judges were instructed to "hear the cases between your brothers, and judge righteously between a man and his brother" (Deuteronomy 1:16). This served to uphold justice and provided recourse for any against whom had been sinned.

This week's haftarah introduces "the vision of Isaiah the son of Amoz" (Isaiah 1:1). Like Moses, the remarkable prophet rebukes Israel for their sins to encourage them to return to their God and live righteously. Isaiah places himself in the position of an advocate and calls to the heavens, "Hear, O heavens" (Isaiah 1:2), to be a witness in the case concerning Israel. God created the heavens, the planets, the sun, moon, and stars. These have not faltered and faithfully perform their service to their creator. In fact, the psalmist describes how the sun rejoices to do God's will every day with the eager anticipation of a bridegroom: "[He is] like a [*chatan*] bridegroom leaving his [*chuppah*, "wedding canopy"] chamber" (Psalm 19:5).

As a second witness, Isaiah calls to the earth, "Give ear, O earth, for the LORD has spoken" (Isaiah 1:2). It is an established practice in courts of law, based on the biblical pattern, to call a minimum of two witnesses to verify the evidence in a case. We also see this applied in resolving matters personally, as in Matthew 18. The most desirable option is to settle the issue individually, face to face, with someone who has acted unjustly toward you. "But if he does not listen, take one or two others along with you, that every charge may be established by the evidence of two or three witnesses" (Matthew 18:16).

Isaiah is echoing the words of Moses, recorded in the book of Devarim: "Give ear, O heavens, and I will speak, and let the earth hear the words of my mouth" (Deuteronomy 32:1). This would startle his audience and demand their attention, for they were perfectly familiar with the words of the Torah. They would realize that, in effect, he was calling Moses and God himself to be witnesses. Indeed, God was in the heavens, and Moses was his representative on earth. His Word of Torah is the product of this union of heaven and earth. Man, too, is the union of heaven—his God-breathed spirit—and of the dust of the earth. All these factors are powerful witnesses to the truth of the words of this messenger of God.

Immediately, Isaiah reminds the people that they are children of God, who says, "Sons [*banim*, "children"] I have reared and brought up" (Isaiah 1:2). But, sadly, the children have rejected the Father's teaching and have rebelled against him and abandoned his ways. The prophet then proclaims, "An ox knows its owner" (Isaiah 1:3).

The Midrash comments:

God says to His people, "You must learn from the animals how to serve Me." Even an animal, who lacks the ability to reason, knows his master—the one who bought him and who feeds him. An ox always comes to its trough for food, but God's children, whom He faithfully sustains and lovingly guides and teaches, turn their backs and will not come to Him.[5]

A rebuke often is difficult to give as well as to receive. Isaiah, in the manner of all true prophets of God, concludes the admonition in the haftarah with a word of hope and encouragement: "Zion shall be redeemed by justice" (Isaiah 1:27). Redemption will come. Justice will triumph, and Zion will be redeemed. This is the promise of God and the hope of all who repent and return to him, just as rebellious children turn from their sin and run back to the arms of a loving, merciful father.

VA'ETCHANAN

ואתחנן – "And I Besought"

DEUTERONOMY 3:23–7:11

The fast day of Tisha B'Av (9 Av) is a somber day of mourning on the Hebrew calendar. It is a day for pleading, beseeching God for his grace and mercy, and the deliverance of his people from the schemes and attacks of the enemy. The book of Lamentations is read. On this day, we recall the two historical invasions of Jerusalem that destroyed the First and Second Holy Temples in 586 BCE and 70 CE, respectively. These horrific events seemed to earmark Tisha B'Av as a particular day of attack for Israel's adversaries as, during subsequent centuries, further tragedies of persecution and terror were inflicted on this very day. For example, Tisha B'Av in 1492 marked the culmination of the Inquisition and expulsion of Jews from Spain. Also, on this date, the declaration of the Crusades was made by Pope Urban II in 1095, and in 1942, Hitler activated the first death camps at Treblinka.

THE LIVING TEMPLE

Sarah Y. Rigler, an accomplished author living in Jerusalem, makes the following astute observation regarding the focus of Tisha B'Av:

> We misrepresent the tragedy of the day by describing it as the destruction of the two Holy Temples, as if the catastrophe is the loss of a building. The American people do not mourn on 9/11 because of the destruction of the Twin Towers, they mourn the thousands of lives lost in the conflagration.

> Contrast a person who mourns the absence of the majestic towers to the New York skyline with a person who mourns the loss of parents on the 98th floor.[6]

Similarly, the tragedy of the loss of the House of God, the Temple in Jerusalem, was not simply the disappearance of the magnificent structure, as heart-rending as that was. It had far deeper spiritual ramifications. It was the physical connection point of heaven and earth. As Sarah Rigler describes:

> The Temple service was a [God-ordained] procedure that kept the aperture between the [spiritual and physical] worlds open and functioning. The Divine Presence manifested itself in the Temple and through the Temple. When the Temple was destroyed, that palpable Divine Presence removed itself from our world. It was a loss as real and as searing as death.[7]

She compares this loss to the heart-rending loss of her earthly father, who died before her son was born. She mourns the fact that her child will never know "how the room lit up when my father entered. Nor will he know the security and support offered by his grandfather to so many others." She continues:

> In the same way, we who were born into a world without the Divine Presence have never experienced the spiritual luminosity that radiated through the aperture of the Holy Temple ... Divine hiddenness has replaced Divine revelation ... We are relegated to "believing" when once we simply knew. Tisha B'Av has made orphans of us all.

Her heartfelt and insightful article enforces a deeper appreciation of the words of Yeshua: "Destroy this Temple, and in three days I will raise it up" (John 2:19).

He loved the Temple, his Father's House. He marveled at its physical beauty and was deeply absorbed in its spiritual reality. He wept as he prophetically saw the complete destruction that would occur forty years after his death and resurrection.

We can be eternally grateful that in Yeshua, by the Holy Spirit imparted to us, we can cry out in loving wonder, "Abba, Father!" In Messiah, the Living Temple—the living place of connection between heaven and earth—the relationship is restored and securely established. Our

Father is not hidden but revealed. We can intimately know him, and we are no longer spiritual orphans. Although the world is still in exile and things are not set right as of yet, we can still participate in the mourning of Tisha B'Av, but one day when Yeshua returns, the mourning of Tisha B'Av will be transformed into joy. *Baruch HaShem*! Bless his holy Name!

HEAR AND DO

The portion Va'etchanan includes two of the most recognized passages in the Bible—the Ten Commandments and the *Shma*. The first presents the quintessence of biblical morality. The second is the declaration of faith in the One God:

> *Shma Yisra'el, Adonai Eloheinu, Adonai Echad.*
> Hear, O Israel, the LORD our God, the LORD is One.
> (Deuteronomy 6:4)

Rabbi Shlomo Riskin of Efrat, Israel, explains that God's ineffable name, translated as LORD, implies eternity, the ground of all existence, ultimate redemption, and steadfast love. The name *Eloheinu*, our God, is a plural noun and implies power and creativity. Each of these names is linked to the other in an inextricable bond.

The first of the Ten Commandments begins, "I am the LORD your God, who brought you out of the land of Egypt, out of the house of slavery" (Deuteronomy 5:6). The reality is enforced that he is the God who sets us free, who brings liberty to the enslaved and oppressed. By vanquishing Pharaoh, he demonstrated that he is the only Lord. No human being has the right to "lord it over" another person.

The commandments then proceed to describe the fundamental standard of *tzedek*, God's righteousness. If adhered to in love of God, this standard of righteousness produces the greatest harmony and happiness amongst those living according to its precepts.

The *Shma* expresses how we demonstrate our love for God: "with all your heart, with all your soul, with all your might [or means]." Bible commentator and ethicist Moshe Chaim Luzzatto succinctly captures the bond between the *Shma* and the commandments:

> Whoever sets the LORD always before him and is exclusively concerned with doing His pleasure and observing His com-

mandments will be called the lover of God ... the love of God is not a separate commandment but an underlying principle of all the commandments.[8]

Therefore, true love of God implies doing his will not out of appreciation of his wonders and might but out of complete, heartfelt surrender to him.

Regarding the commandments, the renowned Maimonides submits:

> We are to dwell upon and contemplate His commandments, [and] His wonders and deeds, so that we may come closer to understanding Him and thereby attain absolute joy—this procedure constituting the love of Him with which we are charged.[9]

This "procedure" is outlined in another passage of Deuteronomy where cleaving to in love and intimacy follows obedience to the divine will: "You shall walk after the LORD your God and fear him and keep his commandments and obey his voice, and you shall serve him and hold fast to him" (Deuteronomy 13:4).

THE SPIRIT AND THE LETTER

Moses made it clear that the precepts he was teaching the Israelites were to be applied and faithfully lived out in their daily lives. They are not simply "good ideas":

> Now, O Israel, listen to the statutes (*hachukim*) and the rules (*mishpatim*) that I am teaching you, and do them, that you may live. (Deuteronomy 4:1)

The injunction is repeated in Deuteronomy 4:5 and 5:29. Another exhortation follows in chapter 6:

> You shall diligently keep the commandments of the LORD your God, and his testimonies and his statutes, which he has commanded you. And you shall do what is right and good in the sight of the LORD. (Deuteronomy 6:17–18)

Nehama Leibowitz poses the question: "Is this phrase [v.18] perhaps merely a summary of all that has been stated previously? Surely one who strictly obeys all the commandments in the Torah *ipso facto* fulfills the admonition to do what is 'right and good in the eyes of the Lord'?"[10] She looks to two of the foremost Torah commentators for an answer. Initially, the inimitable Rashi (France, 1049-1105) who definitively states,

> "That which is right and good"—This implies a compromise beyond the letter of the law.

Then, the Ramban (Nachmanides, Rabbi Moshe ben Nachman - Spain, 1194-1270) who agrees with Rashi and elaborates:

> [God] loves that which is good and upright. This is a very important principle since it is impossible to record every detail of human behavior in the Torah embracing man's relations with his neighbors and friends, his business affairs, national and local welfare.
>
> [Therefore] He included a general injunction to do that which is good and upright in every matter, accepting where necessary even a compromise in a legal dispute and going beyond the letter of the law.[11]

Leibowitz connects this concept of "good and right" with the concomitant principle of "holiness," based on the injunction in Leviticus: "Ye shall be holy, for I the LORD your God am holy" (Leviticus 19:2). She asks, "Is it conceivable that one who observes loyally all the moral and ritual observance of the Torah should fall short of the standards of holiness and uprightness?" Again, the Ramban offers an answer:

> Since the Torah warns us against immorality and forbidden food but permits marital relations and the partaking of meat and wine, the immoderate person might abuse these dispensations, overindulging in permitted sexual relations and in eating and drinking, maintaining ... that this was not specifically prohibited by the Torah. He would be "a fool by authorization of the Torah" (*naval bireshut haTorah*). For this reason the Torah adds ... a general admonition to be holy, to sanctify oneself through minimizing his indulgence in

even permitted enjoyments, in food and drink and sex. The Nazirite abstainer is called "holy" by the Torah. Similarly, every man should sanctify himself until he attains a higher state of holiness.[12]

This indicates that one can keep the "letter" of the Torah, in a legalistic and literal fashion observing God's commands, and yet violate its spirit. By not doing whatever one does in love and reverence of God and love and respect for one's neighbor, one grieves the Spirit of God and, in essence, as the Ramban points out, is dangerously fooling oneself.

The grave importance of acting according to the spirit of Torah, in essence, the Spirit of Holiness, rather than the "letter of the Law," is highlighted by the sages:

> Said Rabbi Yochanan: Jerusalem was destroyed only because they acted in accordance with the letter of the Torah and did not go beyond it. (b.*Bava Metzia* 30b)[13]

Or, as Rabbi Riskin wisely emphasizes:

> Ritual observance not accompanied by ethical behavior [doing what is right, good, and holy in the eyes of God] is what God calls the ultimate abomination. ... Ritual must be a means to an end—the end being a God of love and compassion shining from [our] hearts and actions."[14]

EKEV

עקב – "Because"

DEUTERONOMY 7:12–11:25

> Because (*ekev*) you listen to these rules (*mishpatim*) and keep and do them. (Deuteronomy 7:12)

Obedience is followed by a stream of blessings, as Moses encapsulates: "He will love you and bless you and multiply you" (Deuteronomy 7:13).

It is important to note that the "you" addressed in this context is in the plural form. The community, the nation, the people as a whole, is being exhorted to obey the Word of the God of their forefathers, Abraham, Isaac, and Jacob. If they hear his words and grasp them and live according to them, his presence will be with them, and his love will be poured upon them in blessings of every kind. God promises that "you shall be blessed above all peoples" (Deuteronomy 7:14). Their families and livestock would bear young, they would suffer no illness or disease, and they would overcome all enemies who came against them. They need have no fear, "for the LORD your God is in your midst, a great and awesome God" (Deuteronomy 7:21). What powerful promises, what rich blessings, all hanging on the fulcrum of one little word *ekev*—because, as a result of, *if*—you obey these ordinances and carefully guard them!

STRAIGHT VERSUS CROOKED

The same principle is echoed in the next chapter: "The whole commandment (*mitzvot*, "good deeds") that I command you today you shall be careful to do, that you may live and multiply" (Deuteronomy 8:1). What is the alternative if one chooses not to observe? Moses says:

> You shall remember the whole way that the LORD your God has led you these forty years in the wilderness, that he might humble you, testing you to know what was in your heart, whether you would keep his commandments or not. (Deuteronomy 8:2)

He reminds the Israelites that the tests and difficulties they had faced were to make evident the motive of their hearts: obedience or rebellion. God always sees and knows a person's heart; any tests, and our reactions to them, serve to illustrate to us the true state of our own hearts. Are they yielded in loving obedience to the will of the LORD our God, or are we harboring sinful attitudes of rebellion?

The title of the parashah, Ekev, bears multidimensional meaning. One aspect is based on the related word *akev* ("heel"), from which Jacob's name (*Ya'akov*) was derived when he was born holding onto the heel of his twin brother, Esau (Genesis 25:26). Additional meanings are "footsteps," as in Psalm 56:6, "they watch my steps" (literally, heels), and "supplant" as in Genesis 27:36, when Esau cries out, "Is not he rightly named *Ya'akov*, for he has supplanted (*akav*) me?" This carries overtones of cunning and trickery, which is applied in the English usage of the word, for example: "Don't trust him; he's a heel!" In other words, "He's crooked."

Ya'akov had to face the consequences of his actions. He needed to run for his life, and his steps carried him into exile. There he himself was bitterly deceived by his cousin Laban when his intended wife, his beloved Rachel, was supplanted by her sister Leah.

The Prophet Isaiah offers the hope that our crooked (*akov*) ways will be made straight (*mishor*). *Ya'akov* will become *Yisra'el* and *Yeshurun* (*yashar*, "straight"). God adjures Jacob:

> Now hear (*shma*), O [*Ya'akov*] my servant, [*Yisra'el*] whom I have chosen! Thus says the LORD who made you, who formed you from the womb and will help you: Fear not, O [*Ya'akov*] my servant, *Yeshurun* whom I have chosen. (Isaiah 44:1–2)

God saw his servant's heart—yielded and willing to obey—and assured him that he had known him and been with him even in his mother's womb. He need not be afraid, for the LORD was there, who now named him *Yisra'el*, Prince of God, and *Yeshurun*, straight and upright.

Any flaw or crookedness of the heart that might have been was corrected in this servant of the LORD, and from his line would come the "Seed" of Messiah, who would triumph by crushing the head of the serpent under his heel (Genesis 3:15).

Yeshua indeed overcame the wiles and lies of the adversary and the power of death, and to the resurrected Lord, the Father said, "Sit at my right hand until I make your enemies a footstool for your feet" (Hebrews 1:13). At the right hand of power, Messiah is ruling while all enemies are being bound to form a footstool under his feet. Before him they must surrender, and in his authority we also can "tread on serpents ..., and over all the power of the enemy, and nothing shall hurt you" (Luke 10:19) *ekev*, "if," we hear his commands and faithfully obey.

THE BLESSINGS OF BREAD AND TORAH

The sages of Israel say that one should find occasion to bless God one hundred times a day. They base this on the verse in the parashah that says, "What (*mah*) does the LORD your God require of you?" (Deuteronomy 10:12).[15] The word *mah* is reminiscent of the word *me'ah*, one hundred. We may also consider God's miraculous provision of bread (manna) in the wilderness. The people asked, "*Mahn hu*?" "What is this?"

It is in this connection with daily bread/food that we find one of the two blessings that are demanded in the Torah: "You shall eat and be full, and you shall bless the LORD your God" (Deuteronomy 8:10). The traditional blessing, *Birkat HaMazon* ("Thanksgiving for Food"), is thus recited after a meal.

There are two blessings we receive from food for which we can offer thanks to God. One is the sheer pleasure we enjoy when eating tasty food, along with the companionship often associated with a meal. In anticipation of this, a rabbinic blessing also is instituted to bless God before a meal. The second, and more important blessing, is the nourishment the food provides to our bodies, which sustains our lives. Therefore, after the meal, as our bodies absorb and digest the food, we are told to remember and to gratefully bless the LORD who is our Provider.

As vital to our existence as our daily bread is the provision of God's Word for our spiritual sustenance. Yeshua powerfully emphasized this truth when he quoted a verse from this portion: "Man shall not live by bread alone, but by every word that comes from the mouth of God" (Matthew 4:4; Deuteronomy 8:3). The sages conclude that one should, therefore, also say a blessing before studying the Torah. Why should a blessing be recited before studying God's Word? Rav Kook explains that just as food has two benefits, so does Torah study. The first is the knowledge we gain and can apply in practical areas of our lives. Of the second, he says,

> The second benefit lies in the very act of learning Torah. Torah study in itself is a tremendous gift, even if it does not provide any practical application. When we learn Torah, the soul is elevated as our minds absorb the sublime Word of God. … When we bless God before studying, we acknowledge the spiritual elevation that we enjoy in the very act of contemplating God's Torah.[16]

The sages reinforce this spiritual value, which outweighs even the physical deeds that result from one's study and application of God's Word:

> One who studies Torah for its own sake [out of pure love for God and his Word] is raised and uplifted above all actions. (*Avot* 6:1)

On the other hand, the sages affirm that God richly rewards those commandments that we perform by using our feet, such as going to communal worship and prayer or to a lecture, visiting the sick, and escorting the dead [at a funeral], or comforting a mourner.[17] To disregard the opportunity to do a good deed (mitzvah) in concurrence with God's Word is like treading something of value underfoot and grinding it into the dirt with one's heel.

This connection with our walking, directing our steps in obedience to the will of the LORD and running, as it were, to carry out a good deed, and the consequential blessing of God is indicated at the conclusion of the parashah:

> If you will be careful to do all this commandment that I command you to do, loving the LORD your God, walking in all his ways, and holding fast to him, then ... every place on which the sole of your foot treads shall be yours. (Deuteronomy 11:22–24)

You will also be enabled to stand upright on your feet before anyone who might oppose you without fear. The LORD will make straight paths for your feet if they follow the dictates of a heart devoted to his service:

> So you shall keep the commandments (mitzvot) of the LORD your God by walking in his ways and by fearing him. (Deuteronomy 8:6)

RE'EH

ראה – "See"

DEUTERONOMY 11:26–16:17

"*Re'eh*! See! I am setting before you today a blessing and a curse" (Deuteronomy 11:26). The generation Moses was addressing had indeed seen much. They had experienced the power of God's Presence and had witnessed his miracles of deliverance, provision, and protection. Now they are given to understand that the power of choice was being placed fully into their own hands. The realities of blessings and curses are set clearly before them. One would result in peace, abundance, and happiness, the other in discord, poverty, and misery. Ultimately, one choice leads to life and the other to death. The resounding call of God to his people is, "Choose life!"[18]

It is clear that the emphasis of receiving blessing is not that it is a reward earned through obedience to the commandments of God. Rather, the enactment of a mitzvah (good deed) is in itself part of the blessing. The sages say, "One mitzvah leads to another." One good deed prepares the way for another. It is in the doing of good that the blessing is enjoyed. The chief motivation for our obedience and our "good deeds," however, should be to give pleasure to our Father in heaven.

One's daily walk in his path of goodness and righteousness leads to a more abundant life, as he has promised:

> It may go well with you and with your children after you forever, when you do what is good and right in the sight of the LORD your God. (Deuteronomy 12:28)

"And the curse if ..." (Deuteronomy 11:28). An act of disobedience carries in its aftermath the loss of self-worth. Guilt incurs a diminishing of self, which leads to further acts of disobedience. Each step carries one further from God and deeper into idolatry of one form or another—a path that leads inevitably to death.

The curse occurs "if you do not obey the commandments (*mitzvot*) of the LORD your God." The Hebrew word *tishm'u* (obey), as a variation of *shma* (hear), most commonly means to listen, to hear the voice of God. When one becomes stiff-necked and stubborn in rebellious disobedience, one becomes spiritually deaf. On the contrary, the *Etz Hayim* commentary quotes the Sefat Emet[19] as saying:

> The reward of an observant life [yielded in obedience to God] will be the ability to hear God's voice among the conflicting messages competing for our attention in a noisy world.[20]

THREE TITHES

The Hebrew word for "tithe" is *ma'aser*, the root of which is *eser*, meaning "ten." A tithe is thus literally a tenth of the yield of one's harvest. Three types of tithes are described. Each serves a particular purpose and, although directly connected with one's material income, reflects a different aspect of one's life.

1. The first tithe, *ma'aser harishon*, is given to the Levites and priests, those who have devoted their lives to the LORD's service. This reflects the building up of one's spiritual life, individually and communally. We pay taxes to the government to enable the provision of important services they provide. Likewise, those who serve the community of believers in the kingdom of God in a spiritual capacity are worthy of support.

2. The second tithe, *ma'aser hasheni*, is to be "eaten" by the giver in Jerusalem! "There shall you eat before the LORD your God, and you shall rejoice" (Deuteronomy 12:7). God's selection of a site for his Holy Sanctuary would be a gathering place for his people forever. This second tithe is to be set apart and invested in the provision of food and drink for oneself and one's

family. It is to be shared in the community as all rejoice and worship him together in the place he has appointed—his holy city, Jerusalem.

The Hebrew verbs *samachti vesimmachti* indicate, "I have rejoiced, and I have given joy also to others." The Talmud teaches that, as we celebrate our blessings before God, we need also ensure that those less fortunate can rejoice before him. This applies particularly to the celebration of the festivals in Jerusalem. As we apply our "second tithe" to the deeds involved in the celebration of each *mo'ed* (appointed time), in gratitude and honor of the LORD our God, we can give thereof to enable the needy to do the same, which serves to further our own blessing.

In our day, Jerusalem, the City of God, has been re-established as the capital of his people Israel, and once again, worshipers can go up to celebrate the festivals in the place of God's choosing. This is a mitzvah many are fulfilling today as they hear the call of his voice. They are enjoying abundant blessing as they do so.

3. The third tithe is called *ma'aser ha'ani*, the tithe for the poor. This takes the form of one's *tzedakah*—free-willed charitable giving.

TZEDAKAH – ACTS OF GIVING

All our giving should flow from deep gratitude in our hearts toward the giver of all things. God himself is our example. The desire to give more and more, in ever-increasing measure, is the essence of his love toward us.

The sages say that one who does not give charitably is like an idol worshiper. It is written in *Tzror HaMor*:

> Why is he like an idol worshipper? For one who does not give charity thinks along these lines: "I exerted myself day and night, using my brain, and collected this wealth. Why should

I give it away?" He does not believe that God gave him the riches, and so it is as if he had served idols and denied God.[21]

Rabbi Zvi Miller describes two aspects of *tzedakah* (charity or righteousness): the physical act of giving the gift, and the willingness of the heart to give, i.e., the manner in which it is given. Both aspects are equally important in God's sight. Rabbi Miller states, "Avraham is our model. He was a master of compassion and loving-kindness of the heart."[22]

The outward purpose of *tzedakah*, the act of doing a righteous deed, is to give assistance to those in need, to share the blessing wherewith God has blessed you. The inner purpose is to prevent your heart from becoming hard and your hand from "closing up." Again, God is our example, as is expressed in the final blessing recited in *Birkat HaMazon* (*Grace after Meals*):

> Give thanks to the LORD for He is good; His kindness endures forever.
>
> O God, You open Your hand and give to every living thing what it desires.

Whether tithes or *tzedakah*, giving should be considered a responsibility and not dependent on one's feelings or mood, which are inclined to vary. We are stewards of all that God entrusts into our care, including our material means. Every opportunity to give of one's assets to further a good cause or bring relief and aid to one in poverty or need is an occasion for sharing blessing. True righteousness, therefore, is a combination of heart and action. It is *chesed*, loving-kindness, expressed in deeds of giving—an active caring for another.

SHOFTIM

שׁוֹפְטִים – "Judges"

DEUTERONOMY 16:18–21:9

> On the evidence of two witnesses or of three witnesses the one who is to die shall be put to death ... The hand of the witnesses shall be first against him to put him to death, and afterward the hand of all the people. So you shall purge the evil from the midst of you. (Deuteronomy 17:6-7)

It is on the basis of these verses that the angry "witnesses" brought the woman caught in adultery to Yeshua and demanded his verdict on her fate. Their charge was based on the letter of the Law, but Yeshua's reply epitomized the spirit of the Torah. He said, "Let him who is without sin among you be the first to throw a stone at her" (John 8:7). He bent down as he responded to them and wrote in the dust with his finger. The words he wrote, which we are told they "heard," remain a mystery. However, one by one, they slipped away until no accuser remained. A thought-provoking connection arises with the scenario and the verse in Jeremiah that every man there would have been familiar with:

> O LORD, the hope of Israel, all who forsake you shall be put to shame; those who turn away from you shall be written in the earth, for they have forsaken the LORD, the fountain of living water. (Jeremiah 17:13)

Perhaps Yeshua wrote their names in the dust, "beginning with the eldest," or perhaps he was writing a record of their sins? We don't know. They were, however, convicted and hopefully learned something from this gracious rabbi from Galilee that might well have turned their hearts back toward their God, the "hope of Israel." We also can hope that, in addition to "hearing" his words, their eyes may have been opened to see the Living Hope before them.

THE DEAD PUT TO DEATH?

The phrase above, "the one who is to die shall be put to death" (Deuteronomy 17:6), is rendered *yumat hamet* in Hebrew, which literally translates as "the dead shall be put to death." The opposite of "death" usually is considered to be earthly "life." In fact, the occasion of death is the opposite of the event of birth. Life is that which happens in between and which continues after. Someone once said that when viewing a tombstone, one sees the year of birth and the year of death; all of a person's life is the dash in between! There also is a quality of living that can be termed "dead" or "alive," and it is this to which this puzzling verse refers.

If a person chooses to sin, to turn from the path of God, despite his knowledge of God and his will and commandments, he has effectively "delivered himself up to death." This concept is expressed in the Talmud:

> The wicked are called "dead" while they are alive, whereas the righteous are called "living" even after they are dead. (b.*Bechorot* 18b)

A life of sin does not accord with the concept of true living. The two basic purposes of our life on earth, which reflect the will of the creator, are (a) to enter a covenant relationship of love with our Father God and (b) to live according to his will in order to realize *his* purposes on earth. That's the bottom line!

Everything we do and all we are—all our works, relationships, thoughts, plans, activities, dealings—are contingent upon these basic purposes. The two tablets of the Ten Commandments (*Luchot haBrit* in Hebrew, the "Tablets of the Covenant") delineate the outworking of these purposes. The whole Word of God revolves around them. If we "hear" and choose to live according to them, we are truly alive; if not, we are "deaf" and dead even as we live.

Yeshua, as Messiah, illustrated this truth in his life. He proclaimed, "The thief comes only to steal and kill and destroy. I came that they may have life and have it abundantly" (John 10:10). He invites us to die to the old life of our egotistical self that follows the ways of the world and to enter his life—true life as a son or daughter of the Father. The life that is abundant and eternal. The psalmist describes that it is only through Messiah, the Good Shepherd of our souls, that we can stand strong and live:

> For you have delivered my soul from death, yes, my feet from falling, that I may walk before God in the light of life. (Psalm 56:13)

JUDGMENT AND MERCY

The concept of judgment expressed in the title of the parashah causes us to anticipate Rosh HaShanah, the Day of Judgment, and Yom Kippur, the Day of Atonement, which now are on the horizon of the annual festival cycle. In this regard, David Blumenthal records the words of Levi Yitzchak of Berditchev:[23]

> The Holy One, blessed be He, will judge the community of Israel on the Day of Judgment with the greatness of His merciful love and grace ... We arouse that quality of merciful love when we, here below, act in grace [toward our fellow man] ... judging him or her positively. ... This is the meaning of [the first verse of this portion], "Judges and police shall you set for yourself in all your gates" (16:18); to wit, that you yourself must set in order and prepare the judgments on High by the gates which you open with your deeds.[24]

This time of the year, as the Days of Awe—the high holidays—approach, is a time of reflection on the issues of life. We remember that the line between life and death is precariously thin, physically and spiritually. As Blumenthal points out:

> It's a time to reconsider the underlying moral balance in which life and sanity hang so delicately, to measure oneself against such words as "purity of heart," "true forgiveness," "sin," and "judgment."[25]

In truth the "judges and police" we set in place should be positioned at the "gates" of our selves, particularly at the gates of our eyes, ears, and mouths. When we are quick to judge ourselves and to guard our thoughts, words, and actions, we will be more disposed to judge others favorably and with compassion. Most hostility flows from self-pity, self-righteousness, and unforgiveness—an attitude of self-justification: "I am right, and they are wrong!" As a result, there is no softening of the heart through mercy, loving-kindness, and compassion, and no grace is given. Levi Yitzchak poses the startling question: "Imagine if God thought like that! Who would ever be forgiven?"[26]

Yeshua summed it up well when he taught his disciples to pray: "Forgive us our debts, as we also have forgiven our debtors" (Matthew 6:12).

KI TETZE

כִּי תֵצֵא – "When You Go"

DEUTERONOMY 21:10–25:19

The parashah continues with the enumeration of the laws given to the Israelites by Moses in Moab as they stood on the brink of their entry into the promised land. This is one of Moses' final teachings, and this particular portion contains more laws than any other. The reading can, therefore, be somewhat overwhelming.

LAWS AND MORE LAWS

One can, however, keep in consideration a prevailing theme that underlies the laws: the inherent dignity and worth of every human life. For example, the most marginal individual—a female captive, an orphan, or a pauper—is created in the image of God and should be treated accordingly. This basic respect is due even in the treatment of the corpse of a criminal who has been executed for a capital offense. We read that the corpse of one impaled on a stake "must not remain all night on the tree, but you shall bury him the same day (Deuteronomy 21:23), for an impaled body is an affront to God.

At the execution of Yeshua, by crucifixion on a "stake," his family and friends were present, and they hurried to place his body in the tomb before the arrival of Shabbat (John 19:42). In modern Jewish tradition the deceased is buried within twenty-four hours whenever possible. To honor the dead, however, "burial may be postponed to enable relations to attend the funeral or, where it is possible, to donate the organs of the deceased for transplant. Also, burials do not take place on Shabbat or Festival days."[27]

Some laws, to our modern minds, seem extraordinarily harsh. An example:

> If a man has a stubborn and rebellious son who will not obey the voice of his father or the voice of his mother, and, though they discipline him, will not listen to them, then his father and his mother shall take hold of him and bring him out to the elders of his city at the gate of the place where he lives, ... Then all the men of the city shall stone him to death with stones. (Deuteronomy 21:18-19, 21)

Apparently, there is no record that such a stoning was ever carried out. The sages of Israel found mitigation of the hard sentence in a careful reading of this and similar laws. In this case, stoning would apply only when both the father and mother were present and were in perfect agreement. There would need to be evidence that the parents had taken reasonable steps to teach and impart values of decency to their son and had not, preceding the charge, simply ignored or excused his behavior. Renowned poet and author of a commentary on the Scriptures, Ibn Ezra (Spain 1089-1164), adds, "The son can be charged only if his parents' behavior has been exemplary. Otherwise, they have no right to bring accusation against him."[28]

BIRDS AND LONG LIFE

Listed among the laws is one that is referred to in rabbinic literature as "the least of the commandments." It tells us that if one happens upon a bird's nest containing fledglings or eggs and the mother bird is sitting over them, "you shall not take the mother with the young. You shall let the mother go, but the young you may take for yourself, that it may go well with you, and that you may live long" (Deuteronomy 22:6-7). The latter promise of a long life is linked to one of the ten "great" commandments—to honor your mother and father (Exodus 20:12; Deuteronomy 5:16). These are the only two commandments in the Torah that carry the reward of a long life. The common factor is reverence for the parent-child relationship, whether human or animal. This indicates that one's attitude toward animals might be a reflection of one's attitude toward one's fellow humans, particularly those closest to one. (I am reminded of the title of Gerald Durrell's entertaining book *My Family and Other Animals*!)

The particular commandment under discussion in the parashah has given rise to much deliberation and debate. The *Etz Hayim* commentary informs that the Hebrew phrase employed, *em al habanim*, "mother sitting over children," is a common expression for total, cruel extermination in war.[29] In caring, God-honoring societies, the killing of innocent women and children, in any situation, is indeed considered a grievous and ruthless crime. Cruel treatment of defenseless animals also marks one as merciless.

The Talmud records a poignant story in relation to this law. A father instructed his son to climb a ladder to collect eggs from a bird's nest in a tree. He reminds him to be sure to chase away the mother bird first. While obeying both commands that promise long life, the boy fell from the ladder and died.[30] This tragic event raises the question of God's mercy and providence. It led one of the sages, Elisha ben Abuyah, to despair of God's goodness and even his existence. The wise Rabbi Akiva interpreted the "long life" as eternal life in *olam haba*, the World to Come, and not necessarily physical life on earth. For others, it reinforced the reluctance to emphasize the rewards as motivation in one's obedience of God's commands.

May our chief motivation in obeying the will of our Father be to honor him and to express our love and reverence toward him. In his teaching, Yeshua constantly lifts our eyes from the physical situation to the reality of our Father in heaven and the perspective of eternity. For example, he emphasizes the importance of the spiritual, familial relationship and the fact that our obedience to the Father's will brings him glory:

> For whoever does the will of my Father in heaven is my brother, and sister, and mother. (Matthew 12:50)

> Not everyone who says to me, "Lord, Lord," will enter the kingdom of heaven, but the one who does the will of my Father who is in heaven. (Matthew 7:21)

> Let your light shine before others, so that they may see your good works and give glory to your Father who is in heaven. (Matthew 5:16)

We are responsible for our actions—the doing of the deed. The effects and rewards are in our Father's hands.

GRACE AND MORE GRACE

The haftarah graciously balances the concentration of legal requirements in the portion. This Fifth Haftarah of Consolation is an outpouring of God's loving-kindness, comfort, and encouragement. Shout for joy; fear not; you shall not be shamed:

> For your Maker is your husband, the LORD of hosts is his name; and the Holy One of Israel is your Redeemer, the God of the whole earth he is called. (Isaiah 54:5)

The spousal motif, the covenant relationship of husband and wife, is beautifully employed here. God's vast love and faithfulness toward his people is bound to this covenant of *chesed*, one that precludes loyalty and kindness and keeping faith with one another. His faithfulness is ever new and can never be shaken. His responsibility and adherence to the covenant are constant.

Although God's thoughts and ways are so much higher than ours and often far beyond our limited human understanding, his commitment to us is beyond question. His care for us is unwavering. We are not alone and abandoned to the wiles of the enemy, as Yeshua himself proclaimed:

> Behold, I am with you always, to the close of the age. (Matthew 28:20)

KI TAVO

כִּי תָבוֹא – "When You Come"

DEUTERONOMY 26:1–29:8(9)

The "dark night of the soul"[31] is a familiar expression, and most of us have experienced times of sadness and despair; occasions when the future looks bleak, the present is devastating, and hope seems gone. The phrase describes inner "darkness" rather than outward difficulties. One can endure and overcome the toughest physical trial when one's inner soul remains strong and clear. A far more painful and challenging condition is the draining of hope, the weakening of resolve, the disabling depression—the "dark night of the soul."

SIN AND DESPAIR

Life is filled with challenges on every level. Tests and trials are normal, and we often can face them with confidence and success. There are times, however, when we sin and fail, and we taste the bitterness of disappointment, which ultimately, if left unchecked, can lead to dark despair. Sin, hopelessness, and despair are all steps away from God. Immediately we take a step in the wrong direction through a wrong choice, a yielding to temptation, through "turning a blind eye" and compromising on righteousness, we move ourselves away from God's presence. Unless we take action to remedy the situation, it becomes easier to slip into denial and drift further away.

We eventually find that the path becomes a slippery slope over which we have less and less control, and we slide into the ever-darkening pit of hopelessness. Once there, we no longer have the strength or motivation to pull ourselves upward to escape it. Nor could we without the grace and mercy of our God who is true and faithful to respond to our weakest cry. He has made the way to return from the pit of sin and despair, to be lifted and raised up into the light once again, and to enter the hope of his loving embrace.

THE WAY OF RETURN

Our Father knows that man, in his fallen condition, has a heart inclined toward evil. This *Yetzer HaRa*, the evil inclination, is a reality we need to recognize and to battle against throughout the course of life. Fortunately, the Almighty has provided us with the weapons and resources we need to succeed in this battle. The principal choices we need to make are, first, whether to receive and take hold of them, then to train ourselves in the use of them, and, finally, to effectively employ them.

The first and greatest "weapon" against despair and separation from God is *teshuvah*, repentance. The possibility of recognizing our sin and repenting of it and turning away from it in order to return to God is a capacity that our Father has planted within each of his children. As David Blumenthal describes:

> The capacity God has given us to return to Him negates despair. Knowledge and practice of this is the counter to the black night of the desolation of the soul.[32]

Ideally, we should walk in repentance daily. The more we practice repentance, the more quickly we will be able to recognize subtle temptations, identify "snares of the enemy," and have the strength to expose and renounce them and turn away. The more constantly, then, we can keep our eyes focused on the Beloved of our souls and enjoy the warmth and life-giving light of his presence.

Yeshua, our Messiah and resurrected Lord, paid the price and bore the pain of sin in the affliction of his flesh and sacrificial death. He opened the way into newly created life. When we choose to lay down our life of Self, with its egoistic demands and sinful indulgences, and to receive the life he offers, we are enabled to stand with secure confidence in him and to withstand all the trials and storms of life. As we come to examine and to employ this gift more regularly, we realize that repentance is not a heavy, somber, self-afflicting habit; it is a powerful, liberating, effective exercise of the heart, mind, and spirit—a gift for which we can be joyously grateful. Through repentance we regain our hope, our purpose, and our joy, no matter the physical circumstances we are enduring.

There is great celebration in heaven when we return to God from our fallen state (Luke 15:7, 10). The Father and the angels rejoice. The Talmud states:

> In the place where one who returns to God stands, not even the completely righteous can stand.[33]

It is rare, if not impossible, to find one who is "completely righteous." God's holiness sets an extremely high standard, and all who yearn to serve him wholeheartedly and bless him with our lives will suffer the reality of our own weakness and will know the disappointment of failure. Rather than allowing a failure to crush us, however, we can quickly rise up with the weapon of repentance and turn and run back to our merciful Father. We can learn from the experience and move forward all the more determined to serve him in faithfulness. We also can rest in the understanding and the reassurance the Father has given us, as expressed by his prophet Micah:

> He will again have compassion on us; he will tread our iniquities underfoot. You will cast all our sins into the depths of the sea. (Micah 7:19)

Then, as one dear saint declared, "Then he puts up a sign: No Fishing!"

"DON'T WORRY, BE HAPPY!"

The title of this hip-hop, happy Jamaican song carries more wisdom than one might initially consider. Exaggerated anxiety, prolonged tension, and elevated stress are all diseases of our modern lifestyle. They flow from the existence of curses in one form or another, which can generally be traced back to rebellion against God in the garden. Every little weed of sin has roots that tap into a larger root, which feeds into an even larger root that emerges from the life-choking weed that is the sin of rebellion against God's will. The separation from God that results is a condition that incurs God's curses and the curses of man. It is wise to be aware of the difference.

Every "curse" that comes from our loving Father is intended as an instruction, a correction, a wake-up call. Similarly, a good earthly father will punish and instruct a beloved child for his good. This rebuke, in effect, becomes a blessing. The curses of man, on the other hand, stem from evil intent and are designed for harm. When one is in a rebellious and sinful state, removed from God, one becomes more vulnerable to the curses inherent in man's fallen and bent condition. We can surmise that during the Israelites' journey through the wilderness, they suffered no attacks from the snakes and scorpions that inhabited the region because the hand of God protected them. We read in Numbers 21 that the people became impatient and rebelled against Moses and God: "Then the LORD sent fiery serpents among the people, and they bit the people, so that many people of Israel died" (Numbers 21:6). The Hebrew verb *veshalach*, translated as "sent," indicates being released from the hand. When we remain yielded in the hand of the LORD, no curse can come to rest upon us:

> Like a swallow in its flying, a curse that is causeless does not alight. (Proverbs 26:2)

During the Hebrew month of Elul, we are offered a special time and opportunity to draw aside spiritually to press in to the presence of our Beloved to make a clear and thorough assessment of the state of our souls. We begin by confirming our covenant relationship with the LORD, as the acronym of the name Elul indicates: *Ani Ledodi Vedodi Li*, "I am my Beloved's, and my Beloved is mine" (Song of Songs 6:3). We confess our love and commitment to him. We examine where we have failed him or taken him for granted, and we confess and repent. Then we can rest in the knowledge that we are forgiven and can stand confidently before the "Judge of all flesh" on the Day of Trumpets and the Day of Atonement (Leviticus 23:24, 27). We can eagerly anticipate another year of devoted service in joyful worship of our God and King.

As the parashah's opening verses describe, we can bring to him the offerings of the first-fruits of the labor of our hands in gratitude for his blessings, and we can shed our worries and happily celebrate before him.

NITZAVIM

נצבים – "You Are Standing"

DEUTERONOMY 29:9(10)–30:20

The ability to stand upright and erect is a singular ability afforded to human beings on earth. Being able "to stand on one's own two feet" is seen as a mark of maturity and capability, of taking responsibility and succeeding in one's undertakings. It is an ability for which we can gratefully offer daily thanks and blessing to our Father, and yet we most often take it for granted.

WE ARE STANDING

The heavenly beings described as "standing" are the angels. They stand in praise and adoration of the Almighty God and are swift to bear his messages and execute his will. We do not hear of them sitting on thrones or taking a lunch break! They also are created beings, mighty and wondrous, but unlike humans, they are not referred to as beings created "in the image of God." Their function is vital in the kingdom of God, but it is specific and limited.

The Midrash considers that, at the time of creation, God counseled with the angels as to whether he should create humanity in his image. Some agreed, but some advised him against it.[34] Perhaps, knowing man's potential wickedness, they did not want him to suffer the pain this would inevitably entail. So great, however, was the desire of God's heart for relationship with a people that he decided to persevere with this crown and purpose of his creation. In doing so, he realized that he would forever bear the responsibility for their creation, just as a parent bears responsibility for the birth of a child. He would place himself in the position of incurring judgment when his children disobeyed and rebelled and misbehaved. He took an even greater risk—being rejected by his children, whom he loved deeply and unconditionally. As David Blumenthal describes:

> He opened Himself to the possibility that humanity would reject Him ... [that He would become] a Being contemplating only itself, isolated and alone, unfortunate.
>
> [God] wants to love us and we do not always want to be loved. He wants to relate to us and we are not always worthy receivers.[35]

Our Father God is unfailing in his love and in his desire to express that love. Humanity, and each individual, has been given the choice to open their hearts and minds to realize and receive it and to respond in openness and love in return. Almost beyond reason, however, people can choose stubbornly to go their own way, turn their backs, and refuse the expression of love and affection. Sadly, this closing of the heart toward God is often reflected in a "closedness" toward the "other"—those with whom they are in relationship. On the other hand, hearts yielded and filled with love toward God, overflowing with his love in return, will be open vessels of that love in relation to all others he brings into their lives.

The parashah recounts how the people of Israel are gathered together as they prepare to cross over into the promised land. They are told, "You are standing today, all of you" (Deuteronomy 29:10). They were standing together, bonded as one by the covenant of God. Before him and for his purposes and by his enabling, they can stand upright and strong in unity and hope to go forward as one. They have been given "eyes to see" the reality of the One true God and "ears to hear" his Word of truth and loving instruction. They have been given a heart to love and respond to him, but they have also been given the option of choice. Each one bears the responsibility of choosing—to either love and serve God and, thus, one another or close one's heart and reject him and one another. The way of the first choice is life, blessing, and joy, and the second, death and despair. How often he exhorts us to "choose life" (Deuteronomy 30:19)!

REFLECT, REPENT, RETURN

The portion of Nitzavim is always read before Rosh HaShanah during the Hebrew month of Elul. It is a time of reflection, a time to carefully consider one's life, attitudes, and relationships. It also is a time of repentance for the times we have "missed the mark" and the ways we have fallen short of our desired goals and standards. It can be a daunting undertaking that can cause us to feel that our aspirations are unattainable, and our weaknesses and faults are beyond correction. Can we ever change? Can we make progress and grow in our knowledge of God our Father and in our relationships with our loved ones? Can we stand tall and free and secure, in integrity and wholeness, and confirm our identity as deeply beloved and royal heirs of the kingdom of God?

There is a basic requirement that offers a glorious affirmative in response to our questioning. It is one that is embroidered in gold letters on many curtains that cover the ark containing the Torah scrolls in a synagogue and is a daily and weekly reminder to those who stand in worship:

> *D'u Lifnei Mi Atem Omdim*—Know Before Whom You Stand.

Before we can stand before him, we need to return from the place of separation, the "corner" in which we have placed ourselves as a result of our sin and disobedience or our fear and anxiety. This act of returning is *teshuvah*, repentance. The sages praise even the act of *hirhurei teshuvah*, the *desire* to turn and improve.[36]

God will honor the desires of our hearts that are for good and are in accord with his will. He will begin to remove the "stones" from our hearts and the barriers that have separated us from him and one another. As soon as we choose to change, he "runs" to our aid to strengthen us and to enable us to make a full return to his waiting embrace. We can then return to him with all our "heart and soul" (Deuteronomy 30:6). With his help, our relationship of love with him will be restored, along with the relationship of husband and wife, of "fathers to children and children to fathers" (Malachi 4:6). God desires to liberate us from every fear and bondage, to give us the power to be all he created us to be and to do all he has planned for us to do.

KNOW BEFORE WHOM YOU STAND

The Hebrew word *lada'at,* "to know," means to have intimate knowledge of something. It is not only learning about or storing up facts on a subject; it is also an experience that involves one's emotions. A giving and receiving, an inter-connectedness, a dynamic relationship that is alive and growing and requires one's awareness and intentional cooperation. Does that describe our relationship, our "knowing" of our God and Lord? Our relationship with one another?

This is the challenge and the question we need to be asking ourselves at this season preceding Rosh HaShanah and the Days of Awe. Our response will affect how we stand before the Judge who is King when the gates are opened and we stand on the threshold of the New Year. May we pass through the gate as those washed in the living water of his Word and dressed in the purity of his robe of righteousness (Isaiah 61:10). Let us then enter with thanksgiving in our hearts for the eternal life we have received and with shouts of joy in the victory gained in the full forgiveness and blood-bought atonement of the one who is love incarnate.

L'SHANAH TOVAH!

TO A YEAR FILLED WITH HIS LOVE AND GOODNESS!

VAYELECH

וילך – "And He Went"

DEUTERONOMY 31:1–30

The title of the portion refers to Moses—*vayelech Mosheh*, "and Moses went" (Deuteronomy 31:1). The same Hebrew verb is used in Proverbs 9:5, "*Lechu* ... You [plural] go...and eat of my bread." The one speaking here is Wisdom or the Word of God, and in the context of the book of Proverbs refers specifically to the Torah. In this verse Solomon compares the Torah to bread and wine, nourishment for the body. God's Word and instructions are, likewise, nourishment for the soul.

The verb *lech*, "go," indicates that the procuring of Torah is proactive. Just as one must take action to obtain one's bread to physically sustain oneself and to remain strong in body, so one must "get up and go," diligently work, to procure one's spiritual sustenance.

The sages maintain that the study of Torah reaps rewards even if one studies alone at home. However, when one makes the extra effort of "going" and seeking teaching, and one learns with and from others, "his reward is doubled and redoubled, for he receives the reward for going and the reward for having fulfilled the commandment [to study Torah]."[37]

The LORD richly blesses the heart that is hungry for more knowledge of his Word, which essentially stems from a longing to know more of him. He is faithful to reward those who earnestly seek, and he promises, "Open your mouth wide, and I will fill it" (Psalms 81:10).

FEAR NOT!

The portion of Vayelech is comprised of only one chapter, Deuteronomy 31. Most often, it is combined as a double portion with the preceding portion, Nitzavim. In either case, it demands our attention as it prepares us for Moses' imminent death and for his last, great Song that begins in the next parashah.

Moses went before the people to bring his final words to them. He offered them great encouragement at the prospect of facing the enemies that inhabit the land into which God is bringing them:

> Be strong and courageous. Do not fear or be in dread of them, for it is the LORD your God who goes with you. He will not leave you or forsake you. (Deuteronomy 31:6)

What more assurance does one need? If we could grasp and digest and fully believe this one reality, then every enemy, every obstacle, every evil thing that looms and threatens to destroy us would shrink and be overcome. The LORD is with us in and through it all. The Almighty is our shield and our help, the LORD of Hosts, the creator of heaven and earth. We need not "fear nor be dismayed" (Deuteronomy 31:8). We can press forward in confidence, rejoicing always!

The hearing and receiving of the Word of God are imperative to the preservation of, and the walking in accord with, this knowledge of God. Throughout the years in the wilderness, Moses had written the Torah, all the words he had received from God, and he now presents the scrolls to the Levites and the elders of Israel. He instructs them to keep the Torah beside the ark of the covenant that encased the original stone tablets, where it would be a testimony and a witness against them (Deuteronomy 31:26). Moses knew prophetically, no doubt with great sadness, that Israel would rebel and become corrupt and "do evil in the sight of the LORD" (Deuteronomy 31:29). In an effort to mitigate this eventuality, he shares the command of God:

> At the end of every seven years at the set time ... the Feast of Booths ... you shall read this [Torah] before all Israel in their hearing. (Deuteronomy 31:10-11)

He explains that *all* need to hear, including the children and the strangers who were with them, to ensure that they would learn of God and to engender a fear, reverential awe of him that would encourage them to "carefully observe" the commandments and directions he had given them. When they feared him and walked in his ways, his presence would remain with them, and they need have no fear of any opposing enemy.

BRING YOUR WORDS

God's people are often exhorted to repent. At specific times, such as the month of Elul, the Ten Days of Awe, and Yom Kippur, repentance is focussed on more intently; however, it also is considered a good practice to "keep a short account with God" and to constantly recognize and confess any sin or weakness. He knows our weaknesses and empathizes with our well-intentioned failures. When our hearts repent of any sin that has separated us from his presence, we know we can return to him. In *teshuvah*, repentance, we humbly and gratefully go by way of the ultimate sacrifice made by Yeshua at the crucifixion stake, and we bring our words. Words of confession and words of thanks and praise. This requires the combined action of our feet and our mouths—we need to turn from our transgression and return to him, and we need to speak our words of prayer.

God gave us his words; now, he waits for ours in response. No matter how awkward or seemingly insufficient they may be, each prayer has God-ordained power and is of great value. The most powerful component of prayer is our *kavanah*—our intent and the heart-attitude prompting the words. This is what our Father sees before all else; then, he inclines his ear and hears.

It is written, for example, in Psalm 145:19, concerning the prayer of the righteous: "He also hears their cry and saves them." When Rachel cried out to God for a child, "God hearkened to her and opened her womb."[38] Also, in response to King Hezekiah's heartfelt prayer for healing, God says, "I have heard your prayer; I have seen your tears. ... and I will add fifteen years to your life" (2 Kings 20:5-6). Another righteous servant of God, to whom he hearkened, was Cornelius, "a devout man who feared God with all his household, gave alms generously to the people, and prayed continually to God" (Acts 10:2). The Apostle Paul reminds us of the importance of prayer:

> Rejoice in hope, be patient in tribulation, be constant in prayer. (Romans 12:12)

Moses lived for one hundred and twenty years (Deuteronomy 31:2), and he was to die on the date of his birth. The Midrash reflects that God assured him, "Death is a favor to you. You will have even more glory in the Next World."[39] The sages concur with the resurrection of the dead, as affirmed consistently throughout the *Siddur*—Jewish Book of Prayer. Moses, and all true servants of God, will die and rise to live again in *Olam HaBa*, the World to Come.

Yeshua confirmed the reality of eternal life. He proposed the startling concept that he himself was the bread of life come down from heaven. He was a reflection and embodiment of the truth of the Word of God. He exemplified the truth to be found in the Torah, that, once digested and lived out, leads to eternal life:

> Truly, truly, I say to you, whoever believes has eternal life. I am the bread of life. Your fathers ate the manna in the wilderness, and they died. This is the bread that comes down from heaven, so that one may eat of it and not die. I am the living bread that came down from heaven. If anyone eats of this bread, he will live forever. (John 6:47–51)

HA'AZINU

הַאֲזִינוּ – "Give Ear"

DEUTERONOMY 32:1–52

> Give ear, O heavens, and I will speak, and let the earth hear the words of my mouth. (Deuteronomy 32:1)

This dramatic opening to Moses' ultimate communication with his people distills the understanding that God, who is enthroned in the highest heaven, is approachable. In fact, as the sages maintain:

> God is near in every kind of nearness. For though the distance between heaven and earth is so infinitely great, yet when a man ... prays, God listens to him, for the petitioner is like a man who talks into the ear of his friend.[40]

Moses knew that this was the last day of his life. He gathered the people of Israel, and his final words to them poured forth as a powerful poem—a song, a *shirah*—one that prophetically describes the purposes of God on earth and the future destiny of Israel.

As with the previous two portions, this penultimate portion of the Torah also is comprised of one chapter, as the last will be. The number thirty-two is written in Hebrew as *lamed-vet, lev*, meaning "heart." Chapter 32 is indeed an outpouring of Moses' heart and includes a dramatic description of the enduring depths of the heart of God as well as the variable tendencies of the human heart. The latter fluctuates between the potent and prevailing self-indulgent lure of evil on the one hand and the desire, on the other hand, to yield to the will of the Almighty God, delight in his service, and be the bearer of his light of truth and life. Again we are arrested by the fact that a choice is at the heart of the matter. We have the choice—God's will or ours. Stiff-necked rebellion or yielded hearts? Life or death?

IN THE EYES OF GOD AND MAN

Moses' song of redemption can be divided into six parts, each of which addresses a particular phase of the outworking of Israel's destiny and which, together, present an overview of God's plan of redemption for all humankind:

- 1-6: A description of the God of Israel and his relationship with the world in general and with Israel in particular.
- 7-12: A focus on Israel – its origins and destiny.
- 13-18: A record of Israel's prosperity and sins subsequently committed.
- 19-26: A prophecy of Israel's downfall as a result of these sins.
- 27-35: An admonition and a clarification of the purpose of Israel's dispersion amongst the nations.
- 36-43: A song of Israel's restoration and an insight into the future of Israel and the nations.

The essence of this Song of Moses echoes his Song at the Sea when he and the Israelites experienced the mighty deliverance of God and witnessed the demise of the pursuing enemy army as the walls of the sea crashed down upon them (Exodus 15:19). There they sang the first mighty proclamation of the kingship of God—*Adonai yimloch l'olam va'ed*! "The LORD will reign forever and ever!" Now Moses sings of the outworking of God's kingdom and the establishment thereof on the earth, as it is in heaven.

All that Israel will endure is to serve only one purpose—the ultimate realization of God's universal plan of redemption. An awareness of God's workings with and through Israel, historically and personally, is derived through his Word and is relevant to his workings with and through his people in the present.

At the culmination of the song, Moses declares,

> Rejoice, you nations, with His people; for He will avenge the blood of His servants. And will return vengeance on His adversaries. And will atone for His land and His people. (Deuteronomy 32:43 NASB)

All the nations of the earth will see the salvation of God and can rejoice with, and as, his people. Vengeance is his, and atonement is his, and in his great mercy and everlasting love, his land and his people Israel will be fully redeemed.

Moses exhorts the Israelites to apply this song to their hearts:

> Take to heart all the words by which I am warning you today, that you may command them to your children, that they may be careful to do all the words of this law. For it is no empty word for you, but your very life, and by this word you shall live long in the land that you are going over the Jordan to possess. (Deuteronomy 32:46-47)

As always, God's Word through Moses harmonizes with all his Word, which "in the fullness of time" is expressed in the life of his Son and leads to the way of life eternal for all nations. In the light of the wondrous workings of God, our hearts can sing with Moses and with the song of David in the haftarah:

> The LORD is my rock and my fortress and my deliverer, my God, my rock, in whom I take refuge, my shield, and the horn of my salvation, my stronghold and my refuge, my savior; you save me from violence. (2 Samuel 22:2-3)

STIFF NECKS!

The first Hebrew word in the opening verse is *ya'arof*, which means to penetrate or soften and make flexible. The metaphor employed is that of a rain shower that softens the soil and renders it malleable. This prepares the soil to receive seed and to sustain and bring forth life. God's Word is compared here with gentle rain, *matar*.

The Hebrew term for the joint of the neck is *oref*. This is the most flexible joint in the body.[41] When it becomes rigid and loses movement, it is referred to as *kasheh oref*, "stiff-necked," which usually is not a physical description but denotes a person of stubborn will who will not budge from his position. How often is Israel described as "a stiff-necked people" (e.g., Exodus 32:9; Acts 7:51)?

In a play on words, Moses describes the antidote for this condition of self-willed stubbornness: the steady soaking of God's teachings and promises. His Word given from heaven will soften the dry, hardened soil of the heart and make flexible the neck set in its stubborn ways. Only a heart permeated with the truth of his Word is prepared to bring forth the life he promises. Only ears that are willing to hear and eyes that are opened to see will behold the salvation of God and can cause one to proclaim with Simeon, who received the revelation by the Holy Spirit that he would not die before he had seen the Messiah of God:

> My eyes have seen your salvation that you have prepared in the presence of all peoples, a light for revelation to the Gentiles, and for glory to your people Israel. (Luke 2:30–32)

God gave his Word to scatter, as it were, seeds of life and light into the minds and spirits of his people so that they might take root and produce much fruit in the nation of Israel and the lives of each individual. This fruit of light and life would become the light to all the nations of the world. Through stiff-necked rebellion we stifle the seeds of life and cause them to wither. Such is the human condition, and, sadly, much fruit is lost.

In Deuteronomy 32:6, Moses challenges, "Do you thus repay the LORD, you foolish and senseless people?" Rabbi Hirsch points out that the opening particle of this verse in Hebrew, *Ha*, is always written in Hebrew with an enlarged *hei*.[42] This is seen as a constant reminder that rather than blaming God or others when suffering befalls us, we should question ourselves and examine our ways in repentance. We should always ask, "Is this how I repay God for the life he has given me? Is this the fruit I have to offer in return for all he has done in me, and for me, and with me?"

As we approach the end of this year's cycle of reading the Torah of God, we do well to ask, "Have I allowed myself to become hardened and withered in mind and spirit? Or have I allowed the light of his life to grow and shine through me, according to his will and purposes, for his glory and the extension of his kingdom on earth?" May our answer indicate that we have indeed made the decision to choose life!

VEZOT HA'BRACHA

וזאת הברכה – "And This Is the Blessing"

DEUTERONOMY 33:1–34:12

This is the blessing with which Moses the man of God blessed the people of Israel before his death. (Deuteronomy 33:1)

After all his words of teaching, warning and admonishment, exhortation and encouragement, how fitting it is that Moses' final words to the people he led for so many years are words of blessing. Moses stood before the children of Israel as a father, a man of God—*ish haElohim*, one who has gained full stature in the eyes of God, a true role model to which each son can aspire.

PRIDE – A VIRTUE?

Moses' greatness of character is also reflected in the other appellations accorded him, namely "servant of God" (e.g., Joshua 1:13, 22:5; Nehemiah 10:29; Revelation 15:3) and "the most humble of men" (Numbers 12:3). He had a servant's heart in that he lived to serve the Master of the world, the creator of the universe. His intimate knowledge of this One God and King instilled within him true humility and genuine meekness. This humility is not self-effacing and cowering, yet it is the antithesis of haughty pride and arrogance.

Levi Yitzchak, a Chasidic rabbi, comments: "It is forbidden to be prideful. Only this is permitted—to be afraid of no thing and to have pride in the fact that one has a Father in heaven."[43] David Blumenthal adds that the Talmud (b.*Sotah* 5a) also stresses that coarseness of spirit and haughtiness are vices that are sure to bring disaster upon those who live them. He points out:

> [C]hasidism[44] in particular, made the motif of humility central to religious consciousness partly because of its receiving theological emphasis on God as the source of all vitality and action.

What is true pride, then? Levi Yitzchak defines it thus:

> True pride is the pride of knowing that one is chosen, that one is the object of God's special care. True pride, which is a virtue, is the absolute confidence that God will right all wrongs, in this world and in the other; that the haughty will be brought low; that the evil will be punished ... False pride, sinful pride, is pride in anything other than God.

As an example, Blumenthal records a true story of the massacre of a large group of Chasidic Jews in Lublin, a city that was a great center of Chasidism and yeshiva study before the Second World War. The brutal, local Nazi commander had them assembled outside the city limits, where they were assaulted by his dogs and beaten. He then ordered them to sing one of their Chasidic songs, mocking their teaching that it is a great mitzvah, a good deed, to be joyous always. This central teaching was rendered in the song, *Mitzvah gedolah lihyot besimchah tamid*! As the Apostle Paul also taught:

> Rejoice in the Lord always; again I will say, rejoice. (Philippians 4:4)

How could they sing under such circumstances? The commander resumed the attacks. Then one trembling voice rose in a familiar Yiddish melody, *Lemir zich iberbeiten, iberbeiten Avinu shebashamayim*, "Let us be reconciled, be reconciled, our Father in heaven." The song soon faded. Then a stronger voice picked up the melody but with new words: *Mir velen zey iberleben, iberleben, Avinu shebashamayim*, "We will outlive them, outlive them, our Father in heaven." As the song spread, the Chasidim started dancing and singing with a zeal inspired from above. The Nazi commander yelled and screamed in an effort to stop them, but he could not. They paid a heavy price, but the singing and dancing did not stop.

They gave up their lives, but their spirits overcame and indeed will eternally outlive the spirit of the enemies of God and his people. Those Jews forfeited their physical survival, as did so many others, including those in the "Underground" who attempted to resist with force. Blumenthal concludes: "Resistance, military and spiritual, was necessary; pride was a virtue."[45]

A COMMUNITY OF INDIVIDUALS

In verse 4 of this concluding chapter we find the Israelites described as *kehilat Ya'akov*, the congregation or community of Jacob. This is the only place in the Scriptures where this designation is applied. The term more generally used is *kahal Yisra'el*, which stresses the nation's independence and uniqueness. *Kehilah* is the weaker, feminine form of the noun and denotes a smaller branch of the larger nation—a community within a community. Such are each of the tribes, and Moses addresses and blesses each tribe individually.

The unique term also refers to the time when Israel will no longer be one large group traveling together in the wilderness but will be settled in separate communities in the promised land. The responsibility will then be upon each *kehilah* to observe and transmit the Torah, the teachings of God, within its own immediate community.

The inheritance of the Torah was now being transferred by Moses to the "congregation of Jacob" as a whole. It was the *kehilah* that was to preserve it and pass it on to the individuals within it. The focus now was the maintenance and the building up of the smaller communities. Within the framework of the community and its resources, the protection of this precious inheritance can be assured, and the "fire" of the eternal Word can remain lit for the next generation.

A NARROW BRIDGE

Moses ascends Mount Nebo, where he lays down his life and is buried by God himself. Joshua is the brave new leader of Israel, appointed and anointed by God. This was affirmed by Moses when he laid hands on him and conferred the leadership to him (Deuteronomy 34:9).

The haftarah, fittingly, is taken from the book of Joshua, where we, along with the people of Israel, are encouraged by the LORD, who says in effect, "I will not weaken my grip on you, neither shall I abandon you. You need have no fear":

> Be strong and courageous. Do not be frightened, and do not be dismayed, for the LORD your God is with you wherever you go. (Joshua 1:9)

Another well-known Chasidic song tells us,

> The whole world is a very narrow bridge—*Kol ha'olam kulo gesher tzar me'od*
>
> But the main thing is never to be afraid—*veha'ikar lo lefached klal.*

The new life of Israel would often seem like a narrow and sometimes shaky bridge, but the LORD reminds his people that if they keep their eyes straight ahead and are not tempted to go to the left or right, they would remain safe and would be successful:

> Only be strong and very courageous, being careful to do according to all the [Torah] that Moses my servant commanded you. Do not turn from it to the right hand or to the left, that you may have good success wherever you go. (Joshua 1:7)

The Hebrew form of Joshua is *Yehoshua*, from the root meaning "salvation." The time would come when the Torah would be incarnated, and the way of salvation would walk among men in the person of God's Son, *Yeshua*. He who said,

> Do not fear those who kill the body but cannot kill the soul. Rather fear him who can destroy both soul and body in hell. Are not two sparrows sold for a penny? And not one of them will fall to the ground apart from your Father. ... Fear not, therefore; you are of more value than many sparrows. (Matthew 10:28–31)

We can rejoice in the fulfillment of the prophetic words of Zechariah, the father of John the Immerser who, after his encounter with God as he served in the holy place of the Temple, declared:

Blessed be the Lord God of Israel, for he has visited and redeemed his people and has raised up a horn of salvation for us in the house of his servant David, as he spoke by the mouth of his holy prophets from of old, ... that we, being delivered from the hand of our enemies, might serve him without fear, in holiness and righteousness before him all our days. (Luke 1:68–70, 74–75)

CHAZAK CHAZAK, VENITCHAZEK
BE STRONG, BE STRONG, AND MAY WE STRENGTHEN ONE ANOTHER.

ENDNOTES

1. *Tz'enah Ur'enah, The Weekly Midrash*, Vol.1 (New York, NY: Mesorah Publications, Ltd., 2007), 879.
2. Ibid.
3. Ibid.
4. Ibid., 880.
5. Ibid., 990.
6. Sara Yocheved Rigler, "Tisha B'Av: Waking Up to a World without God's Presence," July 7, 2005, Aish.com.
7. Ibid.
8. Rav Moshe Chaim Luzzatto (Italy, 1707-1746), *Mesilat Yesharim*, The Path of the Just.
9. Maimonides (The Rambam, Rabbi Moshe ben Maimon, Spain and Egypt, 1135-1204) *Sefer HaMitzvot,* reference to the third commandment.
10. Nehama Leibowitz, *Studies in Devarim* (Jerusalem, Israel: World Zionist Organization) , 58.
11. Ibid., 59.
12. Ibid., 60.
13. Ibid., 62.
14. Rabbi Shlomo Riskin, "Shabbat Shalom," *Jerusalem Post*, 1 August, 2003.
15. *Tz'enah Ur'enah, The Weekly Midrash*, Vol.1, 906.
16. Rabbi Chanan Morrison, *Gold from the Land of Israel*, 308-309.
17. *Tz'enah Ur'enah, The Weekly Midrash*, Vol.1, 900.
18. Deuteronomy 30:19.
19. Sefat Emet - Rabbi Yehudah Aryeh Leib Alter, Chasidic leader (Poland, 1847-1905).
20. *Etz Hayim, Torah and Commentary*, 1061.
21. *Tz'enah Ur'enah, The Weekly Midrash*, Vol.II, 917.
22. R. Zvi Miller, *Torat Aish*, Parsha Insights, 2003.
23. Levi Yitzchak of Berditchev, Chasidic rabbi, Poland, 1740-1810.

24 David R. Blumenthal, *God at the Center: Meditations on Jewish Spirituality*, 154.
25 Ibid.
26 Ibid., 155.
27 *Etz Hayim*, 1115.
28 Ibid., 1114.
29 Ibid., 1116.
30 b.*Chullin* 142a.
31 From treatise of the same name by sixteenth-century Spanish poet and mystic, Carmelite monk St. John of the Cross.
32 David R. Blumenthal, *God at the Center*, 160.
33 b.*Sanhedrin* 99a.
34 *Genesis Rabbah* 8:5.
35 David R. Blumenthal, *God at the Center*, 162–163.
36 *Pesikta Rabbati* 44.
37 *Tz'enah Ur'enah, The Weekly Midrash*, Vol.1, 964.
38 Ibid., 966.
39 Ibid.
40 y.*Brachot* 13a.
41 Rabbi S.R. Hirsch, *The Pentateuch*, 800.
42 Ibid., 801.
43 David Blumenthal, *God at the Center*, 171.
44 Chasidism – *Chasid* literally means "pious one." Chasidism is an Ultra-Orthodox Jewish movement that arose in eighteenth-century Eastern Europe. It emphasizes the value of devoted study, piety, and joyous spontaneity of prayer and worship of God rather than a dry, intellectual approach to him and his Word.
45 David Blumenthal, *God at the Center*, 172.

www.ingramcontent.com/pod-product-compliance
Lightning Source LLC
Chambersburg PA
CBHW070130080526
44586CB00015B/1637